SHE FINDS LOVE

A novel

L.J. BERNARD

This book is a work of fiction; names, characters, places, and incidents are either products of the authors imagination or have been used fictitiously. Any resemblance to actual events, locales or persons, living or dead, are entirely coincidental.

The Author acknowledges the occasional use of New Zealand place names and wants to address that she may have never been there, and they have been used fictitiously.

Originally published in 2024.

ISBN 978-0-473-72077-3

Cover Design by 'Get Covers'

Books by L.J. Bernard

The Journey Trilogy

Insurmountable Faith

She Finds Love

Not Plain Sailing

ACKNOWLEDGEMENTS

To my children, Meghan and Christopher,

May you both be strong enough to follow your dreams,

love and be loved even through the difficult times.

And to all my friends and readers that continue to encourage me,
your support and wonderful comments are so very much appreciated.

Thank you.

Psalms 138:7

Though I walk in the midst of trouble, thou wilt revive me:
thou shalt stretch forth thine hand against the wrath of mine enemies,
and thy right hand shall save me.

SHE FINDS LOVE!

A riveting fiction story of greed and exploitation,

initiating a woman's courage

to face and conquer her fear of loving again.

She rebuilds her life with prayer,

resourcefulness

and dignity.

She finds independence and *She Finds Love.*

Chapter 1

Easing her way through 'Country Views' residential home with the last of Mason's possessions, she can empathize that he chose this place because it was not like the others, with its little stream meandering through in a relaxing way, offering up a humble likeness to their familiar pond at home. This place seemed agreeable for Gemma's husband to reside in, but it was a sombre situation after the emotional challenge of having to tour through three previous rest homes before deciding. His moving out of home was difficult enough, Gemma struggled to cope with the fact that her husband had to go into long term residential care, for an unknown length of time. She remained hopeful that it would only be while adjusting to his new medication, and to provide time for her leg to heal after having surgery to repair broken bones.

The hospital assessment had read that Mason was a danger to himself, and to others. With a final diagnosis of vascular type Dementia which followed on from her five year struggle to keep him at home. He had an aneurysm which haemorrhaged and he underwent serious brain surgery which left him with ongoing memory problems.

The touring of rest homes had been emotionally daunting and although they had seen some very settled residents, they had also seen poor lost souls wondering around. Today they came laden with his favourite things, and the struggle began to find a place for everything, attempting to fit personal items in his one little room, small but it was the security that Mason needed. Nevertheless, Gemma found it even more distressing, and she loathed the feeling of finality of Mason moving out of home. She battled with the personal void of emptiness and regretted that they had to go through this together.

"Welcome back Mr and Mrs Brownlie. We hope Mason will be very happy living here when he gets to know us all. It's nearly time for the tea trolley to come around, so do come and sit out on the shady deck to meet everyone." Invited Sue the smiley efficient manager of Country Views Rest Home.

Gemma got the feeling that she didn't have time for them, but was hastily doing her job as instructed, this was an institution and although probably quite adequate, it was not the one Gemma tried to get her husband to choose. He appreciated the country outlook, and having a lot of bird life it would be good that he'll be able to feed the ducks and pigeons, which Gemma accepts will be beneficially relaxing for him. One of her priorities was checking out the staff and the amenities, what they offered, and how her husband would be looked after. She had preferred another place; however she accepted his choice as this will be his home for now. She manages to find enough space for his few favourite personal effects before settling outside with a cuppa on the deck.

Helping him to settle in, she straight away commenced introducing him to some of the residents sitting around them; after drinking her tea she hugged and gave him a discrete kiss on the cheek, trying to appear relaxed like everything was normal, when actually her whole body was in panic, it was a huge lifestyle change for them both.

Their intimacy was now very public, and an inner longing to rush back to his room was overwhelming as she says goodbye, before quickly retreating back to the secure confines of her car. A constrictive lump in her throat, she couldn't hold back the tears any longer, as they started to run unrestrained down her face. People speak of how awful it is for the person leaving home, it was life changing for Mason and she felt upset for his lose of freedom; but it was also devastating for Gemma to accept defeat, and the fact that she could no longer manage him, she felt like she had failed him, relinquishing the responsibility of her partner in life, her much loved husband was moving away. Of course it was traumatic for his wife, life without each other, suddenly everything will change.

After struggling through three restless nights, each time the morning shafts of light pushed their way through between the thread bare curtains and Mason was not there beside her, shrouding her in emptiness, today she was so grateful to have a mob of sheep to drench on their lifestyle property. The house was too quite without him, he was always hanging around being a nuisance before, so although she just wanted to sit and cry at the loss, at least the work kept her physically and mentally occupied to stop her from being lonely and constantly worrying about how he was getting on. She was longing to visit but had been told to let him settle in, and not to visit for a few days so he adjusted to the routine without her. Gemma was told that was best for him, but how does she know if they are right. This is a new occurrence, something she has never had to do before and she felt like a deserter. She continually prayed that her man was okay, enjoying just a short phone call each night, as he had nothing to talk about. It was extremely hard after he had been her constant companion for fifteen years, so her attempt to keep busy and round up the sheep, focusing on them was all she could do to take her mind of Mason. One by one she ran them through the narrow end of the rickety old wooden pen that they had built together, when they bought this lifestyle property.

Opening and closing the gate after walking in amongst the sheep and grappling with one arm tightly around each woolly neck she repeatedly forced the drench into their mouths with her free hand, without really being mentally present, it was routine as it was something she had done many times over the years. Feeling wretched with nothing to be happy about today, she reconciles herself knowing that she was allowed to visit Mason tomorrow and she will have that visual assurance she needed, that everything was all right.

After persistently braving twenty-nine out of thirty-five sheep with an aching back she conceded defeat, she's not getting any younger and decided to leave the last six in the pen overnight as she was physically and emotionally shattered. Gemma was just not up to continuing any more today as she still struggled with her leg healing, it ached from the metal rod and screws inserted into the bone marrow twelve weeks earlier. To make it even more problematic the heavy moonboot was soaking wet and her skin was wretchedly cold, so she turned back to their old farmhouse to warm up by the woodburning fireplace she had installed when they moved in.

The evening phone call was even shorter as she told him of her antics with the sheep and advised him she would visit tomorrow. Mason was losing the ability to hold a conversation as he forgot what was being said within minutes of hearing it. Waking to a new day dawning she was excited, so earlier than normal this morning, she leapt out of bed lively and motivated to get the drenching finished so she could rush off to see Mason, she had something to look forward to!

After parking her trusty little Honda Civic in the rest-home carpark, his room was just a short walk from where she parked and she did not have to hobble too far. She knocked on the faded blue paintwork of his door, but no reply was forthcoming, so opening the door a little, she carefully peeped around to find him sitting motionless alone on the narrow bed. Greeting him with the best smile she could produce and plonking herself down beside him, she attempted to be lively and cheerful, but the sadness at seeing him sitting alone like that was painfully gut wrenching. She stretched her arms around his neck and kissed him gently on the lips.

"Hi darling, are you liking it here, is everything okay?"

"Yeah, someone brings me a drink without me asking, the washing is taken and brought back folded and the meals are always the same time every day. Better than I got at home," he murmured with an emotionless face. He sounded like he was repeating what he had been told. Hurt feelings stung her like cold hail stones pelting at her skin. But he was going through a big change, probably not meaning to hurt her and she's accepting that he might be abrupt while letting off steam.

Looking into his eyes she explained, "Well, here they have a chef to cook for you, laundry staff and cleaning staff, everything's not done by just one person, like it was at home." She politely explained with a smile and he did not reply. Perhaps, he's putting on a brave face so she won't worry about him.

"Are you happy here then, because if you're not, we can find another place for you to go to?" she tried to reassure him that everything would be okay, he should know that she wouldn't let him be anywhere he was unhappy.

"It's okay, I'm really happy here," he declared. They decide to have a walk around while he pointed out the room where he enjoys playing housie, telling Gemma about the morning exercises that they all do, he explained that he arrived on the right day to go out on the van trip and he likes the food. She listened unwaveringly for as long as she could endure it, relieved that he had activities and could make friends, while at the same time she found it difficult to fake positivity because she was upset. She longed to keep him in his own home.

Driving home she tried to be happy for him because everything seemed organized and she should not worry, he was well looked after and safe and he had company now, more than she has at home (excluding Ombre' the dog). The car wheels crunch on their lose metal driveway as she pulled off the tar seal road and stopped to empty their yellow letterbox standing out front. A letter from the orthopaedic clinic at the hospital had arrived, advising her of the appointment on the 2nd of December to get an x-ray to check if her leg had knitted back together. Gemma's health was something she hadn't taken time to think about in the last few months, and now the most pressing business on her mind was filling in the eighteen pages to apply for a rest home subsidy from the government, a task that seemed daunting at a time when she was stressed already and the forms were all new to her. The rest home will cost $1000 every week, an impossible amount for her to find, but after making a phone call to the appropriate income organization and looking online to check if they qualified, it looked like they fitted the criteria, and the house would not need to be sold because Gemma, his wife was still living in the family home.

Only one week had passed since he went into the rest home but she has had a constant headache for the last three days, probably brought on by too much worry and stress derived from this life changing event, so she was extremely grateful to be having a few days off work, and that should allow her to cope with all the paperwork, and the myriad of phone calls to update everyone with what had happened. It would also allow her some down time to cope with the seclusion of not having her husband around.

Being alone on Saturday nights felt like the most arduous time of all, so she decided to visit Mason not only during the day, but also in the evening after he had finished tea to have a Saturday evening of snooker with him. The other residents watched on and cheered.

Inevitably, the time went fast and the residential home closed early, she had to leave alone in the dark, to watch TV at home with her devoted dog Ombre' sitting at her feet. Slipping the key in the lock and opening the door she walked into a quiet house, not having the constant banter of interruptions was noticeably foreign to what she had been used to for the last few years. She lay in their empty bed early Saturday night, when historically people spend time going out and catching up with family and friends. Visiting the rest home will become her outing now. She snuggled down in her soft cosy pj's which tightly envelope her body and listened, she could almost feel the isolation floating in the air, encompassing the house. With all the organising being completed and stressing over Mason now subsiding, things were getting sorted. She lay still and contemplated; her thoughts were a confused jumble of regret and relief. Foremost, the regret at how it had ended when he could have continued to stay home, if only his selfish sons shared his care with her or encouraged Mason to use respite to give her a little time out. Relief, knowing he was happy and that she had done the best she could for him, she loves him enough to let him go, knowing that no matter what happens to her now, he will be looked after.

Thinking '*What if something happens to me, who will care for Mason,*' was something she always worried about before he moved into the rest home, it was as if a heavy weight of responsibility for his safety, had now been lifted off her shoulders.

When she fell and shattered her leg, he was left alone while she was in hospital, his sons not bothering to check on him, and it was a dreadful time for her facing surgery and prevented from being home to care for him, thank goodness she has her daughter Bridget who although she works, made time to check on her stepfather and drive him to the hospital to see her. Panic and fear filled her at that time and she could see that without her, (if she had died in surgery) Mason was vulnerable and who would take charge of his hearing aids, transport, who would help him pay house bills, do the washing, look after animals, cooking and shopping, now it was all okay! she should rest assured she has done the right thing, he will be looked after and is safe if she cannot do it for him, and that affords her some comfort amidst the regret and bone chilling anger towards those who have not helped. When she thinks of how his two sons from his first marriage have enabled this move to happen, it was devastating and she was angry that her poor husband should have to leave his home, it was unconscionable when he has family that could have kept him home until the Dementia got worse.

When the 2nd of December came around Gemma made the slow, painful trek through the long hospital corridors on crutches, because she did not have anyone to push a wheelchair for her. It took longer to get to the waiting areas on her own, but with perseverance and prayer she made it safely on the polished floors. One good thing though, she was grateful that because it had been an accident, a taxi was provided, so that gave her Sam, someone for her to chat to there and back which she found drew her out of her worries over Mason, and she did not have to struggle to drive herself the long distance from home to hospital in pain. The x-ray was taken and the results were not good, it had already taken a terribly long seven months to recover from the surgery, but she supposed that might be because she was not able to rest it enough. The surgeon pointed out the breaks on the x-ray, although the gaps have closed a bit he didn't look happy as her leg was very much relying on the metal work to hold it all together. It was fortunate Mason was not at home while she continued to endure physical pain and will need to go back again for another check-up, it was disappointing news she hadn't expected.

Gemma was hopeful that Mason will continue to stay on the Sertraline medication the hospital has now prescribed to calm his moods, so he'll be safe to be around. Her goal is that when her leg is healed he can return home again and they can continue on together without fear of Mason ever hurting her again. She continues to hope that she can show love and care for him again. For now, she has the opportunity to get the much needed rest to allow the broken bones to mend, endeavouring to put her leg up for a little while every day.

Mason has been living in the rest home for a few weeks, while Gemma continued to pick him up and take him to his indoor bowling once a week, where he went before the move into care. Gemma was pleased to assist him in socialising with his old familiar friends and she got pleasure from seeing him strive to hold a conversation with them. After his morning at bowls he and Gemma started going to a café for lunch, it cost money but she thought it was worth it so they could have that special date together. Gemma was pleased that Mason says he loves it at Country Views Rest home, and being there at a time of year when there was a hive of activities covering all things Christmas, meant there had been a lot of festivities and outings going on to keep him occupied. Meanwhile she was struggling with aspirations of cooking Christmas dinner for them both because she understood that reminding him of their home life they shared together could be emotionally difficult for Mason, she does not want to cause him any upset or put herself in danger, so having him home was not an option.

Their first Christmas apart would be hard, traditionally it should be a happy time for them, she was determined that they would still be together on the day and she felt the pressing desire for him to spend it away from the rest home as many other residents would do. For the simple reason that he found it difficult to make decisions, she phrased it carefully, so that it was not a question.

"Darling, I have decided I would love to have Christmas lunch at one of the grassy parks alongside a beach, like we used to do when you came home from rehabilitation six years ago, just the two of us. I will tell Bridget (her daughter) and John that they can't come this year, and they'll probably go to John's parents' house." She explained it carefully to him while he lay on the rest home bed with her precariously perched on the limited amount of edge space, in his small but adequate bedroom.

"We'll have all your favourite food." She smiled.

"When's that then?" he enquired expressionless.

"Oh, it has only just turned December so it's not for a wee while yet, but I thought I'd tell you that we can have Christmas day together at the beach, so you don't need to have it here."

Looking around, "I must get you a calendar for the wall," she spoke aloud while suddenly thinking of it.

"Okay then," he agreed, his face lit up and he came to life cheerfully enthusiastic with a wide grin on his face.

The need to think ahead and be super organized, please Mason and get everything done for Christmas gave her something to look forward to, helping her get through each day. On one of their visits while chatting, she carefully reminded him that he did not have a driver's license anymore and asked him what she should do with the old camper van parked in the garage. Explaining that it was no good for it left sitting, not being used. It was his suggestion, that she should sell it. Surprised and relieved that today he was able to make that rational call. Thank goodness he wants to sell it. It had been worrying her that the warrant and registration were due, plus she would need to pay the road user charges and the costs all add up to a headache she didn't need. She just hoped that it won't need anything replacing to get a new warrant of fitness.

Chapter 2

They hug and kiss in his room for privacy before leaving, she reclines back in the car seat pausing to take a breath, it was upsetting to see her husband in a rest home, and never in a million years did she ever think that would happen! Starting the car she needed the comfort of being home with her dog Ombre'.

"Let's go for a walk to the pond." She smiled at his tail wagging happily in response and life went on.

Lowering himself slowly to the soft grass he dropped to the ground and rolled over, Gemma looked on, her face softened to a slight smile. Ombre's tummy stretched along the green grass, rolling onto his back with his legs in the air, it was quite comical and she could not help but laugh, forgetting any upset about Mason not being home. Although she longs for life to be better, Gemma was grateful to have this little furry companion.

Every little hurdle seemed like a huge mountain to climb, it was silly really, but she presumed it was the colossal life changing event of losing her husband to dementia, and not having him home anymore overwhelmed everything. Next problem, the van was so big that it was near impossible for her to drive. Gemma's arms couldn't reach the hand brake down beside the seat, without her foot lifting off the brake when she bent over to release it, making it challenging to drive all the way to the garage for a warrant.

Oh help, she screamed inside, it was so scary to sort this. The phone rang and her common sense told her to ask people for help, don't always be independent, people need people and even though she found it unthinkable to expect others to help her, people do offer so why not accept? She knew it was the safest thing to do instead of risking an accident, but while chatting on the phone she didn't have the courage to ask for help. Maybe people say kind things automatically, *'let me know if I can do anything'* without really thinking of the inconvenience it may cause them.

If it were family then yes, she would ask but she doesn't want to feel obligated to friends or neighbours. She just needed to believe that she could do this, and it would be okay, everything would get done in time and it was essential for her to be independent and brave now she was on her own. She had always managed and would continue to do so.

The following morning she cried out to the Lord for help, to do this for Mason. Reaching deeply into herself to find enough courage to drive the camper van slowly and carefully down to be evaluated for a warrant of fitness, hopeful that she would not need the handbrake. She carefully pulled into the vehicle station, stopped to breath a sigh of relief, all went well and she didn't see another car on the road, as she cut through a side street. Sitting on the hard wooden bench off to the side of the garage she nervously watched with bated breath to see how much money she might have to find if it needed a repair, quietly in a whisper she prays, *please let it pass.* It seemed to take forever, but in actual fact it was only about 20 minutes.

As she sat looking worried, the mechanic with greasy hands and overalls walked across the room and clicked a form, without looking up he shoved it at her saying, it passed! A massive sense of relief washed over her, simultaneously wanting to jump and cheer, but of course she did not as it would have looked peculiar. She took a breath in and out, realizing just how stressed she must have been.

Days turned into a new week while she attempted to plough her way through all the things that needed to be done around the place. Working part-time and having the added rest home visits to do as well, made for not enough hours in the day. The nights were tortuously long, and she appreciated her adorable dog Ombre', not only for company but also security at night now unexpectedly living on her own. The following day she busied herself with the animals, got some rest for her leg and organized a builder to replace some rotten timber on the carport. An unfortunate necessity as it threatened to fall down with a good gust of wind this coming winter. Another problem sorted, and the sigh of relief escaped from her lungs when she saw it finished. Suddenly after all the hard work of tidying away the rubbish created from the completed carport, contractors had gone and things were getting organized. She decided to drive down to the shopping mall and get a few groceries, treating herself to a nice coffee at the cafe'.

Finally taking time to sit, the pungent aroma of coffee filled the atmosphere as she watched all the people going about their business, she was alone, and suddenly felt the urge to walk away. Deep in thought she headed back to the comfort of her little car, alone and not knowing where else to go. She wouldn't have even noticed if someone was talking to her. Totally swamped and overwhelmed by the number of people she had around her, loads of busy people, happy excitement and most had a loved one with them, lots of chatter and the clanging of metal trolley wheels against cold tiled floor filled the air, a strange environment with so many varied reasons for people to be there.

An extreme embodiment of loss was felt burning within her, she did not know when life would be normal for her again, remembering when she took Mason home from the rehabilitation unit after his massive stroke five years ago, all she saw was a lost soul, the man she loved. Caring so much for him consumed five years of her life and isolated her, she had never considered the impact it would have on her future. An act of unconditional love and compassion had left a huge hole, now her husband was settled and safe again, and she was left on her own, devoid of friends and much of her social network was gone.

Pulling into the driveway she regained a feeling of security and welcomed the familiar crunching of the gravel under the car wheels. A smile slowly crept across her face as she spied Ombre' peering out from beneath the shrubs, obviously pleased to see her, with his entire body wagging just from the strength of his tail, he was her most important little friend. Gemma's leg constantly ached and she was frustrated with it, longing to be well and pain free again.

Later on in the afternoon she had another hospital appointment, and was well enough to drive herself now, so making the solitary drive back to see the surgeon, he pushed and prodded.

Peering over his glasses he looked at her as he explained, "All the metalwork needs to come out, because some of it is prominent (only just under the skin!) causing pain." He had a concerned look and probably thought she would be upset at the thought of needing more surgery, but actually she was relieved there was a problem they could fix.

Getting rid of all the foreign bodies in her leg was what she preferred, it can't be good to have that stuff inside her unless absolutely necessary for life. They settled on April for day-surgery as then she'll have the Easter break, plus the two week school holidays to recuperate after surgery. That was still over four months away to allow more time for the bones to become stronger. He explained that it would take about three weeks to recover after the metal rod and screws were pulled out from inside the bones, and that it may bleed quite a bit because bones produce blood. Fortunately, this time she would be able to weight bear on it because the breaks will have knitted together, and she'll only have to be careful to allow the bone marrow to fill the holes. Gemma will need to continue using crutches to take some weight off. She continues to dream of having Mason return home again when she is well, even if only for visits, at the present time she was fearful of him hurting her and she will proceed with caution.

Now only two weeks before Christmas and during one of their weekly lunch dates she again reminded Mason about their planned Christmas lunch together, and with a huge smile explained how much she was really looking forward to it. They carefully walked towards the rest home office to inform the young secretary that they'll be together on Christmas day, so the rest home would not need to cater for him. The secretary made a note to inform the kitchen staff.

Gemma's daughter Bridget arranged for her and John to be at their cousin's house that day and they were looking forward to that. Consequently Christmas would be extraordinarily special for Mason and Gemma, just the two of them together again, they were both really excited. The shops had started to buzz with Christmas shoppers and they were getting busy, so Gemma decided to buy some nice, sliced ham and pop it into the freezer to avoid extra costs and long queues later on. She also bought ingredients for their usual Christmas cake that she planned to bake on the weekend. Mason preferred homemade because it didn't have too much fruit and she added sweet red sherry which made it stand out from the usual shop bought variety.

Only a week to Christmas so she phoned her elderly dad in Christchurch. He knew what it was like to lose someone, feeling lonely following the death of his wife (Gemma's step-mum), they had a good chat. She sat alone talking on the landline phone to him for ages just as he sat alone in his small unit in the South Island of NZ, he described to her how lonely he felt being without Mae. Gemma understood and cherished knowing that someone else understood what it was like.

Just four days until Christmas and she was satisfied to have a lovely lay in bed morning, she felt calmer and more accepting of how things were now, with excitement mounting she had spent time making lots of Mason's favourite baked goodies. She visited him yesterday and they went for a walk to the shops with the help of only one crutch, Gemma helped him to buy her a pair of earrings for Christmas. Showing him how to take it to be gift wrapped for free, he was nervous and hesitant but the area was quiet without many shoppers. She wanted him to be able to do little things for himself. Perhaps she was banging her head against a brick wall, but she never gave up trying to give Mason a decent quality of life, just because he had dementia she won't stop trying to retain what abilities he still had left and refused to treat him like a complete intellectual cripple.

Before leaving to go home Gemma cheerfully reminded him that she would pick him up on Christmas morning, and he replied that he might be going out with the boys.

"Oh, have they asked you to?" she queried full of surprise, wondering why they would do that. Over the years, they've never had him on Christmas Day, and surely they knew Gemma would want to be with her husband at Christmas!

"No! But they might, came the response."

"Well probably not, because today is Monday, and you haven't heard from them. Christmas is only a few days away on Thursday. So I'll pick you up Christmas morning okay." She suspects that he's wondering why he hadn't heard from the boys. She looked back through the sign-in book on the office desk and no one else had visited him for a couple of weeks. That is incredibly sad!

Time to cut the Macrocarpa tree branches down, they were self-sown in an annoying place and now reached about three metres high. Gemma found it was quiet hard with a small pruning saw but she was too scared to use the chain saw in the shed. Not having a man about the house brought many difficulties, where are they when you need one? Refusing to be beaten, she got out the gorse killer and proceeded to spray it, that should sort it out for good and she won't have to deal with any grow back. Circumstances have changed, and she now aimed to cut down on as much maintenance as possible since finding herself the only one managing four hectares.

A little later the phone rang, it was Country Views Rest Home, an unexpected call and she panicked, her heart started beating so hard that she could hear the blood pounding in her ears as she asked if Mason was alright. Sue, the manager was quick to reassure her he was fine, but explained that she had been talking with Mason, he was agitated and there was an incident in the dining room when he pulled a milk jug out of an old ladies hand and spilt milk on her. She went on to explain that she could not talk with Mason, and that he became angry when staff stepped in to move him to another table. Gemma listened as Sue continued on to elucidate.. that his eyes were angry, *'Like flames coming out of them,'* she was careful not to upset him any further as she encouraged Mason to go with her to the office, listened and tried to sort him out. Sue said she found him to be paranoid!

Feeling defensive for her husband, Gemma explained that he was probably upset about not seeing his sons lately and with Christmas coming he was feeling a bit lonely, she assured Sue that they would be having Christmas Day together. Sue continued to inform her that if Mason became a problem for the other residents or staff, he would have to be heavily medicated or moved into the secure unit that was also on the premises. Gemma's heart started to beat faster as she felt really concerned about that being a negative move for Mason, and attempted to assure Sue that wouldn't be necessary as he was still settling in and she would have a word with him.

After hanging up from the manager, with adrenalin gushing forcefully through her blood stream, she straight away phoned up mental health and spoke with the person who had replaced Doctor Martin that they normally dealt with. Explaining that she believed Mason should have counselling available to him so he could talk to someone about his concerns and muddled thoughts. Not having met this new registrar before, it was difficult to put her concerns across with no face to picture in her mind, but he explained to her he had seen Mason once so did know him, (it was so annoying that they kept changing). He said he didn't want to look at the medication, or counselling as the rest home should make themselves available for Mason to talk to.

How rude, that's unhelpful and passing the buck! When a concerned spouse took time to ask for some help it should be taken seriously, and to expect busy rest home staff to spend time away from their chores to listen when they don't have counselling training was not really what Gemma expected him to say. Just another example of people that had let Mason down along the way.

She hung-up and tried to put it out of her mind, focusing on spending a happy time with Mason Christmas Day.

Feeling relaxed the next morning she leapt out of bed with enthusiasm, it was Christmas Eve! and the weather was beautiful outside. She reminisces over all the activities people will be planning and reflected on all the lovely times she had in the past when her two children were little, Christmas was a lovely time when people got along with each other and were happy, even if they weren't religious.

Gemma needed to take her Labrador Ombre' to get more arthritis pills before the holidays, she was concerned about how stiff he was walking, it was obvious that his hips were not moving as well as they used to. While at the vets getting his annual vaccination and check-up, the veterinarian reminded her that Ombre' was 13 years old now with a warning tone in his voice but reassuring her that his heart and lungs were all good. Leaving the clinic she drove two streets down the road to her daughter's house. Parking under the carport out of the sun so Ombre' could sleep after his ordeal. Bridget made a cup of tea and Gemma set about telling her how they were looking forward to the picnic tomorrow (Christmas day). She started to describe the food she had planned, the two of them chatted a while before she made her way home feeling relaxed and content with the world, remembering to stop at the garage to fill up her container with petrol in the hope of mowing just the small, level lawn around the house.

The grass was growing flat out now, and alas the lawn mowing guy phoned to say he would be too busy to do it before Christmas. Since breaking her leg it was difficult to use the mower and a little risky with the added metal work, she didn't want to risk doing any damage. However the grass continued to grow very quickly with the nice warm weather. Gemma had the idea of putting the sheep up the fenced part of the driveway yesterday. But even the sheep had not managed to eat all of the grass verge and between the loose metal, perhaps it was too different from consuming a paddock, after all they don't nibble on every morsel like goats do.

Arriving home she routinely checked the answer phone and there was a message from Mason, stating not to collect him tomorrow as his eldest son Dwayne had phoned and wanted him to spend Christmas day with them! Annoyed, would be an understatement because she knew that Dwayne was probably at the end of the phone telling Mason what to say. Mason had never been capable of phoning from the rest home, he had to dial out first and had trouble following simple instructions like that, even when she wrote them down for him.

To prevent him struggling to comprehend what to do, it had been easier for her to always phone Mason. His face lit up, thrilled when the staff arrived with the cordless phone for him, he loved getting phone calls. Gemma half expected Dwayne would do something despicable and manipulative (emotional abuse). Mason's young grandson Adam had never been taken to visit his grandad at the rest home. Dwayne always withheld him so he could manipulate his dad.

Yes! she felt angry not only with Dwayne, but also disappointed with Mason for not being strong enough to say no to Dwayne.

Quickly phoning the rest home was emotionally tough to control her temper of how unjust it all was, she waited for the staff to take the cordless phone to Mason, while she pondered over what to say.

"What!" she exclaimed, "It's Christmas day tomorrow, we have planned to be together and go on a picnic, it's been organised for ages." Trying not to shriek at him because she knew he was being pressured.

Mason knew her, he expected her to be loving and understanding about him seeing his family, she has always encouraged his continued contact with his sons from his first marriage.

"Why don't you see them in the evening when we get back from our Christmas lunch?" she suggested. "Then they can have lunch with their son Adam and you could see them all later in the day for tea."

"No, Dwayne wants me to go in the morning, I better had!" he sounded oddly fearful and unable to do anything about it.

The nervous tension in Mason's voice was palpable, how terrible that it was caused by his own son. Disappointment, hopelessness and sadness, as she knew that iniquitous son had not been to see his dad for three weeks. Gemma knew that Dwayne's behaviour was conditioning his father into missing them, it was especially despicable behaviour withholding his grandson who Mason had been asking after, what an evil, conniving son of a b...

Any caring human being would have invited her as well, or at least told her before Christmas Eve. Speaking slowly and carefully so as not to put pressure or stress onto Mason she knew she had to hang up the phone before she fell apart, (it's not his fault) and she wished him a nice Christmas day, promising to phone Country Views to see if she could visit him when he returned there later in the evening.

Gemma hung up with a heavy heart, from deepest longing and the weight of painful disappointment tears of despair poured out as she walked from the kitchen to sit on the bed, the tears began to flow over her cheeks like a river trickling over smooth rocks unchecked and directionless, she was uncaring and unable to stop them.

Chapter 3

Gemma's heart was broken and her rising chest hurt with every fall as the throbbing blood pounded in her ears. It was so unfair, she was a good person, had always been there for her husband, so why couldn't he stand up and be there for her? Her heart knew the answer, just as Mason knew that she had selfless love for him, he found it easier to let her down, trusting that in any crisis he knew she would always be there for him, he knew she would forgive and love him. He had lost trust in his boys a long time ago! Neither of them had bothered with him before the rest home, so he did what they asked in the hope that he would get to see them and his grandson again.

Sitting holding her head in her hands, gripping a soaking wet handkerchief, her long brunette hair hung lifeless, Ombre' rested his head across her knees, she loved him, he was always there and acted so human-like in his capacity to care for Gemma, he seemed to understand when she hurt. All she wanted now was sleep, Gemma was emotionally cried out, and after the huge disappointment lying back on the bed a dismal tiredness enveloped her as she reached out for comfort, patting his thick fur, Ombre' lay on a sheepskin rug beside the bed. Fatigue took hold.

Gemma recalls how every Christmas for the last fifteen years Dwayne, the son with the muscle building fixation and very little hair in his forties, had always refused to visit and join Gemma and Mason along with his brother Peter who was of average build and masses of fair hair and four lively children for a nice Christmas lunch. Gemma always went to a lot of trouble for Mason to see and enjoy Christmas day with his two sons, partners and especially the grandchildren on such a notable family day. But Dwayne always maintained he was too busy with his partner and then later on his newborn son was the excuse. Although Gemma and Mason are a married couple she will spend Christmas day at home alone for the first time. During the marriage, her life had been rife with cruel and uncalled for injustices as a result of Mason's son Dwayne, it had not affected her as much as it did his father. Gemma felt it had created too much pressure and stress for Mason before he had his life changing brain aneurysm.

Full of despair and unbearable fatigue, she could not sleep but only rested, eventually her face dried and she felt a little restored. She anxiously phoned Bridget praying with fingers crossed that she was home to confide in.

When she heard of Dwayne's horrible controlling behaviour Bridget asked, "Come and join John and me."

Gemma reluctantly declined. "No thanks, I know you have plans to be with your cousins, and it was me that said I wanted to spend the day with Mason, so it's my own fault really." Assuring her that she would be fine but that she would not be answering her phone, as she didn't feel like being available.

After hanging up she then phoned the rest home and left her mobile number in case they needed to get hold of her, requesting that they let her know when Mason arrived back so she could visit later. The receptionist quietly informed her that Dwayne specifically stated that he would not be taking Mason back to the rest home until after visiting hours had finished and the rest home was closed. She would not be able to see her husband on Christmas day.

Lethargically replacing the phone she drifted outside frustrated and upset, she was determined to mow the lawn, her mind was a blur, at least that would look nice on Christmas day to keep her spirits up. She decided that staying busy was the way to go, her entire body was tired and sad, and knowing that the lawn guy was rushed off his feet at this time of the year she decided it would help him out. She considered booking a flight away somewhere for next week, she felt lonely. Then, later on pondering over it as she stood admiring the tidy lawn, she realized that it was impractical as she just didn't have the money to waste.

The Christmas Eve Church service was a ritual of hers, it was always so lovely and sealed the true meaning of Christmas before everyone spent time with family the following day. She had participated in that outing for many years on her own while Mason enjoyed being settled in front of the television, he was not so keen on going out at night once he had settled.

So she planned to have just a steak pie and mixed vegetables from the freezer, thinking that it would be nice and quick before setting off at 9.15 pm. She had something to do, and even though she had a purpose she still felt the chill of isolation. Driving down the road to the church, her body was fraught with tension like a tight rope in a circus show, emotions threatening to overcome her during the quiet time driving, she was feeling lost and upset about tomorrow, forcing herself to think of Christmas as an end to the year and attempting to be optimistic for a new improved life for everyone next year. Alone and feeling betrayed by her partner, the one she had fought health professionals and battled to keep him at home for five long years after his brain surgery and they had advised her not to take him home, praying and providing for him she now felt dejected! Unable to prevent her doubts, she asked herself were all those years worthless wasted years. She sat in a pew, hoping that the happy singing of praises with a dutiful smile would lighten her load while nursing a broken heart, one hour later she did not feel any better and so didn't linger to chat with the friendly caring parishioners. She made a hasty retreat into the safety of her trusty little car, turned over the engine and quickly escaped, the tears threatening to flow yet again. She could not wait to get onto the road as her throat tightened and it came about, as she entered onto the main road home she fell apart, cried out loud, distraught, her chest heaving with sobs so much so she had to pull over to the edge of the deserted rural road.

Rejection and disbelief flooded her heart and soul, she was so disappointed that they notified her on Christmas Eve, it was too late to make any plans now, she was alone! She tried to feel the joy of Christmas but the season was lost on her, Gemma's mind perplexed and full of questions after standing by Mason through all his strange moods, she began to question if he had ever loved her which of course he had. She reminisced over how kind and loving he was before his fall from the roof, before he got sick and was unable to think straight. Whirling in a soup of emotions and questions she cried with regret and confusion, maybe he saw too much of his family and ex-wife when they never included her at family celebrations, she was compassionate and never complained, now she questions if she should have.

Oh, what does she need to do next, when should she visit him again, how can she face him anymore now he had let her down so miserably. Feeling lonely and knowing that it was so unjust as she was always there for him. Why wasn't he here for her?

Arriving home distraught, she briskly wiped away the tears before opening the door to her precious devoted little friend Ombre', trying not to let him perceive any distress, she had concern and love for him, he looked old with white whiskers under his chin and deserved to retire from looking after her. They enjoyed a hug before he ran off to collect her old slippers from the bedroom for her, what a clever little dog. Gemma was glad that she had given him his arthritis pill with his tea before going to church and now he was more energetic. Bless him, and she wrapped her arms around his tummy and confided in him.

"It is just you and me against the world, isn't it darling. Thank you for staying here with me for so long Ombre' please live longer as I really need you," she pleaded.

The day faded into the darkness, gone and she never wanted another like it, after spending a lot of time crying and trying to avoid thinking of the loneliness about to be hers tomorrow, Christmas Day.

Grudgingly waking up Christmas morning after extremely little sleep, there was no rush to get up at all, the first Christmas that she didn't have to cook. Last night before going to bed she removed two small bread rolls and a few slices of ham to thaw out for a solitary lunch today.

She did not remove any of the salami or the pastrami slices she had bought especially for Mason to enjoy on their anticipated picnic, secretly hoping inside her heart and soul that he would come to his senses and tell Dwayne that he could see him later after their picnic together, but love was optimistic and blind, and deep down she knew she was not wanting to face reality. Mason had always been unable to say No! to his first born spoiled and controlling son.

Gemma was tempted and longed to phone her husband to wish him a Merry Christmas, although she was upset about them not being together she couldn't blame him, he was a confused man with dementia and he was being controlled, but she was upset and couldn't wish him a nice day without her getting upset. Gemma resisted putting any pressure on her husband. Going about routinely having a shower, deep in thought about what family reunion they would be planning today. She reached for her faded blue jeans and sneakers, paired with a printed shirt. Disappointment consumed her along with other negative emotions unable to avoid. Gemma wondered what kind of person Dwayne's partner Victoria must be, that she would take Mason away today of all days, and not invite his wife, they had always been welcomed into her and Mason's home.

Concerned for Mason's welfare, she hoped he was happy and it was a little reassuring to know that at least she could trust the residential home, they would phone her if Mason got sick or did not return in the evening. She had their number on her mobile, taking it with her to stay in the lounge with the curtains closed so no one would know she was home alone, determined that she did not want anyone there while she felt so despondent, but also reminding herself what the doctor explained to her, that Mason was unable to act reasonably, and was incapable of putting logic into action, he had brain damage and she knew it was not her husbands fault.

It was Dwayne scheming again; Mason was in a confused state of mind. She ambled around the large farmhouse they had bought and fixed up together oblivious of what she was really doing, the memories were everywhere and she had nothing planned to do, she was not going to be with Mason! and her stomach felt quite sickly. Gemma had not been up long, she kept checking the clock and it seemed like ages but really wasn't. After checking the animals and aimlessly wandering around she decided to lay on her bed and try to read a book, she couldn't focus and when her pillow was well and truly soaked with tears, and she had been reading the same page many times over she decided it was lunch time.

She rose from the bed to make a cup of tea, opening the fridge door and came face to face with the little individual sponge and boysenberry trifles sitting in the fridge that were lovingly made for their day together, sadness gripped tightly around her heart with all her love for Mason being held so painfully inside, unable to be relieved by his embrace, she craved his comforting arms around her, not food!

People everywhere were enjoying lunches together, she was alone and forgotten with her tear stained pillow, seemingly only important to her daughter. Her entire body underwent something she had never encountered before, through all the really tough times it had never felt as hopeless as this betrayal now eating away at her, maybe it had been the build up of Mason having to go into a rest home, it had been a tuff few months of grieving over his departure.

Facing todays disappointment was the final straw, it was the total disbelief and let down that this happened after high expectations, planning and all her effort, she had been so excited and enjoyed cooking to make today special for them both. Gemma found that to not be with the person you love at Christmas time was terrible, and she will remember it when she hears of others who go through similar circumstances for one reason or another. Christmas lunch together was tremendously important to Gemma, it being compensation for all the days of missing him while he had been in the rest home, plus it was their first Christmas apart in fifteen years!

What the family was doing, separating them would remain etched in her memories and in her broken heart with the devastating disappointment felt so profoundly. Gemma hoped that the grief would serve to teach her empathy for others who suffer lost love and betrayal especially recognising elder abuse, with Dwayne forcing Mason to make a choice between family members when he was mentally incapable of making decisions with a diagnosis of dementia. No matter where Mason's mind takes him, she would always love him forever and ever. Gemma was grateful for prayer and the love of her dog to get her through Christmas day without her special person.

Sitting quietly she thought of how warm Bridget was inviting her to join them for lunch, what a loving gesture that was. With it being unplanned she hadn't wanted to intrude on her daughter and John when they catch up with cousins, she would also feel pathetic and in the way. With a shattered heart it was difficult to remember the people that care for you, a fact that was sometimes hidden by deep despair. Life was so unpredictable and not only did Masons life change five years ago with his brain bleed but Gemma's did as well.

It was challenging for her to focus on the joy that Christmas time usually brings, her loneliness somehow accentuated today. No words could express how she felt as she sat and reminisced over their past Christmas's together and the happy times spent, it was impossible to do in an attempt to feel happy while sitting with the curtains closed, the murky chasm threatened to engulf her. Gemma was lost in her own thoughts and beholden that the year would ultimately finish, while in her present emotional state she found it impossible to find any good in the knowledge that another year would soon commence, she did still hold out hope for the unknown future.

Gemma was ambushed by anxiety and the sound of pain escaped from within her as her whole body cried out for answers, asking why? Determined to shake herself up and be positive she decided to treat it as a learning experience, some day in the future she would be non-judgemental and have empathy for someone going through extreme situations, accepting her anguish, trusting that another day was just around the corner and forcing herself to believe that when life was at its worst, that was when it started to get better, that would be the glimmer of hope and advice she would offer someone else.

She felt another kind of pain, hunger. She had not eaten since breakfast and her stomach prevented her from indulging in self pity any longer, it drove her toward the kitchen to prepare a nice ham salad for one, with a double serving of ham. Gemma carried it into the sitting room to eat in front of some boring TV programme. Hanging out for the phone to ring, it didn't. She mainly craved company, and she wouldn't answer it if it did ring. Gemma was undecided when she would be strong enough to visit Mason again feeling very alone and hurt that her husband would allow this to happen. She again reminded herself to be compassionate, he didn't have the depth of understanding to even think outside his tiny world and could not comprehend what she was going through, she understood that, but she had trouble accepting it.

The rest home had advised her that Dwayne wrote in the visitor's book that Mason would not be home until very late, and when they requested a return time so his wife could visit him Dwayne refused to write one, a deliberate act to prevent her from seeing her husband. So she tried to convince herself to forget about driving all that way, even though her heart wanted her to, she told herself that driving on Christmas Day was too dangerous and not worth worrying about for one day, the compensation would be having a nice cold Sauvignon Blanc in front of a movie.

Monotonously watching hopelessly boring television, sipping on a glass of wine with her devoted little friend who was attached to her like a shadow, following around unable to be separated from her.

She praised the Lord for her dog, she was very grateful as she would not want to be without him. She wondered how she would have coped emotionally if completely on her own. No one could ever really comprehend the depth of emptiness and the existence of such horrible people unless having experienced it, the soul destroying torment was so intense that it broke many barriers of suffering within her.

Chapter 4

Quick to phone him the next morning after a good sleep, she leapt out of bed, no longer able to prevent or stop the desire to speak to her husband, wanting to check if he was okey after being with Dwayne for Christmas Day and she was afraid in case they had tormented him by saying she didn't want him.

When Mason spoke to her the main thing on his mind was they had insisted over and over, all of the family were adamant that he should not be living in a rest home, he declared loudly down the receiver that there was nothing wrong with him. Maybe this was their way of putting pressure on her to take him home. The doctors asked them to offer to help care for him, in the hope that they could keep him at home when she broke her leg, they refused!

If they were really outraged enough and truly believed what they were brainwashing Mason with, then why wouldn't they offer to have him move in with them or at least have him to stay sometimes, the opportunity was always available but no one wanted him.

Mason was in a rest home because they refused to offer any help while Gemma was healing and now their excuse was, there was nothing wrong with him, against all medical advise they knew best.

That was the plan, why they took him home Christmas day was giving Dwayne's family the chance to drive a wedge between her and her husband. As much as she wanted Mason home, Gemma's orthopaedic surgeon had warned her that she could not risk a fall before her leg surgery and she had finally put her own health first, choosing not to take any more risks and to protect herself from amputation. Mason had proven to be untrustworthy; he couldn't be relied upon not to lash out and the frontal lobe brain damage was proof that he could not control his temper. Gemma had opted to protect herself; he was just not worth losing her leg for.

Dwayne and his mother (Masons ex-wife) continued to manipulate Mason so he would blame Gemma for the situation he found himself in, influencing him so it placed strain on their relationship and making Mason feel uneasy with his life, even though he was happy at Country Views rest home.

Well, it showed Gemma how horrid, money seeking the whole family appeared to be, she was hurting and could not help feeling that if Mason wasn't allowed to be with her on Christmas day then why should she take any risks with her health, they obviously did not care for her wellbeing. Once again Gemma patiently explained to Mason that the doctors recommended he go into long term residential care because he has Dementia and she also explained to him that she didn't have the medical ability to put him into care as his son were telling him, he chose to go into the rest home himself when he discussed it with his doctors.

The day after Boxing Day and Gemma woke with renewed determination that life was going to be better for everyone from now on. Determined to work on improving her leg strength she phoned Bridget and asked if she wanted to go to the gym with her so she could use the exercise machines.

"Sounds like a good idea mum, I think I better had after all the Christmas food I've eaten." She laughed.

So swinging past her house Gemma picked her up, finding her daughter dressed in striped tights and tee shirt looking like a fitness fanatic, they laughed as they looked and felt the part while they checked out some new machines, finding one where Gemma could sit and not weight bear, but still work on strengthening the leg muscles, it was a lot of fun as they discovered how the equipment all worked. A great adventure and a distraction from life in general.

Pushing herself to the maximum while trying not to think of chocolate she found that having Bridget there with her to compete against, made it easier to work harder. Gemma was actually building up a sweat, and focusing on looking fantastically fit after the leg surgery this coming year was helping to spur her on.

She now had a goal, was fearless, couldn't be hurt or controlled, she was in charge of her future and the challenge was to look her best.

The broken leg had been a physical struggle to cope with during the past year as it was an extra hurdle that she didn't need and not being able to go for walks often left her without a way of coping with stress. Before going home she called in to sit with Mason, she felt the nagging desire to again clarify to him what happened, reinforcing she loved him. Sitting down beside him on the bed she quietly explained.

"I told Bridget we were going to be together Christmas day, why didn't you tell Dwayne you were having that day with me? I was alone," she explained.

"Oh," he replied, straight faced and looking confused.

It was obviously too much for him to understand, her heart melted and she wrapped my arms around his slim body and held him for ages, it was not fair to blame him, he didn't understand the silly games they were playing and couldn't speak for himself. Her heart softened towards him accepting that it was a lost cause.

New Year's Day approached and nothing out of the ordinary was planned as she was feeling very tired, she couldn't comprehend if her weariness would ever go away and was certain that it was a good thing she had animals and farm chores to get her up every morning and they made the time pass, before putting on the electric jug for a cuppa and questioning what she had available for lunch, 12.45 pm and the phone rang.

Reaching for the cordless in the kitchen, "Hello."

"Hi, its Country Views rest home here, is Mason with you?"

"No! What's wrong?" letting out a shrill, the sound of panic involuntarily rising in her voice.

Something is! if they don't know where he is. Here we go again, more for her to sort out and recollections of that traumatic night when he was in someone else's care at the rehabilitation unit and went missing in the perilous cold of the middle of winter, it all came flooding back with a rush of blood through her veins.

"Well, he wasn't here for lunch and we don't know where he is," the nurse went on to say.

"Phone his son Peter, he's within walking distance of the rest home. Has anyone signed anything in the book?"

"He has written that he's walking to Peter's and that he left at 8.45am, but we phoned there and his son Peter said that he hasn't seen him today, and we also phoned Dwayne and he said he didn't have him either."

"I'll drive around and have a look for him." Now feeling frantic and wondering what had happened.

Gemma had no luck finding Mason, so then continued to drive to the rest home and asked them to keep her informed before heading off home again, she reassured the home that the boys are probably *lying* and that they must have him. Gemma knew very well that they think they are a law unto themselves and she was always sceptical of anything they said, especially from Dwayne and his mother.

It was now 2.30pm and the registered nurse phoned Gemma again to explain that she was knocking off work soon and Mason was still not back, in a questioning way like, what do I do.

"If he wrote in the sign-out book that he was going to Peters but they say he never arrived there then there is an issue, you need to report him as a missing person to the police," she explained calmly but sternly.

"Okay, I'll phone the manager." She hung up.

Hanging up the phone Gemma wandered around helplessly wondering what to do. It wasn't until 6.00pm that the phone rang, it was the police.

“We have tracked down your husband, his son Dwayne has admitted that he and his mother have Mason, and they have travelled out of Auckland today to reminisce and visit the places that he used to go to when they were married thirty years ago, they have been told to bring him back and should be at Country Views rest home about 10.00pm.”

Gemma was shocked, despair weighed heavily on her heart at the thought of her poor husband being taken in an attempt to brain wash him with past experiences that in reality would just confuse him, they knew it was wrong or they wouldn’t have tried to cover up the truth. They took him, it was just like kidnapping because he was taken without the ability to understand what they were up to.

Simultaneously feeling despondent but also with tears of relief that he was safe flowed down her blotched checks, her hands began to tremble as her body lost the will to fight on, this was not living. Continually fighting for Mason to be safe and to have a peaceful existence without confusion, she wanted him to be allowed to be happy without his ex-wife and son pulling and pushing him this way and that.

It was tortuous to feel such passion for someone just to be unable to express it in any constructive way or any verbal exchange that Mason could comprehend, with his confused state of mind and an obvious lack of emotional understanding. Yes, they were just ordinary people, but harbouring extraordinary situations and outside interference that singled them out from other couples, Mason’s life was being manipulated out of his control and that was affecting any chance of his wife seeing him today, when she needed to cuddle him and check for herself that he was okay after being involuntarily confronted with his past thirty years, and a dreadful marriage he had walked away from.

Gemma searched out some peace after all the worry of today, quietly slumped on the park bench overlooking the paddocks, she loved this place they had made together, looking out as dusk carried the last of the sun down behind the hills and the cloudy sky began to take hold, far-reaching paddocks with the sound of Pukeko rustling their way through the Toi Toi rushes and the complete solitude alone with no people, no problems or pain, nothing to disturb or aggravate her desire for peace. In the knowledge he was safe for now, she watched the starting of rain dimpling on the top of the drinking trough which sat sunken in an empty paddock, Ombre' lay silently at her feet.

"Lucky that you're here with me eh Ombre," she says while bending to hug him, a whispered sigh of relief escaped her lungs that Mason was safe once again.

Another day in January and another challenge to be conquered all alone, she turned to the internet to find somewhere she could sell their camper van as Mason suggested, now that he was no longer allowed to drive. Scrolling down, she discovered that there was a car yard that handled all the prospective purchasers and took them for rides which would save her the trouble of dealing with men that just wanted to take advantage of a women's inability to drive the large vehicle. First of all, she had to get it to the sales yard for that to happen!

Gemma agonized for a few days over how she could drive it to the yard, determined to stay independent and capable but knowing full well that it was not safe for her to drive, at the same time not wanting to impose on neighbours, not only a pride thing but also safety because she was a woman living on her own. She had never asked for help before as she always had a husband around so she prayed for a solution, unsure how to deal with this dilemma Gemma decided to sleep on it and face another day tomorrow. Upon stirring the next morning the decision had been made, to be brave and not to risk having an accident by driving something that was way too big for her to manage, that would be a foolish thing to do.

So, she was determined to ask the lawn mowing guy due this week, that way because he was practically a stranger and she didn't have to see him very often it would not be as awkward. When he came to the door to collect his money she offered him a cup of tea, (which she never does), he accepted and sat down at the end of the kitchen with her opposite, poor man probably thought he was getting the sack. After explaining to him the situation his face looked relieved that was all it was about and said he would be happy to drive the van for her. She agreed to follow on behind in her car to bring him back to collect his truck which he would leave in her driveway. She concluded there were nice people around, she just had to learn to ask.

While going about cleaning out the glove box of the van and preparing it for sale she removed the car seat covers to wash them, she spotted an envelope concealed on the driver's seat under the cover. Opening it she found a letter signed from Rose, disbelief and disgust pervade her body as she began to read, horrified as to what may have been going on.

Steadfastly doing everything she could to care for and help Mason to recover from his massive stroke, his ex wife had been writing sweet love letters and reminiscing of their life together, fantasizing about how happy they were together and wanting him back. Gemma's hand tightly gripped the letter, stunned and frozen to the spot she stared down at it, all the time knowing that the terrible thing was she will never be able to ask Mason about it. There was no date so how long ago had she given Mason this letter? remembering that it was hidden. It looked old so possibly even while they were newlyweds. What a stupid woman, not moving on with her life after years of divorce, either living in hope of getting back together or just wanting to destroy his marriage out of jealousy. Tearing it in half she added it to the rest of the rubbish where it belonged.

Having her husband in a rest home and taking him for doctors' appointments, visits to the hospital, she was also finding it difficult to be allowed to make the necessary decisions with him and getting access to manage the household upkeep, things like annual adjusting of the joint mortgage when it needed to be done, so she decided she needed to see a solicitor. After speaking to Ms Simmons on the phone she arranged an appointment time.

She sat behind a chunky old desk, had short curly hair and very red lipstick, she looked to be in her fifties and appeared to understand the issues, she was efficient and explained that after Gemma's call her secretary had managed to access Masons medical report from the doctors, thanks goodness as here sat the evidence, wording from specialists that Mason should not make decisions for himself because he lacked the ability to understand consequences of his actions. Exuberant with relief Gemma's energy level went through the roof, unable to think or breathe because something was going right for a change she looked forward to seeing the medical documentation.

Gemma's intention was to apply to the court to be property manager/welfare officer to continue to do what she was already doing but to make access easier. All morning her mind was a blur with apprehension of the unknown. Finally, something positive was happening and it gave clarity that she would get them back on track, stopping the outside interference and stress Dwayne had been creating lately with his comments to Mason on how to manage their finances. Gemma wondered what happens, would she be able to be legally recognised to make decisions on Mason's behalf, does she qualify in everyone's eyes to be allowed to continue to manage their financial affairs at home and continue to talk alongside Mason with his doctors? Settling into the office chair, without speaking the medical report sat on the solicitor's desk, Ms Simmins handed it to her and watched as she began to scan it anxiously, could the doctor possibly have ascertained what it was like to live with Mason and will the report have the necessary impact to help her to protect and continue to provide for Mason?

Gemma began to explain how Mason behaved differently after falling off the roof in 1999, there was a look of concern from Ms. Simmins as she paused heavy in thought before adding that she felt we needed to get further medical records, not just with the hospital diagnosis of Dementia and from the rest home doctors that treat him now. She was questioning if some information had been withheld because of confidentiality and decided to make further inquiries before submitting the application.

Ms Simmons looked at her and explained, "It might be that your husband has kept something from you for fourteen years, nearly all of your married life."

Gemma instantly doubted that, but then had second thoughts.

"Let me look into this further and if nothing comes up then no harm done, but we need to be sure of his health," she explained.

Gemma nodded and was unsure of what issues could be withheld. Everyone experiences disappointment in life but this possibility was crushing to think that all this time she may have been putting up with abuse, not understanding that perhaps he could get medication or perhaps he had been warned of possible behaviour changes and kept it secret.

Back at the collage she works in the next day they sang '*When you walk through a storm*' and singing it with all of her heart she gained courage and strength to go forward, forgive and forget what had or hadn't happened. They must face the present.

With her metal filled leg constantly aching, she was anxious and disappointed with it not getting better after all the water walking and gym work, this morning's appointment with the orthopaedic surgeon he pushed and prodded, looking very stern and serious, he was convinced that no more improvement was possible and the booking for surgery in April was confirmed to remove all of the metal work.

The next morning waking up feeling very depressed and acutely aware that she needed to seek out some inspiration, now totally apathetic to even gather enough energy to make herself do it. Deciding to settle on the sofa and opt for watching a church service on television she was emotionally drained, today everything felt hopeless, tired of the constant financial struggle and rejection from Mason, and acceptance of the fact that he couldn't recognise the lies being told to him she was convinced he didn't understand when Dwayne was manipulating and playing with his emotions.

It didn't help that it was now school holidays and she had no work to go to which left her with no one to socialize and chat with and no extra money to spend so she couldn't go anywhere, exhaustion crept along her limps, dragging heavily like she was slipping down a hole and she struggled to stay positive, plus the dread of bumping into his family at the rest home when she visited Mason didn't help.

Gemma despised them now for instigating the whole situation of her poor darling having to leave home, she understood that she shouldn't feel that strongly, but she could not help it.

Chapter 5

Watching the church programme on television, it talked about tomorrow bringing a surprise, her life could only get better and she decided to pray with heart felt genuine need, she rattled on loudly with out reached arms, crying out for help to cope with the fatigue, physical pain and emotional distress created by Dwayne and his mother and the loneliness of not being able to love and cherish her husband.

Resounding from the kitchen her cell phone dings with a text message as it shuffled along the bench top, it read *'I'm in the area, can I visit, Susan'* surprised relief floated over her, texting back, *'Nice, good to catch up.'* Just what she needed to jump start her into action, she was feeling a bit melancholy today. After a fleeting shower in and out of the water, she ran around with the vacuum cleaner just picking up the little bundles of fluff flying around the polished floors and stopped to look in the mirror. Her long brunette hair hung lankly around her shoulders so she grabbed a handful and quickly smoothing it spun the elastic band over the lot, fixing it tidily into a ponytail. Pulling herself together she looked forward to seeing her friend. Gemma was aware of the days that she did not work and socialize being difficult, she was determined to stay strong and notice all the good things in her life, revitalised on the strength of a txt message it had given her the jolt to face another day.

She doubts Sue will ever know how important that insignificant chat was to her, she listened and chattered, and that was enough to pull Gemma out of her own thoughts and realize there was a world beyond the four walls that constrained her.

Her devotion to Mason and his care was devouring her, mentally draining away the strength to go on, her energy level seemed to be measured by her mind, she was emotionally tired and lonely, dragging herself around while still in physical pain and finishing everyday chores unable to snap out of the grey mist that was her life. She knew that she must keep going, things would get better once her leg surgery was over.

Gemma Instinctively knew that she needed help, scared of physically falling with the metal in her leg and lonely, she decided to see the doctor next week. Speaking to him she explained that she did not feel anger or regret, and that it was difficult to feel any emotion, just an inner desire to stop it all.

Gemma had now convinced herself that suicide was forgivable, it was not a sin that could not be forgiven except the destruction it caused others was cruel and selfish. Trouble was, other people were not on her mind, being in her lost state of isolation no one else was considered in her distraught confusion, she had been through too much, counselling was booked for February.

Without her faith that it would all work out in time, she could not conceive how anyone could get through the life that she had, the awful flashbacks of rejection, despair and facing death when Mason had strangled and attempted to kill her, panic and helplessness of the situation she found herself in was only made survivable by believing that something good would happen for her in the future, she held onto her faith for a better tomorrow.

Monday she went directly home from work without making the usual rest home visit and later on after eating, she phoned Mason.

"Hi darling, how did your day go?"

"All I did was the puzzle book that you gave me." Was his sullen reply.

"Well, I'll pick you up in the morning and we can buy some goodies for lunch, go for a ride and eat at the new marina to watch the bird life and traffic," she paused to let him think. "Do you remember we used to do that after bowls on a Tuesday?"

"Yes, but I'm going out with Dwayne he has something arranged."

"But it's Tuesday!' she almost screamed, and that's our day out," she said in a controlled whisper, upset at their time together being extinguished yet again.

"I think I got mixed up," he said.

"It's not your fault, Dwayne knows I have been taking Tuesdays off work for a long time now. He's taking you out on purpose to stop me from seeing you, he kept you all day Saturday and again on Sunday. When can I get to see you?" she spoke slowly and paused after each statement, to allow for his slow processing.

"Why don't you ask the staff to ring Dwayne, and tell him you're going with me tomorrow, you're the father he's the son." She persevered.

Believing it was time to put her foot down and not to keep putting up with this crap anymore, she needed to speak up, she loved him and missed him.

"I don't want to ring him," he says quietly.

Perhaps it was too much of a task for him now with dementia as he seemed to be very nervous, maybe it was beyond his ability, or he just obeys what ever Dwayne tells him, out of fear that he would stop visiting.

"I have to go and have a shower now," he spoke slowly like an old man when actually only sixty-five.

"Bye then darling."

Both sadness and frustration consumed her at the nonsense of not being able to see or take her loved out because his son prevented her yet again from seeing her own husband. The frustration burnt deeply, with a gnawing in her gut it was breaking her heart not to have their Tuesday date, and perplexing to hear how sad he sounded. When will this torture end, all because she loves him and wants to have a fun day out together once a week. *Love and devotion,* that invisible thing we all seek, it was the weak link in life as loyalty made for vulnerability. Dwayne was deliberately trying to separate them; he never took an interest in his dad while he was at home, never wanted to help him repair the old house or potter around together. Gemma desperately needed to quell the angry fire within her and decided to sit with a cup of tea and pat Ombre'.

Following a sleepless night she rose early on Tuesday morning, she couldn't stay in bed even though it was warmer in there, she was still fuming about the day off work, the day she and Mason always spent together. She can't stand not seeing him and missed him terribly. Jumping in the car she made her way down to Country Views rest home early to try to get a quick cuddle with him before he went out, it was 8.35am when she reached for the faded blue door, knocked, no answer so she tried the doorhandle but it was locked, fear shot through her like a streak of lightening, he can't have already gone surely. She has not seen Mason for two weeks because of Dwayne taking him away when he knew she would not be at work, sudden panic surged through her entire body, a fear of what if she can not see him and he has another aneurysm, that fear was continually in the back of her mind especially when the family were stressing him about not living in the rest home. Gemma never liked to waste any of their precious time together, they don't know how much they will have. Quickly walking toward the reception to find him, she didn't have to say anything as the upset look on her face portrayed her disbelief and anxiety.

"He's gone out," she says with a serious face as Gemma approached the reception desk.

"Already? That's early for Dwayne to travel here and take him in rush hour traffic just to make sure I can't see him," she growled.

"Dwayne phoned this morning and demanded that we had to tell Mason to walk to the local park and he's getting picked up from there," she said quite solemnly.

"So, he's standing in a park freezing, while he waits to get picked up, instead of being here in the warm. That's just to make sure I can't see him. Okay, well I don't want my husband standing alone out in the cold where anything can happen to him," she franticly blurted out, knowing that she was the next of kin and could have a say.

Going on to say that it was neglect and abuse on the rest homes part to allow that to happen on a cold foggy morning. Seeing that she was terribly upset the receptionist informed her where to find him.

Without speaking she frantically drove over to the park where she risked running into Dwayne, and found her poor loved one standing alone in the cold, the fog leaving damp droplets of moisture dripping off his limp hair and he was not appropriately clothed to stay dry and warm.

"Why are you over here instead of in the warm rest home?" she called out to him.

"Dwayne said you were a bad wife even when I was at home and now you hardly ever come to see me."

"What!" she was stunned. "Why was I?"

She wonders what lies he was telling Mason; Dwayne was attempting all forms of emotional control (elder abuse) and lies to win over his father, trying to get rid of Gemma. What an evil toxic person, why would anyone hurt and confuse his poor vulnerable father who had dementia.

"My son told me." Mason stated.

"You shouldn't listen to him, I haven't been able to see you because he takes you away all the time, like today, and I think you should go back and wait for him in your warm room because he might take ages. I don't think it's particularly good of him to make you stand out here on this freezing cold morning, do you?"

"Okay," he replied, sounding relieved and quickly without hesitation turned to head back to the warm rest home. Before he walked away she called out to him trying not to allow her voice to crackle from upset, she was wild at the cruelty and selfishness of his son, the lack of care spoke volumes of how little Dwayne cared about Mason's wellbeing.

"I'll see you after work tomorrow, I miss you, bye darling."

"Bye," he says with cold quivering lips attempting to smile.

She dare not take him back in the car because he will only cop it from Dwayne if he finds out, he sometimes seems afraid when speaking about his son. Even through this nagging deep loss and knowledge of the injustice of it all, she was angry, very angry at the manipulation that was going on without her poor husband being aware of the abuse. Even amidst this stew of emotions there were no tears today, she was wild but able to see Mason, and she was grateful she was able to get him back to the warmth and safety of the home. Seeing him was a bonus filling her heart with warmth and joy after the initial disappointment finding his door locked, just to see him again even though the situation felt hopeless with the lies being told to Mason, it was something special. Goodness knows what other lies he's being told in an attempt to make him angry with her. Mason didn't realize that she hasn't seen him much lately because they made it impossible to do so. He had lost the ability to reason and was cognitively impaired as to the days, they made him believe everything was his fault.

On arriving home she phoned the rest home to check he was okay and yes, he did get picked up by an angry Dwayne when Sue, the manager called him into the office to tell him of another incident where Mason and another resident Barry competed in a snooker game. Barry won and Mason protested loudly, and when he didn't get his own way he threw the cue stick across the table nearly taking Barry's eye out.

Again Dwayne was told by Sue that Mason does have an issue with aggression. They have seen it themselves at the rest home. Dwayne loudly disputed that his dad was aggressive insisting that any past incidents were all lies told by Gemma. She went on to agree with Gemma that Mason should not be standing outside on a cold foggy morning when it was completely uncalled for and she will prevent it from ever happening again. Gemma thanked her for looking after Mason before hanging up with mixed emotions of relief and worry dominating her mind over what her husband was going through with Dwayne.

In an attempt to see him again she started rushing over to the rest home during her one hour lunch time at work, because she did not trust that he would be there later. She could often only seize a short time with him between his lunch time and hers. Also popping in to see him before heading home after work she had a cuppa with him and that helped a little if he was there, although it was never a long enough time for it to register in Masons brain, which meant the memory of his wife visiting had gone by the next day and he was constantly told by his son that she did not visit him at all, it was all very confusing for Mason. Next time when Mason accused her of not visiting him, she walked Mason to the reception desk and pointed out all the times her signature appeared in the visitor book. He was genuinely surprised and the receptionist backed it up nodding profusely so that couldn't be disputed, no matter what Dwayne says.

When he first arrived at the home he was so happy but now he was continually anxious from being constantly told that he shouldn't be there, that there was nothing wrong with him and Gemma did not want him. Mason continued to get bombarded with rubbish for long days every weekend when Dwayne took him from the rest home early in the morning, brain washed him all day and did not return him back for any rest until late both nights. Someone like Mason who had a brain injury tired easily and he needed an afternoon sleep to function well, which he was intentionally prevented from having on the weekends while he was being drilled into believing lies.

Her poor husband looked tired and stressed, and in a panic not knowing what to do as she could only get short encounters with him, she phoned an Aged Persons organisation to get him help. She was told that if Mason was not happy, he wouldn't go out with Dwayne and that he could speak for himself. She suspected that they have also heard from the so called caring son Dwayne and they believed whatever stories they have been told.

She just wished someone could see what was happening to Mason, doctors have classified him as being easily lead, and also having cognitive deficits that rendered him incapable of understanding consequences of his actions. Maybe organizations did not have access to those psychiatrist and medical reports as they would be confidential, and Dwayne would make sure that no evidential reports were made available to them.

Every Saturday she was prevented from seeing Mason, so she focused on doing lots of gardening to take her mind off him. Gemma was beside herself not knowing how to rescue her husband and she couldn't sleep for worrying about what he was enduring, only the warmth of the sun soaking into her skin could provide a little relief from the cold miserable situation. She continued to speak with a counsellor and decided to find an absorbing hobby, something to help her have a life beyond worrying about her husband being harassed, she again contacted the organisation for helping the ageing population and attempted to press on them that they please visit Mason, stressing that they should see if he needed help even if they don't believe her. She was going to look for a dance class to take her mind of it, even though it may be intense and her leg slow to react, she had to try as it might be helpful to ease her worries.

Mason and she loved to dance and she longed to gain that back again, remembering how they were back in the early days. It should strengthen her leg and hopefully help lessen the recover time after future surgery. Persevering in her pursuit to spend more time with Mason she continued to phone the rest home every Saturday and again on Sunday in the hope of seeing him.

Sometimes receiving sympathy in the staff member's voice when they sadly explained, sorry he has gone out with his son and other times she got an impatient reply such as the caregiver that said.

"Why don't you phone his cell phone instead of the rest home, we have other people to look after?"

After apologising to her for taking some of their time and explaining that her husband can not operate a cell phone and did not have one. She then thanked them and politely hung up feeling embarrassed and upset. Countless Saturdays followed where he was not there all day, disappointed she continued to persevere and finally, a Saturday arrived that when she phoned to see if Mason was there, he was! Throwing on some tidy clothes in excitement she rushed around to the rest home. Both faces glowed with wide smiles when she walked in and sat down beside him, he reached to grip her hand in his and they sat holding hands together on his narrow bed. They didn't talk much, both welling up with emotions, words weren't needed, they attempted to just laugh a little about things happening at home with the animals, but it was bliss, there was an unspoken warm closeness between them that they both felt as he squeezed her hand, his eyes were glassy and watering.

Gemma was overwhelmed, she never knew if he would remember who she was when she could not see him for weeks on end. He was welcoming and happy to see her, and when she left she knew that she would get a good night's sleep tonight even without him being home, she drove home with a smile and a warm flush to her face like teenagers have. On Sunday morning before heading off to church to gain strength to keep going, full of hope she quickly phoned him to say good morning, I love you! The staff informed her that he had gone out with Dwayne, she was disappointed but not surprised anymore, and tried not to feel angry by the scheming, just satisfied and hopeful Mason might have an opportunity to see his grandson if he was there.

Chapter 6

With new determination she resolved to find away of accepting her loss and decided to make the time alone work in her favour, time to read and relax, convincing herself that it was possible she might be able to see Mason this Tuesday, because they have a three day long weekend, she remains hopeful of seeing a bit more of him. Common sense told her she was doing the right thing by not bringing him home, even though she often thought about just packing his stuff and absconding with him, on those deeply dark days she would sit outside overlooking the paddocks and contemplate what was the best thing to do, common sense prevailed and she ended up accepting the doctors advice and explanation given to them both was the correct one. Mason needed care and he was in the right place for him to receive that, as much as she missed him she was unable to care for him at the moment while she was unwell herself. Taking him home would be a selfish move on her part.

Another week disappeared and Saturday morning found her very unwell, dragging herself to the gym to work on improving her leg but even a refreshing swim did not help with the lack of enthusiasm, getting dressed afterwards she went to comb her wet hair and paused catching her reflection in the mirror. Dark sunken eyes, sallow skin, clavicle sticking out, she hadn't really given herself time to pay attention to her appearance lately. Maybe she was working out too much, or perhaps eating too many noodles to save money.

Her life was sad as she continued to persevere with constant pain, heartache, little sleep and continual uneasiness about Mason's happiness; it was starting to show both in her appearance and disinterest.

Phoning the rest home she was told Mason was taken out early yet again, straight after breakfast. Nothing surprised her, she felt despondent about the rushing around to visit him through the week during her lunch hour, it was stressful all for a few minutes together, and always on tender hooks wondering if he would be there. Leaving the gym she decided to treat herself to fish and chips plus coleslaw for some extra vitamins, pulling up at a local park she sat and ate while watching a little curly haired boy and girl playing on swings before the inevitable drive home alone.

The crunching of the lose metal under her tyres was a welcoming sound, she made a conscious effort to just sit and read a book, but to no avail. Resting her feet on the footstool didn't really work either as she just couldn't relax, what was wrong with her? walking over to the freezer she removed a packet of frozen sausage rolls and dropped them onto the bench to allow time for them to thaw for her tea, she had a nice lunch and wouldn't bother to cook.

Tossing and turning, sleep was an all night struggle and getting a sufficient amount was challenging, she could no longer snuggle into her familiar position wrapping her legs around Mason like she had done for fifteen years, and her mind was a constant turmoil worrying over the unknown lies he was being told. It was traumatic to know that her husband was being told she didn't want him, and she could feel his pain added to the torture of it being fallacious.

Her body was wary when she rose in the morning and already reluctant to face another day, she prayed for help, that everything would come right. With her energy levels at a drastically reduced rate she was a bit depressed, just wanting to cry all the time and feeling lonely to the extent of again battling with the idea of bringing her husband home. Gemma just wanted it to stop, she wanted a normal life and she wanted her husband to be happy. Thank goodness she was to see a counsellor in a few days' time because deep down she knew that bringing him home would be a backward step, she must keep moving forward. Spending everyday on her own, even though she talked to Ombre' her life was so dismal. Today had to be a stay at home and get well day, so with rain pouring down outside, she had an excuse not to do any physical outdoor work.

The plan was for a day inside to maybe do some baking for the freezer, first of all she needed to move the sheep to another paddock where it would be higher ground in the rain.

Arriving back through the kitchen door dripping wet she didn't have the ability to care, she dropped all of her wet clothes into the laundry tub and went to find a cosy track suit to hang out in. Hardly even talking to Ombre' as he devotedly followed her around and then lay down on the kitchen mat beside her while she made a cup of tea. Gemma's body and emotions had shutdown as his big brown eyes looked up and blinked, a pressing reminder that she hadn't bothered with him today, poor wee thing he knew something was very wrong.

Gemma's mind wasn't really on the baking, she found she had to really focus on what she was doing. It was her favourite chocolate chippie recipe so experience made them turn out okay. The phone rang and she answered it, pleased to be able to speak with Bridget and a little life flickered on inside her. Oh thank goodness it was a life saver, she listened to Bridget's happy chatter catching up on the week's happenings and Gemma's mood improved before they said goodbye, a bit of warmth managed to seep into her cold deflated body.

Her appetite returned and she felt like cooking something nice for tea, after not eating properly all day. She had been snacking on cups of tea and biscuits, knowing full well that was not good but unable to pull herself up, she decided to fry some mince, throw in some onions and add frozen vegetables with a leaf of silver beet from the garden. She lit the fire to eat in front of, watching the flames flicker and everything came right as consciousness gently pulled free of the fog.

After her long talk with Bridget, and all the time she baked biscuits Ombre' had slipped into a sound sleep on his sheep skin rug, all was right with his world as he relinquished his responsibilities.

Another hopeful Sunday morning and she leapt out of bed all keen and excited to visit Mason today, this week had dragged along slowly with life appearing to be boring even though she had plenty to do. All she wanted was her husband and she was lonely.

Walking into the rest home and knocking on Masons door, which was slightly ajar, it slowly opened with a screech to reveal an empty room. Panic as adrenaline started to surge through her, she rushed off to reception to look at the sign-out book! Recognising Masons scribbled and confused sentence, which told her he had gone for a walk down to the mall. Oh, she could drive down and pick him up. Wandering around the mall she could not see him anywhere, but it was almost lunch time so she suspected that he would probably return to the rest home for his lunch, if he remembered to wear his watch, she headed back up the road to hopefully catch up with him, even though it was close to his lunch time, she longed to see him after coming this far. Gemma missed him terribly and wanted to tell him how much she loved him and to see his smile again to cheer her up.

Striding through the entrance her heart pounded with excitement as she saw him sitting with the phone, it was so good to see her gorgeous guy. As he looked up, his face was pale, serious and he did not look well, maybe it was just because of the walk back from the shops she reassured herself. Seeing Gemma he hung up rather abruptly, which aroused her suspicion, who was he talking to?

Smiling at him they walked back to his room; she asked him if he would like to go for a ride after his lunch.

"No, Dwayne is coming to pick me up soon and we're going to his house." He spoke rather quietly, secretively.

"Okay," she said, now knowing who was on the phone. She was baffled why he had looked so unhappy and pale.

They sat on the edge of his bed with his strong arm around her back, he pulled her in for a close hug, the lovely smell of the aftershave she had bought him wafted around his small room. Gemma was aware of the strength still in his arms from chopping firewood, he hadn't been living in the rest home long enough for his muscles to have wasted away yet. They cuddled and talked for a short time and he assured her that he was happy there, she talked to him about the importance of taking his medication to prevent him from having mood swings and worrying about anything. They talked about how his brain had trouble reasoning and how he became overly anxious over unimportant things like the bridge down the road being in the wrong place for him to cross the road. Subconsciously she was preparing for him to return home.

Gemma wished that the doctor had put him on those calming drugs when he was still at home with her, and she couldn't understand why everyone thought he was managing to live with brain damage just because he had her to look after him. No one had been aware of the degree of agitation he was experiencing even when she pleaded for help, and the comments she had been making about the difficulty in managing him, nothing was believed because the son would contradict her. Until the professionals had Mason spend five weeks being assessed in hospital, only then did it become obvious that he needed to be on medication.

Gemma lived with his aggressive outbursts for the last five years and she wished he had the medication then.

He was becoming restless, jiggling on the bed and he started to fidget, there was an all too familiar rise in tension when he spoke.

"Dwayne will be here soon to pick me up, so you better go," Gemma could feel his stress misting the air almost too thick to breathe as he hastily continued, "you'd better go now! I'm going to lunch soon anyway."

"I'm okay to see Dwayne, don't worry." She tried to reassure him that everything was okay.

"No, he gets mad with me if I talk to you!" he says with enlarged eyes and fearful voice.

"Okay darling, you have a nice day."

They linger a little longer, not wanting to part as he planted a warm wet kiss on her lips that sent a rush of warmth through her. He clung on to her arms, saying one thing but displaying another. Why was he in trouble for talking to his wife, she was shocked that he was so afraid and Gemma pondered why he felt so threatened by his son arriving, it was not right. As they sat wrapped in each others arms she knew they were a loving couple, until his son got involved. She just wished they could have alone time.

Monday morning, and the usual ritual began, she got up as soon as it was light, went to make tea and toast to take back to bed. While watching the news on telly before getting ready for work, which she didn't have to get up for today, it was school holidays. Relaxing and trying to convince herself that everything was better now that she did not have to rush around preparing Mason for the day ahead, she was lucky being alone and doing what ever she wanted to, but who was she fooling. It was not okay. Emotion started to sweep over her, a loneliness blanketed and tears started to pool in her eyes, she misses him not being there with her even though she was always exhausted she still wants to run around after him.

Dwayne always said she molly coddled Mason but she didn't care what he said, Mason was her husband to love. Ombre' lovingly looked up to check on her, his eyes firmly watching for signs, she put the cup down with shaking hands and she sobbed silently wiping away any evidence of tears, so as not to alert Ombre'. He looked up again to check and she turned her head away, hiding her face from him.

"I'm okay," she says to him, trying to sound normal behind a shaky voice, no need to upset an old dog.

Gemma decided to phone Mason and check how he survived the outing with Dwayne, he was captive and made to listen to whatever they told him, unable to stand up for himself. Thank goodness he was on tranquilizers so hopefully he wouldn't get worked up, after being his sole carer for the most of their married life, to have to stop caring for him was very difficult, suddenly feeling helpless and unable to protect him.

Easter drew near and with it the worry of going into surgery to get the metal rod and screws removed from her leg, the reminder was constantly popping into her head. Gemma was unsure whether to ask to have a general or a local anaesthetic. Now living on her own who would look after her senior dog, he can not go into kennels at his time of life with the threat of separation anxiety without her. Weighing it up, someone might need to sleep over if she stayed in hospital after a general. The pressure of listening to pulling, cutting, stapling under a local could be traumatic, anyway they probably insist on a general and she doubted if it was an option. She would just have to find a way to manage Ombre'.

The emotional strain of everything that had happened since Mason collapsed on 21st June 2007. He survived two brain haemorrhages and the brain surgery that followed, the diagnoses of permanent brain damage and the long recovery after their wonderful life together as a married couple with their small flock of animals, they were content before their own lifestyle paradise was changed forever. Happiness flew out the window that day in June and the changes for both of them were massive.

With their lives transformed whether they wanted it to be or not, leaving no choice but to accept what they couldn't fix as years slowly tick away like a tightly coiled spring only releasing one rung at a time. The days were long and things got worse, sometimes the years and special moments flew past, although other times it was a long exhausting journey which often felt unbearable for Gemma, their once ordinary lives were replaced with some strange abnormal one.

Having a sick loved one to care for and knowing that he was now kept safe in long term residential care should help, but it didn't as it brought up other issues. Like the family not wanting to accept that their dad was sick, they didn't want a dad who had dementia. All was well when Gemma coped with him at home and no one had to know how dangerous he was and how poor his memory had become.

For Gemma it was having to accept that her husband was disappearing, she had watched him slowly waning for over five years, but love doesn't stop.

Gemma had spent every minute of every day watching Mason didn't hurt himself, that he had eaten, that he wasn't eating too much. She was responsible for his appointments, his blood pressure, hearing aids and health. He had lost the ability to look after himself and now suddenly he was gone, it had left a huge empty space in her day and in her life, their world. The world she remembers and he doesn't.

Chapter 7

Gemma constantly worried, even at night when all she wanted was to hear his voice, rest and sleep, but the opportunity to speak with Mason was often taken from her, the anxiety and uncertainty of how he was feeling, was he happy and coping and what else could she do to help, many things made her everyday life often seem unmanageable and as weeks turned into months it seemed that Mason's health and cognitive issues were insurmountable, the only thing she could do was to show love when the son would allow it and to tell herself that it could only get better, once she reached the bottom of despair she had to turn a corner when it would be miraculously alright, it had to be.

Trusting that they would get through this time had worked for her in the past, believing and having faith. The power of positive thinking and the acceptance that there was a plan for her and Mason, and believing everything happened for a reason gave her strength.

Sometimes in a whisper she would name all the good things she had, appreciating that everything she needed was provided, even though she would like more happiness in her life she knew that others were worse of. Gemma had no idea how she always managed to pay expenses and was able to provide for them after Mason unexpectedly, suddenly stopped work. Another wonderful thing was Ombre', she can not perceive not having Ombre' here for her in the dark moments, so she was forever grateful and just kept looking after her little ageing dog and continued to love Mason as much as his family allowed.

The morning brought hopeful little rays of light spraying brightly between the thin curtains, her intention was to get up, only a pounding headache had a different idea. It was no use, she needed to go back to bed and endeavour to get that elusive sleep lost to her during the dark.

Rest and healing was required, nevertheless there was always some work to do, her conscience wouldn't allow her to neglect the sheep, she wouldn't, couldn't rest until they were drenched, some needed crutching and she needed to phone the shearer to do that yucky job, selling sheep and spraying gorse, fixing fences and she accepts that the constant routine has been what kept her going. Collapsing into a dining chair she decided that all she could do was make the phone call and ensure the animals were fed, everything else had to wait, she was sick. All of the responsibilities had helped Gemma to face each day and she was grateful for the friendly sheep who relied on her, what would life be like without the usual routine and the charges that she had, would she still persevere if it was not for the responsibility of caring for Ombre', he was totally reliant on her and returned her love so she could never let him down, she must keep going!

Every waking day, Gemma felt she was being swept along by an angry torrent, hoping to stay on her feet to reach the end, with the sons wanting to get their hands on any assets they could and her wanting to scream at them.

"Hey, stop, I'm still alive and we're married you know, this is my home too. It's not my fault that my husband got sick."

Some days she was fuelled by anger to see how his family believed that they were entitled to material things as though their dad were already dead! But the cruelty to Mason was the most abhorrent thing, making it difficult for her to even face or speak to Dwayne. Peter was no problem as she was told that he was in prison for assault and drugs.

The thought of just seeing Dwayne made her sick to her stomach, wrestling with herself, she knew it was wrong to feel that way. She was struggling to stay alive; to pay the mortgage, rates and bills without any input from Mason as his pension went to the rest home. Mason's sons should be laughing as she financed their dad's investment they would inherit one day, but greed blinded them to her trials, all they could see was the big property they wanted. They didn't see the work and expenses involved and probably thought how lucky she was to live on the land, it was so far from the truth as she had little joy in her life now that her other half was missing.

No, they are not just ordinary people anymore! Other people's greed controlled their fate, the future was no longer in their hands, happiness didn't seem to be within grasp, Mason and Gemma were kept apart, people dictated what Mason must do. She deliberated if Dwayne was jealous because she and Mason had come so far, after their struggles to get him well they still cared about each other, even with the ignorant family pulling in every direction. Mason and she had a strong bond, grateful for snatched moments together whenever allowed. It was brutal to comprehend that keeping them apart was all about greed, maybe Dwayne was bitter and upset because his relationship had broken down so he must interfere with other people's happiness.

Sitting in front of a councillor was a new call for Gemma but she wanted some clarification of her difficult situation. After an explanation of what had happened between her and her husband and that he now lives in a rest home after being diagnosed with Dementia, Paul O'Reilly asked her how she felt. Pausing to think how she felt.

"Confused," I suppose she explained. "And angry at Dwayne taking Mason away at the only times that I can visit him."

"Why confused?"

"I feel like I'm grieving but he isn't dead!" Gemma poured out her feelings of how she visits Mason on her way home from work most days which upsets her, seeing him there made her miss him more, she felt the hopelessness of the situation and was depressed that she couldn't change it.

"I also live with pain in my leg every day."

Her eyes started to water and she couldn't hold back the flow of tears any longer as she choked up and they began to run unchecked down her flushed face. How embarrassing, her face glowed more as Paul O'Reilly reached over to hand her a pretty floral box of tissues, she shuffled in her seat, it was uncomfortable confiding her inner most feelings to a stranger.

"If you feel worse after seeing him, what could you do to not feel like that?" he asked.

Endeavouring to stem the tide and not cry she paused to think with a clear functioning mind before replying. "I could maybe not visit him as often," she said slowly, "but I can't see him weekends which is upsetting because I could spend longer with him then."

"Well, that's something you may have to consider, do you have something fun to do, belong to a club or people you can be around?"

"Yes, I joined dance lessons to go to, but I haven't been going because I feel upset and exhausted after visiting Mason, and then everything is a struggle when I get home after work," she explained.

"Maybe try less visits and see if it makes a difference, and you can make another appointment to come and see me. But you don't have to come if you don't feel you need to. It is a situation that just needs time," he suggested.

"Thanks," she got up to leave, feeling a bit relieved just having expressed her feelings, because she plods through every day putting a brave face on and not having anyone to talk to when she gets home from seeing Mason.

Gemma continued to go to the once a month meeting with the stroke club group of ladies, she looks forward to going to see how they are all managing in their various situations, and she felt that sharing problems over a cuppa was more helpful than seeing Paul O'Reilly.

Gemma had been asked around to tea by new neighbours and she assumed socializing a bit would be good, so she explained she was married and her life was complicated (in case they had ideas of setting her up with someone), but friends are good. More than ever she needed to have some fun now to show her that life was still worth living. Loyalty to her husband had the capacity to turn her into a recluse and prevented her from socializing in anyway, she now realized that she has avoided people to prevent them from getting the wrong idea.

Lovely food, and a nice group of people and a request that she help them with their sheep, she had found people to talk to about stuff she knew. They would welcome some animal help and have offered to help her in return. Maybe this was a chance to widen her horizons instead of living in a tiny vacuum of air, it gave her hope to not give up but to keep looking forward. Maybe helping her new neighbours would fill the empty void.

The school holidays were coming to an end which was probably a good thing, finding that too much solitude gave her too much time to contemplate and miss Mason, handling any stressful situation such as finding a fence down, a sick ewe or bills to pay were unwelcome challenges that filled her day. Gemma had no incentive to bake or do up the home anymore without Mason. It was a welcome relief that next week back at work with school colleagues, students and busy routine would keep her mind active and she was looking forward to seeing them all again. On top of everything else, being unable to go for walks without pain had challenged her personal life, being a huge irritation like trying to run with one leg tied to a log, it was yet another lost freedom that had added to her misery and would soon come right.

There were days that she just didn't think about eating, with lost appetite and the struggle to be emotionally strong and positive, life seemed very grey, not pink or yellow like happy warm sunshine, not even black and white. It was just a lifeless grey without any possibility's, she sat at the pond with Ombre' and thought about the summer days, they were hot but she never felt the warmth anymore, and friends seemed far away, she didn't want to burden her daughter with her problems so Bridget was unaware of how dire everything appeared to Gemma.

Stroking his soft fur she anticipated how wonderful it will be when her leg is pain free, attempting to focus on how she will be able to walk her problems away again, convincing herself that she will be emotionally strong again, with focus and prayer she will again believe there is a light at the end of the tunnel and that rainbows do still exist. Thoughts of it being just her and Ombre' struggling, and that no one was interested in her and Mason unable to be together would disappear when able to go walking once again. As much as she tried to be optimistic the tears rolled down her face as she searched for a thread of positivity, to pull herself back from the depths of despair and the deep hole that was threatening to swallow her. She flung her arms around Ombre's neck giving him a big hug while tears dripped onto his back, he stayed still and accepting.

She clung onto a thread of positivity, she was back at work next week having people to laugh with, and she'll have to find her smile and be strong for others, she would be busy and won't have time to reflect on how Mason is a different person from the one she married in what seemed like a hundred years ago, they have different lives now. Mason has peace, security and companionship just an entirely different life to the freedom he once had. Gemma's world is full of insecurity's and fear of the unknown! one of solitary existence with the love of an ageing dog and pain devouring her. She had an emptiness from losing her dear husband to a rest home, he hadn't passed away but to Gemma it felt like he had.

Reaching into the bright yellow letterbox that was symbolic of a happy new start for them both when Mason cemented it into the ground, she pulled out a single letter and stood still while opening it, it was so nice to receive a letter even if it had the District Health Board logo on the front of the envelope.

The Orthopaedic hospital has written to advise that it was all go in a few months' time, an April/May appointment will be possible and this was written confirmation that the metal in her leg was unsatisfactory to leave in. She was confident of Easter plus her school holidays, which would work best financially, and the need for someone to be home with Ombre' still had to be sorted. If she can't be home the first night after surgery, she needed someone to look after him.

Saturday morning and she was eager to say good morning to Mason on the phone, even though she tried to refrain from phoning him because he was not receiving any help with his hearing aids and was finding it increasingly difficult to hear on the phone. He says he can't cope and was getting more frustrated not being able to understand what was being said. His hearing aids were another one of the many things that she made sure were right for her husband, things that were never evident to his sons because he could always hear, when actually it was work behind the scenes making sure of the cleaning, servicing and batteries.

"Hi, its Gemma here, can I speak with Mason please?"

"No, he's not here he's gone to the beach with Dwayne."

"Oh, okay can you remind him he has an audiologist appointment on Monday afternoon, and I will pick him up about 2.00pm please."

"Yes I'll do that, bye." Well that was another disappointing start for the day.

She made do with some baking and spent some time in the garden with Ombre' feeling inspired because she will see him on Monday.

Monday morning and the phone startled her, only 8.15am so her heart leapt with alarm, what's wrong?

"Hi, it's just me, I'm going to the beach with Dwayne today." Mason says.

"Oh, that's nice you phoned, did the nurse help you?"

"I think so," he said.

"No, you can't go to the beach today because you have an appointment to check your hearing aids," she let out a stress filled sigh. "Do you have to go to the beach again? You went on Saturday and you've been going on at me to get you an appointment all over Christmas?"

"Oh did I?" he said.

"Shall I change the appointment then? And when do I get to see you?" she cried down the phone in rattled frustration.

He could hear the upset in her voice, this was unusual as she tried to protect him from knowing she was upset, but today waking up to yet another disappointment of not being able to see him was too much. She got through the weekend by looking forward to taking him for his appointment today. Why did she have all the health hassles of caring for him while the demonic one got to take him out.

"No, don't do that he yells in a panic, I need them fixed! I'll tell Dwayne another time then."

"Okay, see you soon." Hanging up the phone she couldn't believe how stressed she was and decided to try Omeprazole to try to ease the acid going on in her stomach. Gemma knew this was bad for her, she needed to slow down as her blood pressure was rising with anger towards Dwayne, that self-righteous son of a b.... He must have found out that she was seeing Mason today and had attempted to stop it, they went to the beach on Saturday and Dwayne needed to work sometime. It's ridiculous nonsense!

The reality of what Dwayne was doing pierced her mind as she proceeded to pick Mason up earlier than necessary, suggesting they go on to the mall and have his favourite curry and rice, he thought that was a great idea and enjoyed the treat as curry was something they didn't have at the rest home. They had a lovely chat and laugh over lunch. Everything was wonderful and it worked out well before taking him to his appointment, they enjoyed each other's company and life was normal again.

Making the most of the time they got together was fantastic but going home it hit her hard, the constant torment of fighting to see Mason was so wrong. Sick of always competing for him when Dwayne never took any interest in having a father before, if he were more amicable he could have had lunch with them.

Chapter 8

The following Sunday was a long weekend and Gemma was hopeful that the boys would be going somewhere exciting and not want to bother with their dad, she phoned Mason up with a sense of anticipation. Not having very much money she couldn't plan to do much but maybe she could get to see him.

"Are you going anywhere tomorrow?"

"No, I don't think so," he says.

"Well, I have to clip the goat's nails in the morning but I'll come after lunch, we'll go for a ride eh!"

"Yeah!" he sounded enthusiastic.

"So if anyone comes to take you out, can you ring me and leave a message on the answer phone so I don't have a wasted trip, okay? I look forward to seeing you tomorrow, bye darling."

"Okey, bye."

Hanging up the phone with fingers crossed, hopeful that he would be there when she turned up tomorrow, she now lacks any confidence in plans being kept when it comes to the son's relentless desire to tear them apart. Fear took hold of her as she parked the car, '*Oh, please let him be there.*' she couldn't bare the disappointment again.

Low and behold he's ready and waiting, and he hasn't seen or heard from anyone on this long weekend, he pulled her close and the kiss was longer than she normally gets. They began to drive off into the wild blue yonder together, she loved those moments when their faces have that wide grin. Its bliss and she began to ask herself if she could cope to have him at home again now that he's medicated, her hopes are cautiously rekindled, but listening to him talk it's not long before she began to have doubts as he tells of his goings on at the rest home in a very loud agitated way, it's obviously not smooth sailing with him medicated or not! He talked about breakfast today, he didn't want porridge and wanted Weetabix instead, the caregiver arrived with the usual porridge and he yelled at her.

"I don't want that bloody stuff! I told you."

She cringed, there is a proper way to explain to someone that you would like to have a change but he hadn't grasped that yet and obviously still had trouble controlling his temper. He continued to explain what happened. It must have been momentous because otherwise he wouldn't have remembered the event with his memory loss.

"What do you want then?" the caregiver had patiently asked him with a hint of fear in her voice, Mason explained to Gemma with a smile, I told her!

"If you stood still long enough to listen you would know, Weetabix!" he hollered at her.

(Poor girl! Memories all came flooding back as she remembers what it was like living with him)

"She then brought me two Weetabix and I wanted four!" he continued to explain with amusement.

"Perhaps you forgot to tell her how many?" Gemma suggested.

"Aarh, maybe." He lifts his head up, thinking about it.

While Gemma listened she recalled the morning he pushed her over because she asked him if he wanted the last piece of toast before she headed off to work. Sometimes he just can't control himself and other times he forgets what has been said and just lashes out, but at least the medication seemed to be limiting his physical reactions or is it just because they are strangers and he's reluctant to abuse them the same way he abused her. His angry disposition was obviously still the same, it was a warning as she is brought back to reality; as much as she didn't want to face it, she would be afraid of him if he were living at home again. That dreadful stroke had a lot to answer for, it changed both of their lives forever but still it was difficult not to love the man sitting beside her, he looked like the same quiet person she married.

Continuing on their drive to a remote West Coast beach, warm air was wafting through the open windows of her small car, grateful to have time together today she just wanted to spoil him. They pull slowly in to find parking at a dairy beside the white sandy beach to buy ice creams, he loves the almond and chocolate ones, there was very little parking left as it seemed others had the same idea on this beautiful day. They are just lucky enough to duck into a parking space as another car was leaving, she ran in to buy his favourite almond/chocolate covered ice-cream and returned to the car to watch his lovely smile spread across his face with such happiness, as he opened it like the innocence of a child's face that reflected all is right with his world, she paused for a split second watching him it took her back, how wonderful it must be to not have any more of life's problems, all swept away with a cold ice-cream. They decide to sit and finish eating while parked before starting to reverse out to leave the area for someone else to use. Turning in his seat he looks out of the rear view window; he yielded once more to the instantaneous aggressive side as he yelled out of the open window at the station wagon that was slowly pulling up awaiting our departure so it could fill the space.

"You can't park there," he screamed loudly at them from the open window. "We are reversing out!"

Gemma caught a glimpse of the poor ladies face; she looked quite shocked and left speechless as to what she was actually doing wrong. Gemma quickly drove out of there feeling embarrassed and fearing escalating road rage. She wasn't doing anything wrong but that was one of the reasons the road transport authority removed his driver's license from him, under the psychiatrists recommendation and concern about road rage, but still Dwayne persists, '*There is nothing wrong with my dad*!'

It was still a lovely day out and she appreciated the time they had, just persevered, was patient and said little.

February arrived and with it some very hot days so she needed to check the water troughs every day for the lambs, they were starting to drink some water as well as milk from their mum. School had started with a broken day for her which meant she had time to pop into Country Views Rest Home and have lunch with her darling before her next students came to class, with Mason living close to school they could snatch precious time together. While signing in at the rest home she noticed yesterday Mason had a visitor but she didn't recognise her name, Gemma asked the receptionist if she knew who that was, she said it was a social worker.

"What for?" she enquired. The receptionist suggested that it might be about getting an enduring power of attorney over his affairs. The manager overheard and came to stand there listening. They both looked very shifty and Gemma wondered what was going on.

"No one has told me anything about it, wouldn't they contact the next of kin?" she inquired quite horrified that they would talk with her vulnerable husband without consulting his wife. His affairs were her affairs also, it was their home and she had an interest in what happens.

It all looked very shifty with suspicious silence so she felt the need to quickly rush around to a solicitor in the next street for advice before it was time to go back to work, feeling panicked like she never has any control over what happens to her anymore. The next day she visited Mason after work and asked him.

"Will you give me the Power of Attorney to continue to manage everything for us, just as I always have?"

"Yes." He replied without hesitation.

Oh thank goodness, and when she left to go home she continued down the road to notify the solicitor (she spoke with yesterday) of Mason's decision, she looked at Gemma oddly, and explained that if he lives in a rest home with dementia then she would have to apply for a Protection of Personal Property and Rights Act (PPPR) because he must be of sound mind to be able to give Enduring Power of Attorney and he clearly wasn't. The court will need to decide who to give it to, so she proceeded to fill in the appropriate application forms to be filed in court.

Starting back at work was good and the week quickly disappeared, after having tea with Ombre' looking on she wondered what Mason had for his tea, she decided to phone him now his hearing aids worked, the staff took the cordless phone down to his room.

"Would you like to come to the wharf market day tomorrow, Saturday? There will be kites flying as well, so that'll be good to look at." She was excited and hoped they could do that together.

"Yeah okay," he said.

Picking him up was no problem and she sighed with relief as he climbed into the car. They both enjoyed the day walking under the brightly coloured overhead kites, Mason was fascinated by the various kinds of animal and fish kites as well as weird shapes and assorted sizes. Everything was wonderful, the sun shone with a good wind for the kites, as they carefully munched on hot dogs turning them so as not to get covered in tomato sauce, it was a fun day together. Dropping him back at Country Views she went straight down the corridor and asked the kitchen for two cups of tea, the kitchen staff smiled and asked about the kites before Gemma found some privacy sitting quietly beside each other on his bed before saying her goodbye. His warm lips touched hers and his tongue pushed to explore further, she had to resist and started to feel a bit upset as this was not the place to be doing that. Driving home a smile spread across her face as she recalled the advance and her face blushed pink.

When Tuesday came around for bowls, she reluctantly drove down the road to pick him up, she had mixed feelings, a time she usually enjoyed was now tarnished by hurt and a huge sense of bewilderment and betrayal because staff have told her on the phone they knew that Mason had been out to his ex-wife's house, she came to pick him up. Not wanting to upset her husband Gemma didn't let on that she was aware of it but it did confuse her as they headed off to bowls, with a plan to find a new place to have a picnic later. He went in to play and they kissed quickly before she headed home to do housework, to return to collect him she had make a flask of tea and packed a picnic rug in the car, calling in to have a cup of tea and chat with his bowling buddies had become a pleasant routine and Mason seemed to enjoy her arriving to pick him up. He never mentions his van that has been sold and was happy being a passenger.

Sometimes arriving early she watched him bowl, he modestly suppresses a smile and she can tell he's thrilled at her being there as he glanced up from his crouched position on the edge of the green mat, smoothly laid out on the rugby club floor, he bowled with great concentration and then his team cheer and make constructive comments about his shot, it's good to take an interest in his game as he stood up to look at her in a childlike manner. Over the past years a lot had happened to knock his self-confidence and getting him involved with bowls was a great move, his Tuesday mates have been invaluable not only for him but as an opportunity for her to be involved in his hobby.

Living away from home created distance between them, a void that was hard to bridge now her wifely duties have been dramatically reduced. Every Tuesday pack-up time he rushed around the hall helping to roll up mats and stack the bowling balls into their boxes, before lining them up on a shelf out back. How lovely to watch his show of independence and she was proud of his growing confidence.

The excitement was mounting at the kitchen hatch with tea and coffee and two types of biscuits to choose from, providing that much needed end of play refreshment. Mason found her already seated at the round table waiting as he carried two cups of tea, handing one to Gemma with a massive smile on his face, he was in a good place emotionally and behaving as a gentleman should, forget any brain damage! When he first started at bowls she was hesitant to intrude on his space but he obviously wanted to sit together and chat among the friends he had made, he was proud to have his other half there beside him and she warmed knowing that, as warm fuzzies ran down her arms.

One time Mason explained to Gemma about the elderly at the rest home who never got a visitor, and it was nice to see that he now understood that fact. Gemma will continue to enjoy these special dates with him and they shall remain in her memories for a very long time to come.

"Let's see if we can buy fish and chips and find a beach to have lunch at today," she suggested when leaving the hall and walking towards the car.

Driving across the Greenheads bridge she executed a quick glance across the water, pointing out the wharf that they used to sit on overlooking the strong steel bridge with its many cars full of ordinary people rushing through life, unaware of how lives can be totally changed by sudden unexpected trauma, sitting close to her man she reflected on their lives. Unable to comprehend how all this had come about, nowhere in her goals and plans when getting married did she ever think brain surgery would feature in her world. How strange we think that we're bullet proof and things happen to others but not to us.

A change of plan, as they discover a local home cookery in a group of beautiful little village shops they had never been to before they forget about fish and chips. The window was full of scrumptious looking food and after purchasing an array of goodies for lunch they follow a street sign pointing to a boat ramp.

"Let's look down here, there might be somewhere nice to sit by the water for lunch," Gemma suggested. There was easy parking and Mason collected the worn out old car rug from the boot to sit on, between them they carried the food and the flask of hot tea and milk. Spreading the woollen rug out to cover a nice patch of lush soft grass they settled. It was quiet, deserted, just the two of them having a special time together. How wonderful that being a Tuesday everyone was either at work or school. Looking out onto the still charcoal grey water, a few ducks were just bobbing up and down on this calm sleepy day, sitting there together in silence, special, memorable and magical it all became too much and the tears wheeled up, pooling in her eyes.

Gemma loves him and she can't understand why he won't stick up for them when it came to dealing with Dwayne and Rose who were obviously in collusion. It was as though he had no fight left in him, like being drained of all feelings and ideas since the life saving brain surgery, and his life was now like a spider just hanging by a thread with no more ambition than to just go wherever the wind took him. He looked happy today. Endeavouring to hold back the tears while sitting in that beautiful place so close to him was perplexing to say the least, she didn't want to spoil the time by asking him and yet all of her life seemed to be melting as was her energy drained at the thought of what will become of them as a couple. She knew she couldn't sit there anymore as the anxiety was too great knowing that his son and ex-wife were scheming against them and any future for them after being married for over 16 years now.

"I'd love to just drive around looking at the beautiful homes after lunch," she suggested to him.

"Okay." He smiled.

Feeling indescribable anguish from the hurt of Mason's betrayal and an unforgivable sense of lost loyalty and bewilderment after she has looked after him, she was the only one seeing him through his confusion, with the copious amounts of patience she had to have, to tolerate his anger and to put her happiness and hurt to one side to help him recover, plus all the hard work to keep the property running smoothly, just share hard physical work and financial strain. Packing things back into the boot of the car they prepared for a drive around the lovely homes, admiring and discussing places they could only dream of.

Chapter 9

Mason never mentioned anything about Rose (his ex-wife) so she tried to put them out of her head, it was not fair to him that people were controlling and taking advantage when he was not in a fit state to speak up for himself. The summer passed without much change and his birthday was fast approaching. Gemma was so excited about taking Mason out to a nice restaurant for his birthday, it was something he never got to do now and she had arranged for Bridget and John to meet them there, Mason says he was looking forward to it as well.

The day ultimately arrived, she leapt out of bed to phone the rest home and wish him a happy birthday before he went to breakfast.

"Hi, can I speak to my husband Mason please?"

"No, sorry he signed in the book that he went out at six o'clock this morning."

"That can't be right, it would still be dark outside, it's nearly April! It's freezing cold outside," she shrieked in dismay.

"Yes, some of the staff said they saw him standing beside the road this morning when they were coming into work," said the receptionist.

"But did he have breakfast? And what about his medication?" A thousand concerns swept through her mind. "Can I be put through to the manager please?"

"Putting you through now."

"Hello, Sue speaking."

"Hi, I don't think Mason should be standing next to a busy road at this hour of the morning and without breakfast or medication." She quickly expressed her concern to Sue.

"Yes, I agree with you and the staff should have brought him back inside, there is no reason why he needs to be standing in the cold,

Dwayne or Rose can pick him up down the driveway in the reception area."

She promised to speak to them when he arrived back later today. Gemma thanked her and hung-up disheartened, it was his birthday! So, Rose and Mason have been seeing each other and staff have respected his privacy and said nothing to her. It was a plan to try and disrupt their marriage, the piece of trash had to pick up a mentally impaired man from a rest home to try to get whatever she can, she was a really nasty lady. Gemma needed to phone the restaurant and cancel their booking, and also let Bridget know. Unable to see her husband on his birthday because he was with his ex-wife and son, she was told that when questioned by staff about the return time they refused to return him until late, after the rest home was closed. It took all of her courage not to cry, so she asked Bridget to please phone the restaurant to cancel the birthday lunch before putting the phone down and bursting into tears of disappointment and bewilderment.

When phoning him later in the evening to see how Mason's Day had gone, the receptionist apologised to her about the morning and explained how they had received a call saying that Dwayne had been held up, so could they get Mason to wait outside to be picked up, staff watched as Rose arrived and ordered him to get into her car. Mason just did what he was told, he was so vulnerable and then Rose took him back to her house for breakfast, he hadn't arrived back yet. Upon hearing this explanation by the receptionist Gemma requested that she phone Rose and see if Mason was okay, he might not want to be there and his rights are being abused.

"Please speak to Mason and check if he needs to be picked up, the rest home is responsible for him and his welfare." She insisted.

Rose answered the phone and said that she would bring Mason back at 6.00pm. She said he couldn't come to the phone, and she refused to let the rest home speak with him.

At 6.00pm Gemma got into her car and frantically made the trip to the rest home to wish her husband a happy birthday and give him a new watch, he was not back. While she waited, the nurse phoned to ask when he would arrive back, but unfortunately she told Rose that his wife was waiting here for him. Wrong thing to say!

"Oh, well I won't be bringing him back until 10.00pm then," she laughingly said to the staff member who was gobsmacked and couldn't believe the rudeness.

So now Gemma knew where Dwayne had gotten his nasty sadistic streak from and she felt very concerned about her husband being snatched in essence, when no one could speak with him, was he being harassed, pressured and controlled?

Dwayne and Rose were taking turns to prevent her spending time with Mason on public holiday's and prevented her from seeing him on the weekends. They had begun a rigorous effort to swoop on him after breakfast and not return him for at least 12 hours, rendering it impossible for Gemma to see him again on Easter weekend. If only they had taken him sometimes when he lived at home and maybe he wouldn't be where he was today, only once had she asked for help to have a day off from caring for Mason and Dwayne had laughed at her and said, '*no way*'!

They made sure to take him on all the days they knew she would be off work to prevent her seeing Mason, so she started popping in after school again and stayed as long as possible even when tired, by the time she got home to cook tea she was feeling very dreary, knowing that it was contrary to what the councillor had advised her to do. She didn't have a choice, she longed to see Mason, and he always welcomed her with the most beautiful smile when he saw her, how could she deprive him of that little bit of happiness.

Tuesday morning and the phone rang causing her to pause and catch a breath, was something wrong? her phone rarely rang. Country Views was phoning to say Mason's not going to bowls today because

Dwayne was taking him to the beach. She demanded them to please take the phone to her husband so she could check with him.

"Hi, it's Tuesday and we always go out darling, you go out with the boys on the weekend. Tuesdays are for us and we have the restaurant booked for your birthday, you missed it the other day."

"Well, I didn't know what day it was, and I can't change it now because he rang and said he's on his way."

"Well, Dwayne knows that you go to bowls and they'll be expecting you as well to celebrate your birthday, it's our day together, he asked you out to prevent me seeing you. I don't see you much and I miss you."

"Oh, he might be here soon."

Her voice breaks as she quickly says goodbye to him because she knew he couldn't sort it; she didn't want to upset him. Her heart was breaking not only with disappointment, but because it would have been a special day for his birthday.

Little b......! That Dwayne should never have been born, he was an unwanted pregnancy and he had caused nothing but misery the whole of his life. She was furious.

Bleakness filled her every day, there didn't appear to be any way of improving their lives together, the many hugs they missed out on now and the laughter they always had when together, those little things no one sees were few and far between as they were prevented from being together by Mason's son and ex-wife. Selfishly controlling who Mason was allowed to love, for what purpose? Why are they so manipulative and unkind to him and disrespectful of Mason's wishes. Gemma just could not understand why they wanted to penalize and confuse an already tortured soul.

Someday we all reap what you sow, and that day they will both get what they deserve, if Dwayne has a stroke like his dad did, which was very likely because of his overweight and high blood pressure, evident by his nervousness and red face, who will he have to care for him now his wife has left him?

Gemma's leg surgery was due on the 21 April 2013 (Tuesday) so she wanted to put things in order just in case, the years have changed things and Mason can no longer live at home on his own. Things needed to be arranged and so she set about writing some changes to her existing will before seeing her lawyer.

The day arrived and she sat with her dog, a feeling of liberation and relief that today she would get all the metal work removed, the long 11 months of enduring the awkwardness and pain would finally end, but she naturally had pre-surgery nerves that today was the day she started her road to permanent recovery to be the way she was before the broken bones.

Gemma had organised one of Mason's bowling buddies to collect him and take him to bowls, she didn't want her husbands Tuesday disrupted, it had been carefully explained to him that she won't be there and she even wrote it down for him to see beside the bed to remind him. The rest home knew who was picking him up. Gemma carefully explained on the note that she would be out of action for a little while, unable to drive the car she won't be able to visit but promised to phone often.

Gemma was hopeful of being home tonight for Ombre' as he was her main concern being completely dependent on her. She knew it would be awful to be away from him, he was left alone. Bridget will arrive soon to take her to the hospital for day surgery so she silently sat with a small carry bag containing a nightie just in case she had to stay overnight. She stood up to put Ombre's bed out onto the porch, she left it as late as possible because his big brown eyes looked up at her knowingly, and she gave him a big breakfast. She prayed that he would not have to sleep outside tonight, and that she would return soon after surgery.

Looking into his questioning eyes, "I'll be back soon." She says to him stroking his soft little head and popping a kiss on the top.

Unfortunately as she sat in the waiting room of the hospital and Bridget went off to work, there was a long wait for her to get in for surgery which meant she would have to stay overnight to be monitored after the anaesthetic. Gemma opened her eyes in recovery to the sound of two nurses whispering while looking at her leg, a concerned thoughtful look, alarmed she forced herself up onto her elbows avoiding the tubes sticking out of her arm, fear of what they have done and to see if she still had two legs, what was all the murmuring about. A pool of red, the bed was covered in blood, her blood.

"Should I call the surgeon?" says one to the other. They both looked very young and this must be very confronting for them.

"No, not yet I'll just put more dressings on and see if it stops."

Well, lets hope it does because she was already feeling sick from the anaesthetic, without becoming anaemic as well she thought. Darkness took over and she had no idea what happened next. Gemma woke up in a ward with two other ladies opposite her so that was progress, all was well.

She lay awake for hours feeling unwell, it had been exhausting and the night was very long on the ward with clinks and clangs of metal beds and wheels on trolleys coming and going, she was tired but nevertheless when you are worried about your little old dog out on the porch in the cold it was even more impossible to sleep.

She was sure that Bridget would be doing her best to care for him while she was unable to be there, but her heart was crying out to reassure Ombre' that she would be coming home to him soon, *'Please let him be strong, I couldn't bear to lose him, please let him be there when I get home,'* she prayed.

When daylight arrived she was anxious to go home as soon as she could be discharged, Bridget arrived to help her with her bag, and waited outside of the room while the nurse checked everything was looking good, she was back on crutches again for a while and a little light-headed she was careful not to rush and fall over, she ignored how she felt as she couldn't wait to see Ombre'. Pulling up in the driveway there was a big welcome from a wagging warm companion, instantly a huge wave of relief swept over her, to see a loyal friend waiting on the porch keeping vigil, the first thing to see as soon as she arrived home. Gemma's heart warmed with love and joy even while her body was cold and sore.

All had gone well, so now onto recovery and she will have options on what her next move should be on how to look after Mason. Friday morning she awoke relaxed and happy lying there feeling the warmth of the sun filtering through the window as it shone onto the bed, she pulled back the blankets to allow sun to penetrate through the cold bruised skin with all of the many layers of bandaging on her recovering leg. It felt comforting and she felt at peace, content that it was all over.

Gemma's thoughts wandered back to last year as she recalls being in this same position after surgery for her leg, but then she was full of anxiety and fear of the uncontrolled anger Mason had in his inability to understand that she was unable to do everything she would normally do to care for him.

Today she was reluctant to think of his companionship and his presence. Maybe because she feared that he couldn't come home if his anger was not managed with medication, she was afraid to cling on to that hope. Feeling safe following this surgery, her life had evolved into a new era of tranquillity and peace and she was reluctant to relinquish it or place herself in danger anymore, she must move on to stop grieving and give him the release he also needed. She loves Mason enough to let him continue with his new secure life in the rest home if that was the best thing for him.

But saying that, come Sunday and Bridget and John have gone away for a much deserved break in Rotorua, Gemma longed to be with Mason as she hadn't seen him for six days now, and only communicated by phone where he didn't really talk much. There was not only physical holes in her bones where the metal rod had been but an emptiness held in her heart, she felt incomplete. She phoned him and while speaking to him on the cordless phone it started drifting in and out, he must be going outside the rest home and the signal was breaking up.

"Don't go out to the ducks darling," she called down the phone but it was too late, the phone cut out.

Oh no! she cursed out loud with frustration longing to hear his voice, if only he could hold a conversation. Should she phone him back or not? No, she tried twice to get hold of him that time, and she would be back to square one with staff tracking him down with the cordless phone outside again. She waited to see if he would get staff help and phone back, upset cold tears flowed freely and trickled off her chin dripping onto her legs as she lay convalescing with her leg up to prevent it from swelling. Alone and helpless, she became overwhelmed along with tiredness and the healing going on in her bandaged wound she no longer sobbed silently. Realizing she wanted her husband, but he was unable to be there with her during her recovery, she missed him and the endless cups of tea he made last time. Convincing herself that things would get better, she knew the early days when healing took time were hard and it was normal to be a bit down after surgery.

Ringing broke into her thoughts and her heart skipped a beat as she quickly grabbed for the phone.

"Hi, is that you Mason?" she cried out with thrilling disbelief and excitement that he was able to think and act on phoning her back just like a normal person, she was so tremendously proud and pleased for him.

"Yes," came the reply from what sounded like a thousand miles away, "I'm using the hallway phone," he explained.

"Oh, that's good." She responded to him without letting on he did anything out of the ordinary, so as not to embarrass him. "The other one gets the signal from the office so you have to stay close to reception next time you use the cordless okay."

"Does it? okay then," he says happily.

Bless him, it was so good to speak with him when he was having a good day, and she knew that it was also to do with the fact that he had not been influenced by the son lately because they knew Gemma was unable to drive. They haven't been brainwashing him with their lies and she was sure that was why he appeared so relaxed and able to think normally.

"I'll be well enough to pick you up on Tuesday for bowls and we can go to the drive through for lunch together while I'm on crutches."

"It's a date!" he says giggling and she could visualize his gorgeous smile and those lovely grey eyes. All arranged, and she could hear the warmth and excitement in his voice and as they both hung up she had goose bumps. If only they would always let him feel and be himself without Dwayne's interfering ways, he sounded so happy.

There will always be a connection between Gemma and Mason, not because of life's trials or family leverage and although nothing will ever takeaway the pain the aneurysm has caused them, simply because they were bonded together not by thoughts and brains but by their hearts and souls and the experiences they have been through together. Once upon a time they were ordinary people who fell in love.

Chapter 10.

Being constantly confused as to what day it is, and his room having minimal space Gemma thought it might be a nice idea to combine some doggy photos of Ombre' and one of Mason and her together, all copied onto a calendar for him. She was not very computer literate but with Bridget's guidance she endeavoured to create this work of art; the photo of them both at a cafe' on one of the many Tuesday outings turned out cheerful and quite lovely, so she added it to this months calendar to surprise Mason with it on her next visit. His face beamed with delight as he helped attach it to the side of his plain ecru coloured wardrobe.

"I'll be able to see us together from bed and also know what day it is." He was pleased.

With it being so well received she set about gathering various photos of them both, of him playing bowls, some of the sheep and Ombre' and allocating them to be scanned onto each month of the year. Attached them together into a calendar and added it to his wall.

Her month of recovery has now passed, during which time memories of the accident last year had sometimes plagued her. Recuperating in that same spot that she lay when Mason was home, now she appreciates the safety of being on her own and not having to repeat the trauma of caring for him while on a walking frame. The memory of being afraid of him would hopefully fade with time, she didn't blame him for being sick and understood that he can't grasp that when things go wrong she can't always fix them. The horror of last year was frightening, she was unable to defend herself and his loud demands to cook his tea or else be pushed off the walking frame were memories she would rather forget. It was then that she understood that she could not manage him on her own anymore, he was becoming too dangerous.

Today she was safe, but alone, and still being very careful when moving about the house, very much aware of the stiffness in the permanent scars and that she mustn't have a fall or slip over while going about looking after the animals, bone marrow and wounds heal and she regains strength. Winter was coming and the paddocks would become slippery so she attempted to minimise the number of times that she ventured gumboot clad into the mud, calling the sheep to the gate for treats to gobble up while doing a quick head count, sighing thankfully when everything was okay and she didn't need to go and find anyone, it was fortunate that she planned to have five months before lambing, she delayed putting the ram with the ewes knowing of her upcoming surgery to recover from, now confident that she can relax and not worry.

Gemma was looking forward to enjoying this long Queens birthday weekend coming up and having time to catch up on housework not done while she convalesced, she wanted to spray gorse if the weather was kind. Hopefully, she would also gain extra visits and outings with her husband.

"Hi, it's a long weekend this week are you going out with the boys?" Gemma inquired over the phone.

"No I haven't heard from them." He sounded a bit down.

Maybe the effort to keep them apart was becoming too much for them, thought Gemma.

"Well, I was going to suggest we go and find the nicest autumn trees to look at in a park somewhere, but now I'm having second thoughts. Maybe everyone will decide to travel and the traffic might be too bad on Saturday. We probably don't want to spend a lot of time stuck in traffic, so there are a couple of new movies out that we could see if you want?" suggested Gemma.

After explaining each movie, they agreed on one and planned to go for afternoon tea before the movie at 3.30pm tomorrow.

"I'll phone you tomorrow lunch time, that's Saturday. If Dwayne wants to take you out then we can still go on holiday Monday, okay?"

"Okey."

"That way you don't have to disagree with him, go with the flow and if he does take you, leave me a message on the answer phone saying you have gone out. Then I'll see you on Monday instead."

"Okay then, I'll write it down," he replied quite cheerfully before hanging up. She smiled and absorbed the vibes in his voice, aware of the warm fuzziness that they both felt, looking forward to their time together and praying that Dwayne was too busy on holiday.

Waking up on Saturday morning, on tender hooks anxiously wondering if she would get to see Mason or not, she hoped that being a long weekend the boys may have gone away. The phone startled her. No! dreading any disappointment. Answering it, it turned out to be her daughter inviting her to tea tonight.

"I'm not sure if I'm taking Mason to the movies this afternoon or Monday."

"That's alright," she said, "We'll put tea off until after the movie is finished and then if you do go tonight come after you have dropped him back at the rest home." She was insistent.

"Okay, that's sounds good, I'll see you both later then, whether I go to the movies today or not!"

Gemma hung up and hesitantly phoned the rest home, absolutely elated finding it was all good to go and she could pick him up. After happy greeting kisses she slid her hand inside his palm, noticing how soft it had become now he doesn't cut firewood.

Reaching for a space on his bed they sat together for a cuddle before deciding to proceed to the KFC drive through for some afternoon food. The car filled with contented silence until arriving at the drive through. Mason eagerly looked at the photos of burgers and chips and pointed to what he wanted to eat. It was all very exciting for him now after rest home meals which were nice but different from takeaways.

The movie was a comedy and they laughed throughout which was a great treat for them both, and after it was a must to buy chocolate topped ice-creams before returning to Country Views Rest Home. The whole afternoon was wonderful and she was feeling relieved and hopeful once again that with no outside interference everything could work out for them one day.

Later, saying good night together with happy hugs and kisses she drove to Bridget's, pulled into the driveway and knocked on the door. She was expected and there was a lovely roast dinner cooking. Chatting with Bridget, they both agreed on visiting Mason one Saturday night to have a game of snooker with him at the rest home. Gemma had had a brilliant day and a lovely dinner with her daughter and son-in-law, life was looking brighter and her leg was healing. Traveling home she sensed that she would be able to sleep contentedly tonight.

Gemma was unsure why Dwayne was indifferent to Mason being in the rest home, when he was obviously safer there than being at home alone all day while she worked, it was perplexing as Mason really seemed settled and happy to have other residents to talk and mingle with, there were a couple of men he got on well with.

Out of the blue, Mason suddenly asked her how much money was in the bank, and that was unusual for him when he never bothered in all of their married life. She made sure he had money in his wallet all the time to help him to feel independent, he never had to ask for money and he knew that she had also left more at the office for him if he went out. It was Gemma's old fashioned values that it was important for a man to have money on him for good self-esteem, she also made sure he had his mail with his bank statements in a side drawer at the rest home. Mason said that Dwayne wanted to take him to the bank, so he needed his bank book from home and that his son was going mad that she sold the van.

Pondering over why the hell Dwayne was stressing his dad about money she carefully went over the situation with Mason again, explaining that he didn't have to worry about money because the government was paying for him to be in the rest home and as long as she worked she would manage and wouldn't have to sell the house. Gemma tried to reassure him there was nothing for him to worry about it was all sorted, also reminding him that he didn't have a driver's license anymore and the money from the van was in his personal bank account that he had the statement for in his bedside drawer, with his memory loss he had forgotten. She fished it out and showed him where the van money had been deposited.

"I remember now, you showed me that before," he smiled and nodded.

No good would come from Dwayne's intrusive behaviour and he could always phone and ask her, he was trying to create mistrust between her and her husband. Then this morning over a quiet cup of tea and toast it came to her, the novelty was wearing off and Dwayne was finding it cost petrol and was becoming a chore to keep visiting his dad. She looked after him at home the last five years after his brain surgery which meant that Dwayne never had to bother to visit because he knew Mason was in good hands. But now, maybe he felt guilty if he didn't turn up to the rest home.

The selling of the van probably upset Dwayne because Mason used to drive himself to Dwayne's house so he never bothered, but since he had his license revoked that could never happen again. She wondered if they want to buy Mason a car with the money from the van, maybe that was why he wanted to know about it. Gemma hoped they won't get Masons hopes up because there was no way he would ever pass a driving test this time around, you only had to have him in the car to hear the wrong suggestions he made on the road and the lack of any anger management would be dangerous. If that was what it was all about, fancy expecting his father who has a diagnosis of Dementia to visit him, instead of Dwayne visiting the rest home.

Gemma stopped fuming with it sorted in her mind as to why Dwayne was being so horrible to her, and she had to admit feeling a little smug that justice was being handed out and all too often she wondered if they had offered help, making a combined effort she could have been able to keep Mason at home.

Her leg was still covered in bruising, black and blue plus a little yellow thrown in for good measure just to prove that it was slowly recovering, she was unable to consider bringing him home while in such a precarious position and if he decided to have a temper how would she get him back to the rest home again. Feeling too exhausted to even go to make a cuppa this morning but accepting that she had no choice, with no one else there to help she had to keep on going and so gradually made her way to the kitchen just to reach for a bottle of water out of the fridge. Returning to lie on top of the bunched up duvet with Ombre' sitting on the fluffy sheep skin rug beside the bed, he looked up as if to say what about breakfast today?

It's going to be a slow start today, she was weighted down with worry, it had become an extreme compulsion to save money were ever possible to fund the mortgage, rates and many bills that she now paid on her own, and with the dreaded power bill on her mind she was unable to relax. Eventually trudging her way to the kitchen for breakfast. Anyway she must pick the tomatoes that are doing really well in the vegetable garden so as to avoid losing any, plus pick the guavas and fill an ice-cream container of them to freeze for making jam later on, everything was about saving money now and she was getting good at squirreling things away and never wasting anything.

Memories of their times together repetitively came to mind, possessing her thoughts, often impossible to get them to leave, even when attempting distractions like reading a book or magazine, she found herself reading the same page over and over and reflecting on Mason and some wonderful times they had together, times spent dancing or just being alone together, private and personal times that his sons could not comprehend because they never saw them as a couple, and her many memories of Tuesdays they now have together especially stand out after the long days spent apart.

Sometimes she felt cheated of the many special occasions they should have had. Prevented by ignorant and selfish people excluding her. Gemma witnessed how hard it was for Mason stuck in the middle, and at those times she felt sorry for him and tried not to complain, she spent the time writing notes down in her diary.

Life on the land together had changed although she holds on to hope that he might spend some time at home again in the future. In reality she knew that her long term future would be without him and emotionally she was not ready for that. He still needed her and the fact that his face lit up when he saw her provided a little piece of encouragement to keep loving this strange person, the husband she remembers was somewhere deep inside the dark chasm that was now Mason's mind, a sad sigh involuntarily escaped as she continued to pick fruit with Ombre' always present.

Gemma's check up at the hospital turned into a long haul marathon along hospital corridors, leaving her completely shattered by the time she got there and back, the good news was it should be the last appointment. Now having the all-clear to start living life again.

Breathing in the crisp air she and Ombre' once again tackle a walk around the neighbouring roads, it had been over a year since they had been able to do so, and it was exhilarating. They briskly continued on their way in silence, only hearing the crunch of the metal road when the odd car careered along, it seemed as though they were both deep in thought and reliving the thousands of times they have walked this footpath, since he was a tiny puppy. There were many times that she thought it might never happen again, now regaining the emotional enjoyment of the freedom and pleasure of walking along side her best friend once again. In that moment everything seemed so perfect, oblivious to every care in the world, they cherished this unique and special moment once again. Ombre' stopped at the top of the hill and looked out over the paddocks, she paused to look at him as he drew deep breaths of air into his nostrils, the wind whistling in his ears and ruffling his coat showing he felt it too! Just in that instant both feeling free and content, he had also missed their walks together.

Her Tuesday date with Mason had come around again and she was slow to rise, knowing that she didn't have to rush around and get ready for work. It was nice having the day off work and she considered taking Mason somewhere special today for lunch after bowls. It would be nice to sit behind big glass windows looking out at the waterside, they haven't been to the Riverside restaurant before so it was not reminiscing so much as she would like to create new memories, a place for her to recall going together. In the past they never had money to spare on lunches out, always being practical and she would bake.

Now Gemma has learnt that life was too short, she knew only too well after all they have been through together, and she didn't care how much Tuesday lunches cost, they needed to have that time together before time ran out.

"Come on then Ombre' lets go and see Mason." Looking up at her expectantly he ran off to the back door and looked back to stand and stare, no doubt wondering why she was not already there.

"All right just wait while I put my shoes on, I'm nearly ready." She called out from the bedroom.

Ombre' knew that the morning she didn't start to get dressed for work and place her lunch and work bag by the back door for school, that he might be going out, he loved to see Mason and then have a ride and sleep in the car. They cheerfully proceeded to the car parked in the garage and he was so excited she reminded him that he was not to jump into the hatchback when she lifts the boot lid, he was no longer a puppy.

"I'll help you!" and he obliged by putting his two front feet up onto the sill with a pained look on his face, he was too old to jump and was happy for her to lift his hind quarters into the car. He watched out the window and recognized when they drove into the rest home carpark. The autumn leaves were falling off the trees lining the drive and littering the tar seal, like rubbish spilling out of a bin, she hoped Mason was there and dread suddenly shot through her as she hesitated to knock on his door.

"Come in." Came the reply.

Warm smiles spread across not only her face but shone to light up her insides, the relief and joy engulfing her entirety as his arms gently embraced her body and he planted a moist kiss on her lips. The smell of his aftershave filled the small room maybe a little too much as she observed that he was smartly dressed ready for bowls and obviously by the greeting she had received he was eager to see her, how wonderful to have this special time together.

The little click was heard as the central locking allowed Mason to open the back door of the car, enabling him to reach in behind the seat and pat Ombre' who was straining for a pat. Mason had started saving a wine biscuit from his cup of tea on a Monday now, so he could feed Ombre', and with wagging tail they looked pleased to see each other. It was intense, he was getting himself into a routine and was able to connect these two things together in his mind, thinking for himself to save a biscuit was pretty amazing compared to what he was like when at home. Gemma hopes the medication will continue to help him get better, if only they could be together again one day.

Mason was dropped off outside the rugby hall to join his mates for a game of bowls while she continued on to the supermarket, stopping off home to sort the groceries and then leaving Ombre' to stay warm before returning to pick up Mason, saying goodbye to his mates before they continued on for a nice lunch.

They hadn't booked, so she respectfully requested two seats by the window and being a Tuesday weekday it wasn't busy. They were both thrilled when the waiter was able to find the perfect spot, overlooking the full length of tide coming in and watching as the tide went out with a couple of boats floating slowly by. Mason struggled to decide on what to order, so she reminded him of his favourite foods and they both enjoyed a wonderful lunch while looking out over the river, before venturing back to Country Views feeling exhilarated and pleased with each other's company, they had made memories, hugged and kissed goodbye. As she gave him the usual $20 for his pocket he quietly explained.

"Dwayne takes my weekly $20 now for petrol money to visit me, so can you bring me more money next time please?"

Not wanting to spoil their lovely day out she didn't answer, wanting to head home to think about what to do. Dwayne earnt good money working full time and she struggled to survive on part-time wages with a mortgage and without a partner's contribution.

Why should she provide petrol money to visit his dad!

Chapter 11.

Sprinting along the corridor to reception to sign out of the rest home after a lovely day. The manager called out; she wanted to speak about another incident that happened in the dining room. Nervously pulling up a chair in her office, Gemma was tense as Sue recounts how Mason demanded to have a certain sunny table at lunch yesterday.

She quickly explained that an old man who had been living there for 10 years always had that table. Gemma's response was that Mason hadn't complained to her about it and he had probably forgotten anyway, continuing on to say she thought that the medication he was on now had calmed him as he did seem better than before he moved there.

Sue informed her that they were still having issues with Mason, assuring her that it was only because of the fast actions of her good staff that no one had been hurt. Gemma apologised for Mason's behaviour and expressed hope that he would continue to improve. (What else could she say in support of not moving him somewhere else). Gemma got up to leave and thanked Sue and her wonderful staff for their help in caring for her husband.

Unbeknown to Mason, Gemma has since discovered that when Dwayne took Mason home one Saturday, his son had organised a solicitor to arrive at the house during the visit there and her poor bewildered husband was totally unprepared for what was about to happen, needless to say he just agreed with whatever suggestion was put to him.

The arrogant solicitor looking for work had gone out of her way on a Saturday to visit a client's house which was very unprofessional, she couldn't recognise that she was not working on Mason's behalf but that the wool was being pulled over her eyes, a jack up. She only saw one side of the picture; Dwayne's side, and he was the one paying her bill. He had finally found a way to dissolve their marriage by using his father's lack of understanding and being easily lead, words were put into his mouth, what a devious son of a b.... to cause more stress for his father who should be able to end his days happily, again he was put in a position of having to take sides.

Gemma had no knowledge of this deception until the following Saturday when she woke to a damp white fog blanketing outside and a sore neck penetrating up to her head.

"Oh! I don't feel well today, and I don't know why Ombre'."

Her head pounded as she stood beside their empty double bed still with the cuddly duvet that Mason loved so much, she peered out of the window, she felt worse than normal. Strolling towards the kitchen, maybe with the damp weather she needed her arthritis medication, reaching for two tablets she stopped, realizing she couldn't swallow them with the glass of water held in her other hand until she had food lining her stomach. Her thumping head never let up and was so painful, she could hear her blood pumping when she stood up. All she wanted to do was to lie down but she couldn't, she knew she had to get something to eat before taking medication to get better.

Reaching for a slice of bread, she leant on the bench and couldn't even put it into the toaster with her eyes closed. Desperately wanting pain relief she started to eat it dry because the builder was expected at 8.00am and she needed to get outside to unlock the gate for him. The slice of dry bread was eaten anxiously without anything on it, she swallowed her medication, carefully made her way down the porch steps tightly gripping onto the corner of the house as she went, walking outside she understood that something was different about her today and she started to cry. Unsure why she was crying, she impatiently wiped away the tears and mentally told herself off for being so pathetic. Feeling lonely, sick and wanting Mason, she had been contemplating running away from everything lately, suppressing a strong urge to escape and make it all go away, maybe she was a bit depressed, pulling herself together she unlocked the gate, she started making her way back through the freezing fog as it formed droplets on her hair, she closed the door. She had time to relax on the bed with a hot cup of tea to let the tablets take full effect.

Ombre' was enjoying himself with a couple of cold sausage rolls quickly thrown to him after seeing them in the fridge, while reaching for the milk. He didn't mind whatever she gave him he was very tolerant and would eat those for breakfast, his big brown eyes watching her painfully slow movements. He was 14 years old and he ate them ravenously enjoying every morsel, she smiled, that was nice to see.

It would be awful if he stopped eating because of old age, he never complained when she was sick and just watched as she went to lie down on the deserted bed. He trusted Gemma and knew enough to understand she would be back on track once the damp fog lifted from the air outside, she was sure to feel better soon and manage to feed him proper dog food later.

The builder was finally here after waiting a month to have a doorway made in the back of the garage. Gemma continued to stay hopeful and happy at the progress of improvements she had initiated around the place, it was slow but on going whenever finances allowed her to fix something, telling herself she should remain positive. The headache was different today, not like her familiar arthritic pain, she wondered if it was a migraine.

A pretty silvery grey dove coos in the huge stately gum tree and she thought of her mum, feeling sure that her mother was trying to tell her something, she passed away the same year as Mason had his brain aneurism and her mum knew she loved doves, which was when one started to appear on the deck. It was comforting to have a sense of knowing and a depth of reassurance that her mum wanted to be with her today.

"I'll be okay mum," she cried out gently to the dove, thinking it was a good thing no one was around listening to her calling out to a bird.

The builder cut the hole in the garage wall with a loud screeching and unbearable noise of metal being sawn through but she just stayed inside the house and left him to it, only venturing down to the garage to see if he was managing okay once the noise stopped.

She left him to fit the single door that Gemma managed to get second-hand off the internet. The garage was erected with just two roll-a-doors at the front and it really was a nuisance to have to open all the time if you just wanted to walk through to fetch something and did not need to get the car out, so the single side door would make it easier. It had taken until mid-day for the sun to come out and she now felt a little better with warming sun rays soaking deeply through into her joints, plus the paracetamol she ultimately ended up taking.

Rushing past the yellow letter box she spotted a large envelope shoved forcibly through the narrow slot. Carefully removing and reading barrister and solicitor on the bottom right corner, adrenaline rushed through her blood stream, thinking that can't be good!

Gemma's heart skipped a beat as she suspected something toward, what are they doing to her now? She felt reluctant to open it, paused while pulling out a dining chair to sit down. Carefully unsticking the flap to reveal a letter which read, '*We have been instructed by Mason Brownlie to advise, you two have been living separately since October and regrettably your marriage has broken down irreconcilably. He thinks it is now time to consider division of assets and to formalise the marital separation.*'

She continued on to read, her heart was pounding and she couldn't believe the word, *separation?* When was going into hospital called a marital separation?

The letter referring to separation had arrived out of the blue and taken her by surprise, it denied belief as Mason had never said anything to her, was always welcoming and loving. She was shocked.

Unbeknown to her now, this envelope would plumet her life into turmoil, many sleepless nights were to follow and an inability to focus on work, why would he want to grow old alone? Didn't he want a devoted wife to help him at this important time in his life.

One who stood by him through thick and thin, and spent nine hours a day sitting next to his hospital bed for a month protecting and feeding him. Feeling small and her needs insignificant it continued on to say Mason and son Dwayne would like to visit the property to decide what he wants to retain. Well, that had not improved her day any, maybe waking up sick was a premonition of a bad day. Gemma will have to consult Ms Simmons next week!

Shock and panic welled up from deep within her, threatening to constrain her throat, she endured actual physical pain while attempting to swallow, she struggled to understand how Mason who had no understanding of what he was doing could potentially end their marriage. This was not just brain damage and an absence of cognition to understand the consequences of his actions! It was also coercion by a family member who stood to gain financially from it.

Stressed to decide on what the best action was, she smiled down at loyal old Ombre' and told him, "I'm going down to the pond to think." In a mental and emotional turmoil she slid out of her slippers and pulled on gumboots, and in a daze walked slowly to the pond with him plodding alongside her.

Choosing to settle beside the pond on a lush green bed of grass he lay down next to her, she wasn't alone. All around her was an aura of peace and quiet, the water was still and the day had cleared with a cloudless sky above, but the tiredness enveloped her with a strange phenomenon of being almost hypnotized with a sleepy inability to move, she prayed for knowledge of what to do and faith to trust that it would all work out, will this stop her from seeing her husband. This was where she wanted to stay with her dog beside her forever, with no desire to return to the house or the world for that matter, she was only half present and the other half not here, it was a strange phenomenon and she was emotionally exhausted.

Their world they made together, her and Mason, the lifestyle they loved, the memory of him being there with her and the mornings they walked here together to rehabilitate him, tears stung in her eyes and she was brought back to the present, nausea and aching pain eating away inside. Why go on? she felt old and she had no reason to be strong anymore. The tears just would not stop flowing and she sat beside the pond until the cold was biting.

Now that explained why Dwayne's visits and taking Mason away weekends had stopped, he had done the brain washing and got his signature on whatever papers he wanted, Dwayne had withdrawn $10,000 from the bank account and so wouldn't need to bother with his dad for a while, until he wanted more. Meanwhile the days don't stop and after a prolonged restless night she returned to Country Views rest home to visit Mason in his room after he had finished his Sunday lunch. Another resident came up to her before she entered Mason's room and started explaining that everyone could hear Mason yelling at old Jack at morning tea today, he had his feet up on a footstool beside where Mason wanted to play snooker. Mason said he did not have enough room to play and kicked Jacks swollen feet off the stool, staff intervened and prevented further incident by ordering Mason to go to his room to calm down. (Just another incident of aggressive behaviour which Dwayne refused to acknowledge)

"My dad's not aggressive." He always snapped back at Sue. This was reported to Gemma when she proceeded to the office to check on what happened.

"I'm sorry, but he is!" Sue always reportedly went back at Dwayne. Apparently Dwayne just walked away with his nose in the air like she didn't know what she was talking about.

During their time alone together Mason showed more affection after Dwayne had either left or had not been for a while, and there was an obvious difference in behaviour. Mason didn't mention the letter, maybe didn't remember it and she was unsure whether to mention it either.

Dwayne is such a b......, a heartless piece of excrement! He was only after his dad's money, his actions in the past proved that. He only became interested in visiting his father since he went to the rest home. Gemma recalled all the father's days that her poor husband sat waiting expectantly just to be disappointed when the day passed without hearing from Dwayne, and now he sees an opportunity to gain something for himself, taking charge by filing for separation and getting Gemma out of the way will be quicker for him to inherit.

Gemma's resolve strengthened to fight for Mason to continue to have the best life, he was entitled to be taken care of. In what way would it benefit her poor husband to lose his wife, home and for the boys to get their hands on his money leaving him to live out his life on his own without visits. If the house were sold, Mason would no longer qualify to have government funding for a rest home because he would be expected to pay for it with the house sale money or buy a place. Gemma's horror dream is of Mason ending up on the street homeless after the sons take all of his assets, how many years could she keep fighting for them to stay together? it was very stressful.

Before leaving to go home a strong desire to run away from all the turmoil was back with a vengeance as she hugged and kissed Mason goodbye, fighting to hold back the tears while slipping into the safety of the car seat and hastily heading for home. The whole situation was made harder for her by not being able to speak with Mason about what he signed, he had memory loss and confusion and she resisted upsetting him, he always looked forward to visits and outings together so it made no sense that he wanted a separation. What did make sense was believing her poor husband was harassed and exhausted into doing whatever his son told him to do, he has a diagnoses of Dementia and would sign whatever he was told to sign with no cognitive ability to understand consequences.

Monday morning she phoned Dwayne's solicitor whom the letter came from and tried to press on her the mistaken understanding that she would believe Mason and she were separated! Making it quite clear that she had documentation stating that Mason has

Dementia and could not understand what a separation entailed, that she suspects it was down to his son Dwayne's manipulation to get his dads assets. Jill Hanover admitted that the first contact was with Dwayne, and Gemma also pointed out that she was not contacted for an appointment by Mason, because he was incapable of initiating or comprehending consequences of a separation, the meeting was initiated by the son without consultation with Mason. Stressing to her that Mason had never expressed any desire to separate and she believed he was being lead into a situation that he would later regret. Gemma expressed how she was stunned with disbelief as it was ridiculous to think that someone going into care has to get a separation, stating that there must be hundreds of married couples with one partner in care. The lawyer was insistent that '*he agreed with everything that was talked about*.'

Ignorance! of course he agreed with everything that was said, he was under duress from Dwayne. Any idea that was suggested to him by Dwayne along with unrealistic dreams and possibilities wearing rose coloured glasses would have been agreed to by her husband. Gemma said goodbye to her because she was obviously blinded by whatever it was Dwayne had told her or maybe they were good friends. Dwayne was also footing the bill.

Whichever one, she was not acknowledging the actual documented facts, that Gemma's husband had a diagnosis of Dementia and could be easily led, without the ability to understand consequences, and would believe and agree to anything.

Chapter 12

Gemma popped in to see Mason before work on Monday morning just in time to have a cuppa, the receptionist welcomed her warmly. She found Mason happily perched on the edge of his bed equipped with his favourite set of tiny jewellery screw drivers she fetched from home some months back. Aware that he has an audience he carefully undoes the nose piece from the old broken sunglasses, his focus depicted intense concentration and contentment as he proudly went about the business of swapping two small plastic pieces from the broken pair, onto his favourite wraparound sunglasses she bought him for Christmas, the old pair were broken when he went out with Dwayne.

She knew that he had light sensitive eyes ever since that life changing day when two ordinary lives were changed forever. She stood motionless, silently watching him repeat an action from years gone by, he always loved playing with screws and stuff and repairing things. Sitting in front of her was her dear husband radiating self-confidence as he achieved this small challenge with great clarity of mind and skill. Oh, her heart swelled with love for him, sadness that this has happened and pride for him in his successes.

"Can you fix them then?" she asked with a hopeful smile.

"Look," he says as he proudly thrusts the finished pair towards her, his lovely smile filling the entire width of his jaw line. He was smiling on the inside.

"Well done," she reached for him, wrapped her arms around the top of his broad shoulders and stroked his greying hair as they bathe in the glory of his success. She loves him! Every day she reminds herself that whatever becomes of her, lack of happiness was not Mason's fault, she hopes to never feel angry with him because he can't understand what's going on around him, he has dementia and needs reminding what day it is. No one ever desires to become the intellectually disabled person he had become, and she just wished that when he and his ex-wife were bringing up Dwayne as a child they had said 'no' to him more often, and taught him to respect his parents. Dwayne was the first born and never learnt to respect and accept that parents have their own rights, loves and dreams beyond him.

Another Saturday brought another more threatening letter, saying that she, Jill Hanover represents Mason Brownlie and she has now been to visit him at the rest home since Gemma informed her that Mason did not request a solicitor, that Dwayne had organised it and separation had never been mentioned between her and her husband. She accepts that she made the appointment with Dwayne but continues to insist that Mason does want a separation and does not want to return home, so the house needs to be sold. *Doesn't want to return home* resounded in her brain, shocked, she knew that those were not her husband's words, it was completely untrue as he often talked about when he is well enough to come home! How outrageous making false accusations like that, what is going on!

More shenanigans from that demonic excuse for a human being Dwayne. In one sense she felt sorry for Dwayne and his family because he must spend so much time obsessing over how to destroy his dad's marriage, the financial greed will surely affect his home life. Wariness continued to take hold of her although anger pumped her full of adrenaline. She continued to question how losing the love of his life, the person who worked 24/7 to rehabilitate him, could possibly be beneficial to Mason. The unconditional love she has for her husband spoke volumes, what is wrong with the Brownlie family. She has been married for 16 years with the last six years spent caring for him and he had never once talked about separation, not in her wildest dreams would she believe it was Mason's wish. None of it made any sense, and she could not comprehend a sick ageing man wanting that.

Life had been hard, and her years of loss and heartache for the man she married had dragged her through heartfelt pain, and being emotionally wounded watching the suffering of a loved one, living in the knowledge that she will need to care for her husband for the rest of his days, treasuring the good memories from the past, bravely tolerating physical threats and controlling behaviour which at times ignited every fibre and nerve in her body, fear bursting into life like a sparkler crackling down the length of its frame until her life force was extinguished. Only through her love, faith, determination and courage did she continue on.

Frantically searching the discharge notes from the rehabilitation unit, along with a large envelope of hospital notes that had accumulated following the five weeks assessment in the secure hospital ward, she sat down and lay them out on the kitchen table to carefully read the twenty odd pages, concluding in the diagnoses of Dementia.

Organizing them into a pile in preparation to take to her solicitor with a cover letter and with a heavy weight of disbelief and bewilderment that this was really happening she continued to plod on. Tonight on the phone she decided to double check with Mason what he wants, calmly, quietly she asked did he remember a lady coming to see him at the rest home.

"Yes, she just turned up."

"Did you want to see her?" Gemma asked.

"No," he said.

"If we sell the house you won't ever be able to come home again. Did Dwayne tell you to sell it?"

"Yes!" he replied. She will take this information to her solicitor, but she had no evidence.

At least she felt reassured that she must fight on for him because what was happening he did not request, it was not in his best interests and he doesn't understand the consequences of a separation.

Waking up to a morning of sunshine filling her bedroom brought with it an air of positivity, she will phone Mason.

“Hi, it’s a lovely day can I take you out for lunch? we can stop off at the home cookery we always went to after Church on Sundays and get your sausage rolls and cream cakes if you want.”

“No, Dwayne is picking me up soon.”

“Are you sure, because you saw him yesterday, won’t you be free today?” She was surprised.

“He made me write it on the calendar.”

“Surely you’re not going two days in a row, when do I get to see you?”

“Yes, he said I have to go with him today because it’s important,” he said unrelentingly.

“Do you want to come home?” (She wondered what’s going on!) And needed to know for sure what he wanted.

“I always want to go home!” he says quickly.

If only that was recorded for Dwayne and his ignorant solicitor to hear. It all seemed out of her hands, Mason was manipulated by his son and agreed to whatever he was told, his son appeared intimidating being a large frame bodybuilder and maybe Mason was too scared to disagree or found it difficult to express his wishes. One of the cruel things about his Dementia was that his memory and emotions were regressing back in time and sometimes when she took him out he referred to her as Rose (who he ended up divorcing). Sometimes he was good, but out of the blue especially when tired, he just got strangely confused, at those times trusting his son was the natural thing for him to do, he was susceptible to being manipulated when they kept him for long days.

“Okay.” You have a nice day darling and I’ll see you later okay.” she said to him fawning cheerfulness, not wanting to distress him as it was not fair, none of this was his doing.

“Bye then,” he said with all innocence.

“Bye.” Trying not to sound deflated but disbelieving that others would go to such lengths to come between a man and his wife, it was just so wrong and she trusted that right would prevail, hopefully sooner rather than later.

A little ray of sunshine penetrating through a gap in the clouds helped to warm her, she was numb. The sunlight also enlightened her soul with the positivity of a better future as she spent time sitting at their pond with her loyal friend, just her and Ombre'. The tranquil sound of birds singing in the weeping willow tree over-hanging the pond limited any negative thoughts.

Gemma focused on stroking his soft fur, noticing it was becoming brittle and hair like, drawing attention to his age, it affects dog hair as well as our own, silver grey was appearing around his mouth. She smiled fondly down at him as they sat in silence, there was no need to speak as he instinctively knew her feelings, with his warm body pressing affectionately against well-worn jeans, just the right amount of pressure that demanded a pat. Tranquillity and tweet, tweet she sighted a Swift lightly skimming the top of crystal clear water as it swooped around the pond collecting insects. The vital thing wrong with this scene was her husband not being there with her, natures beauty endeavoured to ease the dreadful torment plaguing her insides, as she attempted to push sad thoughts to the back of her mind, to allow for much needed rest and space for ruminating over better times she longed to enjoy in their little bit of the world.

Monday came and went with the usual routine and she was anxious for any update on what was happening. She popped in to again see Mason before going home.

After hugs and kisses, "I'll pick you up tomorrow morning, that's Tuesday, if you don't feel like bowls we'll just have a day out and go for lunch somewhere nice eh?"

"No, I don't want to go," he says with a quick short glance before looking away with pleading eyes.

"Why? Did Dwayne tell you not to come out with me?" Aware that he has been home with his son two days in a row to be harassed and lied to.

“Yes.” Came the sad reply.

“That’s not fair is it? You should go out with your wife if you want to eh.”

“My son said we’re separated,” he murmured glumly looking down.

Her heart shattered into a hundred pieces, as she tried to hold herself together for him.

“No, we’re not separated darling,” she replied, “Don’t worry I’ll never leave you.” Reaching her arms around his neck and giving him a big kiss while blinking profusely, trying to prevent tears from falling in front of him.

This was too awful, the stress of seeing him hurting was unbearable and so unnecessary, she needed to protect him.

“I will pick you up in the morning eh. Everything’s okay, bye darling.” Starting to move towards the door to make a hasty retreat, so upset, desperation and helplessness weighing heavily, it was crushing and she could not stand to see the cruelty happening to a loved one.

Tuesday morning, she cannot take anything for granted so phoned to check how he was before turning up at the rest home. She was fearful Mason would not know what to do, he was being pressured into not seeing his wife! and Gemma was afraid for his welfare not wanting to contribute to his stress. This should not be happening.

“No! he says to her after the staff hand him the phone. “I can’t go out because my son will stop coming to visit me if I do.”

“Okay, don’t worry darling, you know that I’m always here for you eh,” she was frantically distraught, heart pounding and tortured.

“Yeah bye.” Was the sad hapless reply.

Now what can Gemma do? How does she help him? And the tears of desperation pool in the corner of her eyes, so sad that he was being tormented by his son, when would this end? Of course he was being forced to do things against his wishes, this was nothing short of elder abuse. Poor Mason, of course in his confused state it was easier to go along with Dwayne which in a macabre sort of way was a complement to her. Mason was confident enough in their love that he knew she would always be loyal and not mad at him. She would never threaten to take away their visits, her poor lost darling! In a normal relationship you marry your partner before you have children, but in today's world of second marriages plus the regression of his damaged brain, he has lived with Gemma for 16 years but his son came from his first marriage, Dwayne was 49 years old so Mason had distant memories of knowing him, Gemma was more of a stranger.

Dementia is a heart-breaking disease and she prayed one day a cure would be found. Gemma's poor lost husband would be happy if left to follow the routine he had come to know at the rest home except Dwayne was heartless and controlling. Gemma feared for Mason's well being with the pressure he was under, discerning that one consolation, his lack of memory may help alleviate the stress a little.

During ongoing visits to see him every day when he was there, she noticed if he had been out with Dwayne there was an aggressiveness about Mason she did not understand. Eventually discovering he was being told lies, when one day he accused Gemma of seeing someone else, buying a new car and stealing the house off him. After explaining to him that was all nonsense that Dwayne tells him to make him get a separation, she also took him outside to the carpark and showed him the old car they go to bowls in, he remembered it. He was reassured that she didn't have time to be seeing anyone else because she was either at work or with him. Kissing and cuddling he soon forgot the horrible things his son was indoctrinating him with.

Another Tuesday finally arrived for bowls and she naturally felt apprehensive now that she knew what Dwayne was doing, intuition told her to phone the rest home first and check if Mason was ready. Stressed and longing to know whether to pick him up or not and longing to be able to be with her husband she nervously phoned. Lately Dwayne had been picking him up at 10.00am and not returning him to the home until 10.30pm on Saturday nights and the same again on Sunday so when he got back to the rest home he was worn down from listening to false accusations. Gemma's heart ached for him, aware of the pressure and the continual brain washing to destroy their marriage was so wrong. Dwayne was inflicting his obsessive controlling ways onto his dad and the manager (Sue) told her Mason was disorientated when he returned to Country Views late at night and unable to find his room.

No, he won't go to bowls, the rest home informed her that he was too tired as he didn't get in until very late last night, Monday, and he won't get out of bed, he doesn't want to go anywhere.

After thanking them she quickly hang up, her hands were shaking and she was unable to stop the flow of tears, she was worried sick about what's happening to her husband and how exhausted and stressed he must be if he will not get out of bed. Covering her face with her hands she sobs, with chest heaving and a sickly stomach, Gemma missed him and was looking forward to seeing Mason who she had been kept from seeing for three days now. It was Tuesday, she looked forward to their date. Having to console herself the best way she could, she told herself that he was being looked after, only it didn't help as her heart was breaking, tearing her apart and she knew this torture cannot go on.

Dwayne continued to take him home early on Saturday and Sunday mornings only bringing him back to Country Views late at night preventing Gemma any weekend visits. Life was very difficult for her not being able to see her husband, fearful for him and any distress he was under, she did not know how to stop it happening. She tried talking to the rest home but they said if Mason wanted to go they can not stop him, after persistent calls about elder abuse, the aged people organisation promised to visit him.

Week after week, between work and looking after the animals at home, her visits to the rest home are often short as she was still prevented from seeing him on the weekends. Gemma always undertook with all of her heart to not let him see her grief and make their limited time together special, not allowing her poor husband to see how much she hurt.

One kind concerned staff member confided with Gemma that Dwayne had been spreading vile rumours around the rest home trying to turn everyone against her, but thankfully they just ignored him and didn't care, Mason always welcomed Gemma so that was all they wanted to know. A lot of perseverance, she never gave up and when Tuesday rolled around again and the rest home said he was there they sat down on the bed beside each other and she tried to undo the damage his son had done; she expressed how much she missed him as this was always their day out together and she enjoyed their dating. He was relaxed and laughed, he appeared to be quite lucid today but went on to explain that Dwayne's partner Victoria was leaving him and she owns most of the house they live in, so Dwayne had told Mason he must get a separation, sell the home and get money to buy a house together with him. Dwayne said he won't be financially able to own a house without his dads help, promising to move Mason in and look after him if he gets money.

What nonsense, after getting any money there was no way he would cope with Mason and still be able to work the hours he needed to. Gemma did not believe for one minute Dwayne was willing or a suitable carer to cater for Masons needs. He had the opportunity before the rest home and refused, she was also certain that Mason would not get his name on the title either. It looked like Mason was being pressured to help out by providing a home, he was unable to comprehend the outcome because of Dementia and of course he would use Dwayne's solicitor to protect his assets, this was a conspiracy. Gemma's thoughts were in total disbelief, concern and anger that the scheming s.o.b was planning to take advantage without any concern for his dad. Mason's welfare came first, at this time of his life he needed people to love him, visit and make every day stress-free for him plus she did not want him to lose everything, to be alone and broke out on the street after Dwayne took everything.

Desperately trying to remain calm for her precious husband even though hurt reached inside her guts crushing her. Powerless to feel well or think normally Gemma was filled with contempt for what his son was trying to do, straining a reply and with all she could manage to get out without being emotional for them both she replied.

"Dwayne's problems with his marriage breaking up is not your problem darling. You do not have to buy him a house." He didn't answer, Mason was told what to do.

Before leaving with her heart pounding, Gemma went to see Sue and inform her that Dwayne had plans to move Mason out of Country Views, and she queried if he could do that. She explained to her that Mason could leave if he wanted to, but if he received money from his house sale he would lose the government Residential Care Subsidy and as long as he doesn't ask for home help no one will be in contact with Mason to follow up on his care or medication or be aware of any elder abuse. He could be well hidden from society unless a neighbour or someone complained about him as he was incapable of helping himself. Gemma wondered how much of this was going on, taking money from the vulnerable without anyone knowing, it could be happening a lot if they can not get help for themselves. The only way to sleep tonight was to try to think of flowers in the garden, trees and pray for Mason to understand what his son was trying to do, she hoped he would have a lucid moment and recognise the deceit. Gemma spent the night praying for strength, digging deep for compassion that Dwayne was going through a marriage breakup, she must stay well to get through this emotional roller coaster.

Work on Wednesday morning took her mind off things for a little while as she concentrated on students' needs, focusing on someone she could help and finding that the camaraderie among the staff was invaluable. Gemma had two very special friends to confide in, one in the library and one who was a scientist. They both listened compassionately, showing genuine concern for her situation, which was so valuable and appreciated.

Chapter 13

It was a short day for Gemma, finishing at lunchtime so she gobbled down a packet of two minute noodles packed into her bag this morning, they were cheap and quick before she headed off to seek free legal advice. Thank goodness there was no appointment needed and it was just a short wait to ease her tortured soul, finding out some facts on what Dwayne could legally do. Just because Mason went into care they could not make her sell the house. It was not costing Mason anything as she paid all expenses and his superannuation went to help with the rest home fees, he received clothing money each winter and some spending money each fortnight. Worst case scenario any settlement would be negotiated with proof of what she contributed.

Gemma put more into their home with the sale of her own mortgage free home she owned before marrying Mason. They also gave valuable advice to phone the mental health crises team. So many phone numbers and suggestions were given to her by kind people that understood her shock but were unaware of law and who does what. Gemma just needing a bit of time to contemplate and clarify what the best action was.

Back in her trusty little car parked at the shopping centre she sat quietly, picking up her mobile phone she phoned the mental health number given to her by the police. The lady on the other end of the phone asked her to phone another number. She hung up, tired from all the emotions swamping her mind she decided it all needed to wait until she was able to communicate more intelligently, when she was not so emotionally exhausted. Gemma stopped off to get a few items from the supermarket and decided to phone their doctor in the morning to see if he had actioned anything. What a massive relief, Dwayne could not force her to sell the house, as apart from the upheaval and lost memories, why should she lose her home because her husband got sick?

Gemma's next visit to Country Views rest home she was told that she could no longer see her husband. Her foot staggered back like someone had hit her, she was gobsmacked, what was going on?

"Why?" In amidst panic for his safety (what has happened, are they hiding something).

The manager informed her that Mason had signed a Power of Attorney over to his sons, Sue went to get the form to show her, in black and white it read that a copy should have been given to Gemma to object to. It had not been, of course Dwayne hadn't abided with that ruling because they waited for the time limit to object, to expire. She can't object!

Reading the pages and seeing the sons' signatures Gemma was stunned, she looked at Sue, bewildered before stating.

"Peter shouldn't have signed acceptance because he has convictions and is not a worthy person to have Power of Attorney, so that is inaccurate! He has a long list of drug, assault and burglary convictions." Gemma explained, hot and stressed. "To give Power of Attorney Mason must be of sound mind, but he has Dementia!" she gasped at how they have flaunted all the rules.

"He doesn't understand consequences of his actions and is easily lead according to his psychiatrist report!" Gemma blurted out, "That is why I have applied to the courts for PPPR which is a fair assessment of who can take care of him and his affairs. Also he was under duress when he signed that form." She paled and her hands shook with anger and astonishment at the flaunting of the rules.

Gemma's heart felt the loss of her husband as her chest tightened and her legs were heavy, feeling like her blood would no longer circulate without the man she loves, filled with fear and panic that he would not understand why she was not visiting him.

Sue replied, "This paper is what she must go by until the court rules otherwise, I sympathises with your plight," she expressed, that she had never seen any animosity between Mason and her and she saw no reason why she shouldn't visit her husband. This could take months to go down legal tracks and all that time she will be prevented from seeing her husband by Dwayne who had POA. It's an unbelievable illegal farce, merely getting her head around it she realized it was no good being upset with the rest home, at the present time Dwayne had the paperwork to stop her from seeing her husband and the rest home had to abide by it. She must take it to court and have it overturned. Gemma's fear was of how long that would take, keeping in mind that Mason would be told she didn't want to see him anymore, with progressive Dementia, time was of the essence.

Driving home in a whirl of mixed emotions, shock and feeling sick with the deceit. She struggled to understand how corrupt this solicitor must be to witness and sign a Power of Attorney for someone who has a documented diagnosis of Dementia and memory loss. It was unknown how long Mason would be able to recognise her as his wife. She knew that the court system could take years if Dwayne objected. It was a nightmare and she cried herself to sleep from anguish, suffering and the shear erroneousness of keeping them a part.

Following a very restless night she drearily walked into the kitchen the next morning feeling defeated, blinded by a bright yellow glow of the morning sun, just rising above the wooden fence bordering the front yard. She had never encountered such an undeniably positive sight before.

Standing barefoot on the cold wooden tongue and groove, staring into the yellow glow as if prompting her to be mindful, to acknowledge a light of hope that was shining down on her, no matter what torment others create she must continue to hope, a light at the end of the tunnel and promises of a better tomorrow, full of knowledge and life experiences to be able to help others. She was destined to go through a demanding time, and learn understanding and empathy, after her years of dark fear and relentless torment, her days would again be full of peace, finding joy in just being alive. This strange phenomenon was telling her, she was not alone and she mustn't give up! Light is untouchable and unbreakable, a brightness to motivate her to press on but also a warning some should fear.

Everything was now changed with the sons holding Power of Attorney they were able to sell the lifestyle block, her home. She was resolved to fight to see Mason, pulling herself together and becoming strong, he needed her to be. Drying her eyes she looked in the mirror, if nothing else today she must make a trip to the bank to find out how much she could borrow, to see if she could buy him out, that's probably a good start. To know what her options were, that would sort out some of her concerns even though it would take courage to find out. Unsure if she could borrow anything, and eager to keep living near her job of seven years if she must move. Can she make an offer to buy him out or was that dreaming, his sons would ask the world or even straight out refuse to sell it to her. Would any bank provide a mortgage for someone in their sixties? And even if she could get a mortgage did she want to go into so much debt now at this time in her life. She remembered how she was mortgage free before falling in love with Mason, which was now prevalent in her mind, making it totally debilitating and unfair that it has all gone so wrong because Mason got sick.

Plans of retirement ran down the drain, consumed with thoughts of doubt that she would ever retire, and grow old without money problems and the continual need for self-preservation. The days that followed were full of panic and she was overwhelmed with the constant subconscious questioning of how wicked it all was. She woke every night with concerns constantly muddled and changing from Mason to herself and wrestling with the fear of how their future would turn out. Perhaps it would be easier to just give up and not exist anymore but then she remembers that intense light shining into her kitchen and knew that she was meant to stay strong.

Pulling a soft paper tissue out of the drab checkered tissue box, dabbing her eyes gently, she confronted an unknown pale-skinned person looking back from the mirror, this amount of stress had taken its toll and she wondered how things got to be like this, when all she ever did was take her husband home from Rehab against medical advise and care for him. Loving partners don't expect a reward for being loyal and caring but she did think that they would die looking after each other and all their hard work done towards their future, would pay off in retirement.

An awareness of a soft warmth pushing up against her bare leg brought her back to now, her cherished dog sensing that she needed his presence, he probably saw the tears. Bending down to hug him and promising to take him for a ride in the car, his tail wagged. Thank goodness her needs are met by this devoted little companion, with his grey chin and ageing fur he was a tower of strength as he continued to hang in there for her, losing him didn't bear thinking about, but in reality she knew he was old and nothing lives forever, she would cherish him for however long she was able to keep him, never permitting a thought of being alone to enter her head.

Again, she drove with a mind in the grip of dark clouds, parking the car she was oblivious to how she arrived at her destination, solemnly but determined she walked up to the bank counter for her appointment, her handbag full of income and expenses documents.

"I'll get the mortgage manager to come and see you, just take a seat." The tall young girl appeared to be a very approachable person and put her at ease very quickly, as Gemma asked to speak to her somewhere out of public hearing she was directed to a quiet office. Her hands were sweating as she took a seat, brought out her pay slips and rates demand that told of the estimated value of their home.

"I would like to know how much I could borrow to try and buy my husband's share of the house please." They set about filling in the blanks of the assets and expenses list before she left, to find out later.

Wednesday was another relentless night of no sleep, speculating if she would lose their house and feeling upset that they have been kept apart for three long weeks now. Using lies and deceit they were taking everything, her husband's love and companionship, the roof over her head plus the joy they both have when together.

Silently hoping that it will be sorted and not go on for too much longer, her heart was pounding too fast even just lying in bed, and she knew that it would eventually impact her health, how can she work if she can't sleep. Silent tears of desperation rolled down the sides of a strained face and into the soft violet coloured pillow, she hoped that she didn't make a sound to disturb Ombre', he needed his sleep. Gemma could just make him out from the dim light shining through the slit in the floral curtains, he was still covered up with his blanket on the sheep skin rug beside the bed and had not moved since both retiring for the night.

Feeling tired and hungry for lunch she watched as the four lively students quickly made their way out of the cosy classroom, thank goodness she would be in the warm staffroom for lunch. Gemma will always remember her student days when she would huddle in a corner somewhere outside trying to shelter from the bitter wind, even though September was officially spring in New Zealand and the four legged woolly babies were miraculously appearing in peoples paddocks, she still found it was a cold wind that blew outside and the sun did not often shine during the day.

Optimistically scrolling through ten emails to see if Ms Simmons had managed to obtain the information needed from the doctor. Gemma had now reached the end of her tether. Ping, and there was an email, it's from her!

Holding her breath she hurriedly opened it; *Dear Gemma we have received the medical report that we needed to be able to proceed with your application for you to be property manager and welfare officer.* Breathing a sigh of relief with the confirmation email and now having further doctor's reports, relief swept over her, exhilarated and hopeful. She couldn't think, as it went on to read.

"Please settle the doctor's account as soon as possible so we can uplift the original." Gemma read it full of anticipation and was impatient to read what the doctor had written. Would it be enough to prevent Dwayne from making Mason formally separate from her?

Briefly it advised, 'Doctor Gilmour goes on to say, Mr Mason Brownlie is fully incompetent to manage financial affairs and is totally unable to communicate his needs in relation to welfare.'

Surely the court will understand now that he was not of sound mind to give Power of Attorney and he needed protecting. An appointment was made with Gemma's solicitor to see her on Tuesday at 2.30pm.

Oh wow, Gemma was happier, she had never felt that excited and relieved about anything in her life, this must be what it felt like to win a million dollars. Anxious and unable to focus she phoned Bridget and told her the good news.

"I know that it's not over and I still have the Settlement Conference to cope with, but the doctor has done a good job of assessing Mason and has seen what I had to live with. Sometimes you think that living in this situation no one could possibly understand. But he did, if he were here now I would hug that complete stranger. The ball is rolling and I will be able to get some sleep tonight."

"I hope that will put an end to the Power of Attorney and you get to see Mason again," said Bridget.

"It will still take time in court, and money to fight it," said a relieved Gemma.

Two months have slowly passed, waiting for the conference hearing date her solicitor had managed to get her the legal right to have time with Mason again. Excited she turned up with treats and presents for him, he welcomed her like she had never been gone, and she joined him at a game of Bingo in the dining room. After a couple of games Mason touched her arm and pointed to his room, so they both went to sit on his bed beside each other, she lay her head on his chest and her long hair fell around her shoulders as he picked up her hands, squeezing them he spoke softly, not wanting anyone to hear.

"Dwayne said he's coming to pick me up today and I asked when, but he wouldn't tell me. So you better go!" he said.

"That's okay, he won't come until after morning tea, so I'll go then, he won't see me. I'll leave out the back door."

"No, he might come!" he sounded very nervous.

"What happens if he does see me, I'm okay with it?" smiling up at him.

He held her hands tightly, "He goes **really** mad at me if I see you," he explained in a very normal and genuine sounding way.

"Why, what does he say?" she enquired.

"*If you keep seeing her you're wasting my time, and I won't bother with you ever again.*" He recited angrily.

Gemma's heart missed a beat as she made it clear, "It shouldn't be a waste of time to visit his father, he can't tell you who to see and you should make the best of your life. Tell your solicitor what he's doing."

"No, I can't he'll get really mad!"

Gemma called for a staff member to come in and told her Mason sounded afraid of his son. Not interested or just unsure what to do the young caregiver responded.

"Best if you just go, and he can go back to Bingo before his son arrives."

This was elder abuse by Dwayne, what should she do to help her poor husband, she wondered if staff need training to recognise and know how to deal with elder abuse in rest homes. Gemma believed what Mason was saying to be true and no one really cared. She could not do anything to stop what was happening to Mason, and it was driving her insane not knowing how to protect him. It was no good contacting the police as then Dwayne would stop visiting and withhold Mason's grandson, which was what he was afraid of. Anyone living in these institutions need visitors and she understood that contact with their family was important. Placing a little kiss on his cheek she wanted to console him.

"Thanks for explaining to me why you want me to go. I miss you and love you very much. I'm sorry that this is happening to you."

He stretches his arm around her shoulders without speaking, and she felt burdened with the weight of the world heavy on her shoulders instead of the joy and warmth of closeness with the one she loved.

"Do you want a separation?" Gemma whispered in his ear.

"Dwayne said I have to sell the house because he has nowhere to live."

"What about me? I won't have anywhere to live?" but there was no reply, he was unable to grasp an understanding of it.

Pushing his emotions she asked, "Is it okay if I meet someone else and marry them?"

"No!" he declared, as he turned to face her with a raised voice and wild look.

"But if we don't have a home together anymore and you want a separation that means I can get a divorce, are you okay with that?" pushed Gemma.

"No, you can't," sounding desperate and getting agitated as he was backed into a corner.

She decided to leave, hoping that he would think about things. Also aware that he would unfortunately be seeing his son very soon and listening to false promises of living some fantastic life with Dwayne.

How can she find out what her darling really wants in life, he had Dementia and believed whatever stories Dwayne told him, he didn't have the mental capacity to comprehend consequences of his actions and now Dwayne had the paperwork drawn up in such a way that he can do whatever he wants with Mason's bank account without another person having to co-sign.

Meeting with Ms Simmons today, she proudly had the full report, ready to proceed now to sign and go over Gemma's application to overturn the Enduring Power of Attorney. All morning her mind had been a blur with nervous tension and apprehension of the unknown, but finally something positive was happening and that brought hope that she could get her and Mason back on track to happiness. She wanted to protect him from all the stress that the proposed separation from Dwayne and his solicitor had been causing, to take away any incentive for Dwayne to manipulate and blackmail her husband.

Thoughts of what might happen ran through her head continuously, would she be able to get PPPR (Protection of Personal and Property Rights, act 1988) and will anyone object, does she qualify in everyone's eyes to be allowed to continue managing the financial affairs at home and pay the bills as she has always done the whole of their married life. Mason had always left the running of the house to her and never paid bills, he did not understand how often they even arrived, and they just miraculously got paid leaving him without a care in the world.

The day slowly disappeared, looking at the clock every half hour didn't hastened it any, but finally it was time to jump into her car and head off to see Ms Simmons. Pulling onto the cobbled parking her mouth was dry, after sliding open the ranch slider entranceway she noticed a sign that read '*We are happy to make you a cup of tea or coffee, just ask.*' Brilliant for settling her nerves before getting down to business.

"Could you make me a cup of tea please?" she smiled to the receptionist." Who replied, "Do you have milk and sugar?"

"Just milk please, no sugar." She went to sit down on the black leather couch.

It wasn't a long wait before she sat across the desk from her solicitor and the medical report from the doctor slid across the desk towards her. Gemma began to scan it anxiously, could the doctor possibly have ascertained what it was like to live with Mason and his lack of cognitive abilities, will it have everything she needs in it to help her to protect and continue to provide for him?

Aware of the stark official room around her as she read, and the airy silence of someone watching and waiting until she reached the part where it said he had a serious brain injury in 1999.

"That's when he fell off the roof," she shrieked loudly, shocked by this news, it took her by surprise, she had no idea!

The solicitor nodded.

"I kept going to the doctor and telling him something was wrong; Mason was behaving strangely and was always impatient and grumpy for no reason. We would agree to do things and then he'd do something completely different, he just wasn't normal in anything he did around the house and he was not the same person I married," she exclaimed, aghast, she now had an explanation.

An enormous lump formed in her throat and she did not know what emotion she felt right then, her hands began to shake from shock and validation.

"I can't believe that the medical records say he had a serious brain injury just a year after moving into our home," she gasps in horror as it hits her that not only did the doctor keep Mason's confidence when she was concerned about her husband's health, but he had never told her either.

The word *serious* ran over and over in her head as this may have contributed to the brain haemorrhages that had changed their lives so dramatically. Ms Simmons went over the forms and put the application affidavit into the court.

It's only Tuesday and Gemma had work tomorrow, how would she be able to concentrate and put this out of her mind, Mason must have been warned of possible consequence of such a head injury and kept it from her. They were newlyweds, maybe he feared losing her.

There were so many questions that she wanted to ask her

husband, but he had dementia and what he didn't remember he would just invent an answer for, she longed for an explanation and was frustrated as she will probably never be able to find out how Mason felt and why he kept the secret, where was his conscience, to condemn her to a life of unknown problems, did he live in fear for his health, that concern was abhorrent to her.

Chapter 14

Wednesday passed in a blur as her head filled to overflowing with memories of the past, all the times he would cancel his days off because he could get extra money if he worked them, she wanted him home but he insisted on working. Was it because he knew he had an aneurysm and wanted to get as much money as possible before his job was taken from him, if the doctor signed him as unfit for work, or he worked because of brain damage, perhaps it was a routine he wanted to follow. Gemma's worst fear was if he knew something was wrong and was afraid to tell her, either out of a need to protect her or was he being deceitful not caring what her life would look like later. Was he able to have surgery and chose to ignore it? (That possibility made her angry!)

So many questions will remain unanswered. They both went through such a lot of pain and anguish because of the brain surgery and horror night when the aneurism burst, that could have taken his life, was it all avoidable and did the doctor keep it from her when she asked him for help?

Gemma was finding it difficult to confront this medical report, along with the threat of losing their home because of all the unanswered questions and the many lost years that she can never get back, the feelings of betrayal from their doctor not helping them both, being told that maybe they just weren't suited together, when she asked for Mason to have a brain scan. Of course he wouldn't request one, because he already knew Mason had a problem and the hospital had already done one, it was patient confidentiality.

Yes, he had protected Mason's confidence but at the expense of their quality of life. What if she hadn't been with Mason to get the ambulance in time, the burgeoning anger and questions at what happened only a year after moving into their home together, and whether all those lost years of confusion and memory loss were preventable if he had had surgery to correct a ballooning artery, it all weighed down with a heavy sadness of what if things had been different. Why didn't the doctor suggest a couples meeting to discuss options, but maybe he did and Mason refused. Uncovering a serious head injury was huge, and she was unsure how to grieve and work through all the anger and questions she had. Was he protecting her and was he scared all those times when he would explode with anger for no apparent reason. It was all so heart-breaking and tears streamed from her eyes just thinking about it, trying to sort through her feelings and memory's it was all too much.

The following two days Gemma was plagued by a sickening migraine, a desire to throw up just exasperated the dark days that continued one after the other, the joy of getting the medical report that could put an end to all of the separation nonsense was pushed into oblivion with the constant pain in her head brought on by the horrible secret now exposed, extreme emotions and legal stress.

Making the decision to do something nice to relax, she booked the hairdresser for a haircut after work, once sitting in the chair the woman convinced her to try foils to brighten her sallow face, Gemma had no idea what a time consuming job that was, after agreeing she found it hard to stay awake, she closed her eyes when the hair was pushed to the side of her face. Drifting off, heavy bloodshot eyes were reluctant to open. She knew if she didn't open them soon she would nod off, it was so relaxing and boring that she longed to sleep.

Two hours later she struggled to get to her feet, stiff after sitting for so long, her mood was such that she couldn't cook tea so headed towards the mall, she was sick and tired of noodles and tined fish. Sleep would come easily tonight as she went through the routine of turning everything off, plus her cell phone as she had a landline available for emergency.

Morning arrived, she was in no rush to get up, at 8.00 am she turned her mobile back on and a message lit up, a missed call from Peter (Mason's youngest son) showing a time of 3.45 am!

Gemma's heart missed a beat as panic pulsated through her. Had something happened to Mason. Why didn't the rest home phone her landline, that loud ring would have woken her. Leaping out of bed and racing to the landline her heart pounded from worry, the sick feeling showing just how much she still loves Mason.

Someone at the rest home answered the phone.

"Hi, its Gemma here, is Mason okay?" she tried to stay calm and speak clearly.

"Yes, he's having breakfast." Short and to the point.

"Oh, that's good, it's just that his son rang my mobile at 3.45am and I thought something must be wrong. Can you ask him to phone me when he's finished breakfast please?"

"Okay, bye," she said hastily and hung up.

"Bye." Hanging up the phone before heading to the kitchen for a cup of tea and toast thinking that was strange, did he just phone her to disturb her sleep? who knows! When Mason phoned with the help of staff she poured it all out to him, relieved to unload her worries.

"Why are they harassing me when there's nothing wrong with you, at that time of night I would have got a heck of a shock, as I did when I woke up this morning." Telling Mason that she was pleased he was okay, she loved him and she would see him later on.

Why people play silly games was a complete mystery, the highs and lows, the feelings of love and hate of years of abuse and upset linger on. She somehow got through another routine week and today she would visit Bridget and John.

Early the following Saturday she hastily leapt out of bed to phone Mason, wanting to tell him how much she loved him and missed him in case he was taken away early to prevent anytime together. He sounded cheerful but explained he was being picked up by Dwayne. There was no way she could get to see him; he will be gone from the rest home from 9.00am to 10.30pm being an intentional act to prevent

Mason and her being happy together. Dwayne will bombard him with ideas of how bad she was, that she put him in care when there was nothing wrong with him and she is a terrible person who was trying to steal his house and money. Weekends of the same old stabbing Gemma in the back will leave Mason bewildered in his demented state, and next week he'll be told not to go out with his wife. This extent of evil and control was not the behaviour of a normal human being, Dwayne obviously had some very serious insecurities and greed issues.

Sunday morning and she awoke to the birds singing outside, after spending yesterday with her daughter and son in law, and Mason sounded happier on the phone, the pressure had lifted a little, eager to leave her solicitor to sort out the paperwork. Mason was alive, so she persuaded herself that she had to move on and forget about the head injury. Gemma had to believe that anything Mason did, he thought he was doing the right thing for them both. Dialling the rest home phone number straight after his breakfast time, before anyone could take him away for the day.

"Hello," Mason says when the cordless was taken to him.

"Hi darling, how was your day out yesterday?"

"Okay, I'm going out soon."

"Again, well when can I get to see you?" she asked with a cheerful little giggle she managed to fake.

"Ah."

"You have to see me on Tuesday, because the boys take you on the weekends eh!"

"Yeah."

"We'll have to start going for walks again darling, now that the winters over."

"Oh yeah," came the lively reply with a ring of hopeful longing running through his voice, he thought it was a good idea. All sounding positive she was feeling hopeful that she might have a little bit of time with him. Everything will work out.

Gemma struggled to cope with the lonely weekends without seeing her husband, so she went back to dancing on a Saturday night, a hobby she always enjoyed and she hoped that she would get fit, occupy her lonely nights at home and then Sunday she would be physically tired and able to focus on church.

Making an affidavit was a new challenge to master but her submission was now in the judicial system, she was objecting to a separation along with proof of Mason's inability to make an application on the grounds that he was not of sound mind, and would not understand the consequences, plus she managed to get a brilliant lawyer who dealt with mental health concerns. Gemma must wait for news of when to go to the court for a round table conference, it was mandatory that before a separation the parties should have a chance to meet with their lawyers and a court official to sort out what each party wanted. Jill Hanover (Dwayne's lawyer) representing Mason can not stop this happening. Gemma put her faith in the court being able to help her and Mason and protect them from evil influences and selfish unkind people. Until then she lived on edge, because of the absurd situation and the unknown! It was a welcome relief that the legal process was under way. Looking and feeling beyond tired but having a chance to see and speak about what Mason wanted with him present at the conference provided some hope, there was a legal requirement to turn up to discuss the issues.

Confronting this mayhem there were no words to describe the emotional roller coaster she was on. The lack of confidence to accurately explain to her lawyer what she needed to say, because of her shattered nerves and sleep deprivation making it difficult to think clearly being an added hurdle. Sleep was elusive again now with legal issues looming, her mind continually played out what she wanted to say, so slipping out of bed and picking up a pen she began to write everything down for Ms Simmons, fraught with restlessness she worried that she might forget something important.

Paying legal fees was also a major concern and the need to get this all done in as short a time as possible, with no choice but to pay for a solicitor as no one wanted to take the case on legal aide. She endeavoured to fight to protect her husband's rights and needs. Although frugal with money she would need to find more. Mason's health was such that she fretted about that as well, she was always under pressure and so was he. Continual disbelief that this was even happening clouded Gemma's judgement, she sought clarity as she wrote points down. Mason had never asked her for a separation, not during the six years since his major stroke when the aneurism burst causing his memory loss and cognitive deficits, feeling certain that while looking after him 24 hours seven days a week the subject would have come up if he had wanted one. No, he never mentioned a separation until Dwayne came on the scene. Negative panic ran rampant through her thoughts, even though she knew what she was doing was right and justice should prevail she couldn't believe everything would go well.

Her mind ran over the facts, why did he not leave her before going into the rest home if he didn't want to be married. Gemma looked at all the scenarios and questioned all aspects, she worked through the brain fog and nights, not understanding what Dwayne must be saying to Mason to persuade him to leave her.

The day of the court appearance her mind was all over the place, unable to follow her everyday routine she just wanted to get it all over with. Foremost in her life, her mind and body were preoccupied and anxious about Mason as she wondered how he was feeling. Gemma had been prevented from speaking with him by Dwayne, holder of The Power of Attorney all week.

Sitting down in the dining room looking at his photo hanging on the wall, thinking over everything that had happened. She smiled as she remembers how she took that photo of him next to the Avon River, on one of many wonderful trips around New Zealand in their campervan, just the two of them and the dog. Life was wonderful then, before his brain aneurysm.

He looked calm, relaxed, his beautiful grey eyes full of life and happiness, all was well with the world and life as they knew it.

However, she contemplates on how it has changed, her heart is broken and tears welled up looking at his photo hanging on the wall, memories of happier times during their 16 year marriage.

Gemma's dear husband Mason now 65 years old with his thick black hair and clear grey eyes has no memory of those precious times together, diagnosed with Dementia in 2016 following five years of her struggling to care for him.

Dementia was like a living death, he was alive but his brain was dying, the rest home was for his own safety and hopefully with medication he will return home when Gemma's leg was better and she was sure of her safety. Residential care had caused great destress between family members who would not accept that she could no longer prevent the move, it was a last resort, a medical decision that he needed care.

After a long five week assessment and after the family declined to provide Gemma with any kind of help from caring for Mason, all glimmer of hope that she might be able to keep him at home was lost, gone, dissolved like melting ice. Other family members went on with their own lives without a thought for Mason, it had been left to Gemma. For five years she struggled to provide everything he needed before breaking her leg which made it impossible to continue.

Mason needed more help than she could provide and life changed for them both. A huge sense of loss and loneliness was felt by the one left behind in the real world, suffering just as much, possibly even more than the person with Dementia, Mason found that life in a rest home following strict mealtimes and routine made life much easier.

Gemma felt hurt during Mason's times of frustration and confusion when he did not understand why they couldn't have unrestricted time together anymore, visiting hours, mealtimes and not being in each other's arms at night was hard to explain to Mason.

Looking into his upset eyes was torturous, it was painful not being able to make it right for him, and always putting on a smile when all the time her heart was crying out, unable to take him home, it was both frustrating and heart-breaking.

At first they both struggled with what seemed like a living death, watching him disappearing into a shell of the man she loved, she understood that he was lost in a dark abyss of his mind, as she sat with his arms around her somewhere the man she married was still there, for now.

Gemma sat reminiscing over the early onset of the illness, there were strange happenings around the house, such as finding the TV remote in the fridge or filed neatly in the bookcase, and they have become fond memories as she smiles at them, there was the time he attempted to pump up the car tyres with the suction of the vacuum cleaner, all the many things that just didn't matter at the time (and family members were protected from), they learnt to accept and laugh secretly about them together on his good days. They both knew things weren't right as his Dementia took hold of him, but they were there for each other in love, sickness and in health.

Today, now living a horror story, he had lost control of his feelings, memories and all reasoning.

Mason's son refuses to acknowledge the time he spent at home when he should have been in residential care much earlier, and Gemma admits that she is angry that he is no longer at home with her growing old together, this was not the retirement they had planned together. Their dreams of future years as little old people doing things together had been stolen from them because of a serious head injury.

Luckily, Gemma retains her memories of them to treasure, only choosing to remember the quiet gentle person she married in what seemed like another life, someone else's life a very long time ago.

Chapter 15

Fortunately, it was only a 20 minute drive to the court, meeting up with solicitors and before going into the hushed room with the huge round table. Gemma caught one glimpse of Mason and her eyes filled with tears, she retreated into a side room and could barely stand, broken because she was not allowed to hug her husband, his solicitor (or Dwayne's really) sternly shuffling him quickly in to take a seat. Being kept apart the way they had been, caused her great concern for Mason's sanity and emotional welfare.

A few months before she had asked Country Views rest home that if anything happened to Mason when out with his son would they request an autopsy be done please, as she did not trust those that stood to inherit, Dwayne's behaviour was extreme.

The manager had looked a bit stunned and Gemma could almost hear the cogs of her mind ticking over as she replied.

"Mason has come back with bruises and once an upset stomach after going home with Dwayne on the weekend," she said reflectively.

"Please make a note of dates and what has happened for future reference." Gemma requested.

"Okay."

There had been too many lies and deceit, Dwayne had made sure that Gemma had no access lately, taking Mason out early and bringing him back late. Not being allowed to see her husband like she had endured, had fuelled the anticipation and longing she felt in that moment, living in hope of seeing the man she loves, only to be let down again by lack of compassion or basic humanity by others, what harm could a hug and welcome do? It was so tangible for her to be able to have a meeting with a third person to assist in clarifying where to go next, and a chance for her to tell Mason that it was not her fault he got sick, living in residential care and being told propaganda and filthy lies. It was Dwayne's greed that motivated this heartless monster to blacken lives, she felt that soon his mortal heart would fail him when karma stepped in, because of the cruel inhuman things he had done keeping a husband and wife apart.

Gemma's thoughts and words of clarification and explanations were written down, to hand to Mason if she was too upset to express her feelings for him around the table of lawyers. Susan, her longtime best friend who also knew Mason, waited outside the family court and although she was not allowed to enter Gemma felt stronger for her being there. In court her poor husband looked down, his face sad, with a blank stare and his eyes darker than she remembers, gone are the lovely grey eyes and he had a strange emptiness, he avoided looking at her. All seated in the court room in comfy chairs and behind a nicely polished table, water was sparkling under the overhead light waiting in a nice practical glass jug with glasses grouped together. She sat at the precipice of the rest of her life, wondering what their destiny will be. Life changing decisions would be made. The sabotage didn't abate as Jill Hanover went into full swing with false unsubstantiated accusations flying just for dramatic effect, and to support her case for a separation.

Taking a big breath and listening intently to her speaking for Mason instead of allowing him to speak for himself in this round table mediation conference. Gemma watched, as the lawyer stated Mason wanted a separation, her husband sat motionless and silent appearing to be heavily medicated, a look that reminded her of executions seen in movies, a look of 'The End.'

The young mediator was not having it and asked Mason directly, "Mr Brownlie, do you want a separation?"

Looking up there was a vague, "Yes, um I can't hear very well with my hearing aids."

When it came time for Gemma to say something, everyone was expecting to hear an argument such as in her affidavit. She had a lot of time to think about life and mastering the art of losing herself in thought for the past two years, fighting for Mason's happiness while he was in the rest home. Many lonely days where spent drowning in a world of black, oblivious of any sleep and copious amounts of wishful thinking as the red eyes and dark circles showed. Gemma looked at her husband, he raised an eyebrow at her and his face exhibited the pent up anger as he appeared to spark into life, he burst forth with an attempt to express his story of how his wife dumped him in a rest home to get rid of him, pieces of distorted information began to spew out, not understanding why she didn't visit him (those times that Dwayne prevented her by using the Power of Attorney, illegally obtained). It was obvious he had been kept in the dark, indoctrinated with lies, and now with Dementia his fragmented and very confused story evolved driven by anger.

Frustrated, Gemma's hands were sweating with tension and upset, rubbing them down the sides of her trousers and in this instant, a split second, she knew! realized that if she won her case to care for Mason whom she loves, and doesn't get a separation she would be condemning herself to a life of this craziness! His son will persist in tormenting them for the rest of her days.

No! Years of fighting for her husbands rights and thousands of dollars spent in legal fees, it had to stop. A sudden revelation, it was time to grieve, to take time at that moment to feel the heart break and have hope of finding light in her life. She wanted to dream of greater things and she will no longer settle for a life of what she had now. Gemma had a desire for more, expects more, deserves more and she will achieve more. This was her life now and she would accept that here her husband sat asking for a separation that his son had told him to do, he chose the son over his wife, and for whatever reason she no longer cared, because what better justice would be served than if she let Dwayne have this angry person.

The best justice served was for Dwayne to be responsible for Mason for the rest of his days. Gemma had seen the light, a ray of light guiding her to achieve great happiness and wealth, a new better life, her life.

"Do you want a separation?" the mediator again prompts her.

After a long pause of watching and waiting for Gemma to answer while she sat and watched this poor demented soul, he would never get better and she would devote her life to someone that could one day kill her, as he tried to do once before.

"Yes!" Gemma turned her eyes away from Mason. "Dated from the time he went into the rest home," she stated.

Both lawyers were astounded! there was a cloud of silence, a heavy pause of unasked questions hanging over the room, then the proceeding continued, it was agreed and the document was signed and witnessed by both lawyers.

"Well, as you have been living apart for more than two years, either party is entitled to file for a divorce," he continues to say.

Mason then leapt to his feet, no anger or blank expression anymore, now alert and replaced with fire. The word divorce shocked him into action.

Declaring with a loud forceful voice, "I don't want a divorce!" he yelled.

Ms Simmons sitting beside Gemma turned to look for instruction, Gemma looked away hoping she wouldn't say anything. It was obvious to everyone there in that room, the truth was out! He does have Dementia and did not understand the consequences of his actions when he ordered a separation. Case solved! It was too late for Mason as they had agreed and signed an agreement to separate, on the date he went into the rest home. He doesn't know if his wife will file for divorce but he was verbally adamant he didn't want one.

Why would Gemma want to waste the rest of her life caring for someone that was happy to make her homeless, that was not the action of a husband. How could he expect her to face every day being his wife with no arms to comfort and love her. It was not fair to ask of her and tomorrow she will be looking at downloading divorce documents. Mason's lawyer was clearly not working in Mason's best interests but for the one who was paying the bill.

In that decisive moment she had regained her life back, no one had the right to control her and she felt relieved of the duty of care and was victorious in the outcome. Good luck to Dwayne who would have to do all the running around to appointments and shopping for his dad now that he will lose the residential care subsidy and have to care for Mason himself. Gemma and Ms Simmons walked out of the District Court building and standing on the outside stairs with light rain glistening as it landed on their shoulders, her lawyer put an arm around her.

"Are you okay? That must have been very hard. You did well," she whispered, nodding.

Not wanting to let on about her body involuntary trembling all over she answered.

"Yes, I'm fine." Her voice sounding a bit shaky.

Gemma had made her decision, it was like a light bulb being turned on, she had no intention of compromising herself any longer, her career, life and beliefs, never doing anything to stir up his enmity but sacrificing her health for the sake of her husbands, well no longer, the heavy cloud and darkness had gone, replaced with the promise of a future. Making the decision to walk away in that instant she now wanted to forget, she left the court. Saying goodbye to her solicitor, Gemma stood and faced her dear supportive friend Susan who had been standing to one side, she was not aware of what had happened but expected the worst.

"Let me buy you a cup of coffee." Without asking anything.

"Yes, I need one, but I'll buy you one for coming with me." Gemma said to Sue.

"No, really let me," she says as they walked to the 'Home Baking café, a bright yellow building which reminded her of their letter box. Mason and she chose it because yellow would show the world how cheerful and happy they were together, and even when Mason lost his memory and couldn't remember his address to tell anyone, he remembered their letter box, small things like that made her want the best for him. Her poor Mason all she wanted to do was see and hug him, she hadn't been allowed. Instead she was drinking hot chocolate to celebrate her freedom. Catching a quick glimpse of each other when they left the court building, he looked drawn and very upset, he had lost everything.

The round table day had changed her goals completely, seeing his hostility and selfishness enlightened her. None of what she did was planned and she didn't know that was what she wanted, until she saw the man he was through new eyes. Gemma was on a high, excited about moving on, she was independent and free of responsibility, a weight had lifted as she had nothing to lose. For once there were no tears, because today in court was a victory for her.

Tomorrow she will give instructions to Ms Simmons to withdraw her application for Protection of Personal Property and Rights immediately as she will be serving divorce papers and putting the house on the market.

Gemma was full steam ahead getting appraisals from different real-estate agents and looking for a house near a beach. Grateful for what she has, not what she has lost. She needed her dog and somewhere to live and the ache was still there inside her (for the moment), she refuses to think about Mason anymore, that time in her life was a closed book. Having the courage to give up material things and completely opening her heart to trusting and believing that everything happens for a reason, all that she needs would be provided along the way in a quest for a better life. Gemma was empowered to strive, work harder and find a life, in the knowledge that when things seem at their worst, that was when it can only get better. She has freedom and she was going full on to live her life; she had wasted too much already.

Driving home from fun dancing on Saturday night the air was so cold and chilly on her skin, but life had changed for her, because apart from the physical coldness of her body she was free and warm inside, she had a wonderful evening and twirled like never before.

The worry and struggle to visit Mason had gone, and even though the house was on the market she did not care, no stress after the years of anxiety. Although she was so programmed that she was now sceptical, wondered if he could withdraw the separation he filed, could he say he didn't understand that it led to divorce. That possibility filled her with horror.

Gemma fought a hard fight to care for her husband and went through every feeling imaginable, her solicitor said she wasted five years of her life, and suffered the loss of her husband but the worst emotion was the betrayal. Now Gemma wants to look after herself, her survival to an old age is the goal, time to look after her and live life to the full.

In the morning she would phone Ms Simmons and check if he could object (which hopefully Dwayne would never allow him to do).

Ms Simmons explained that there was a time limit, so with three weeks now gone without a sound from them, everything was status quo. Full steam ahead, she lay down in the long grass by the pond, looking up at the cloudless blue sky feeling optimistic and enjoying a new perspective on life, an unfamiliar feeling of contentment and happiness. The sky was as clear as her mind, no panic or fear, full of hope and faith that only good would now embrace her, leading her to find a new home.

Confident that as things fell into place, she would return to being that patient happy person that took time to smell the flowers and to get pollen on her noise. Happiness was tremendous with the absence of the tiredness that she thought would never go away, and she was able to sleep again. Gemma no longer sought to visit Mason so there was no more torture. When she danced she felt the beat of music through her whole being, life was beautiful again because she no longer wanted him. She deserved more.

Fretful crying and heartfelt sobbing thumping from within her chest woke her as she sat upright, and she was surprised. It was because she just imagined that Mason refused to sign the Sale Agreement of their home. Gemma was terrified of being trapped, that he wouldn't let her go, and that he would keep her financially unable to move on, trapping her forever. It was just a nightmare.

No, she was being silly as the court would make him sign and anyway Dwayne had Power of Attorney and he wanted the money, he would sign it. Her subconscious just could not believe that everything will be okay after years of nonsense.

There was always the fear of the unknown and uncertainty of her future, but it could never be any worse than what she had already endured in her marriage. It was wrong to think that if you love someone enough his sons would be pleased for their father, she learnt many things on the journey, one of which was that greed was stronger than love in people who didn't understand the value of true unconditional love. Life was already better, she noticed a renewed awareness of everything around her, life was good and the sun shone into the bedroom after the forecast was for rain.

Gemma thanked God for Ombre's companionship, she will never understand why it had happened to her, but she trusted that there was a mighty plan, that it will all work out for the best. She learnt so much during the years of their marriage, the emotional trauma she endured had made her a very strong woman with a new awareness and a depth of compassion for others she would not comprehend if she had not walked through the trials of desperation, fear, and panic. Being lost in a world of controlling people like a never ending damp forest of trees, she now saw light through the trees and with courage and determination she strides fearlessly towards it. The heaviness felt on her brow and pressure like a physical weight had now gone, she trusts the dark days are behind her and she can only see light going forward.

Even breathing in the air as she lay there beside Ombre,' pausing to take heed of the brisk calming fresh air, it seemed different somehow like the air that she breathed when they first married. Unsure of where she will live or when the house would sell, but she had faith that she would have everything she needed, the Lord would provide.

Four weeks later, she is over the moon when the real estate agent presented her with an excellent offer for the house and so she began her search for a home by the sea for her retirement. Gemma had whittled it down to several homes in her preferred location off the main State highway which would take her just over an hour to get into Auckland.

The offer would allow her to buy the more expensive house that was a three bedroom home in lovely condition, compared to a three story run down home that would require a lot of renovation to create a more valuable home in the future. Her desire was for the smaller home that was on an easy to maintain level site with no stairs, has internal garage entry, would be easy to mow the beautiful 1800 sq. metre section just a walk from the east coast beach, it was full of gorgeous established trees including many beautiful camellias that would flower on the dull days, this was her dream home. Gemma signed acceptance of the offer and the agent proceeded to see Mason to get his signature to sell. Oh please let him sign she prayed, hopeful he wouldn't try to hold on to her by not signing, aware of his strong reaction of not wanting a divorce, she held off serving the papers on him until she had his signature on the sale of the house first.

He signed the sale and purchase agreement and because the divorce papers needed to be presented by hand she asked a girlfriend to go around to the rest home straight away while she knew where he lived, anxious in case Dwayne took him away and she couldn't get the papers served. A new life awaited Gemma, with all kinds of dreams and possibilities, a new beginning and it was all so exciting. She put away the past, it was time! Gemma's struggles, being afraid of Mason, amidst hopes for a life going forward, she started to feel sorry for him, *stop!* He was getting the house sold like he wanted after she had explained to him that she would be homeless.

The past had taught her that when you allow grief and sadness, disagreeable people and a mind filled with horrible memory's enter your life, every day was a heartbreak and her body, mind and soul had been filled with darkness and a deep sorrow for long enough. The days of missing him, she replaced with positive thoughts, and creative dreams of what her new life might be like in her new home.

It was all signed up, conditional on her getting a good sale price from the lifestyle property and it would be hers to move into with the unconditional cash settlement went through. Wow, Gemma was so excited and grateful that the Lord had provided her with an easy sale and she received the amount needed.

Vivid plans for a garden full of flowers, dreams of a white picket fence, archway and the love of a dog by the seaside. She confronted life with an optimistic stance and light piercing its way through the bleakness, bit by bit the bad memories would start to fade. Gemma will need to go back and discuss what possessions he would like to keep when she moves out, but most of it can go to the tip as there are only a few nice pieces of timber furniture that she will retain and the rest she did not want. There was no desire to take memories along for the ride.

When approaching Mason, she was surprised that he no longer looked attractive, he had a wide podgy face, his grey eyes having that queer blankness with a deceitful glint, she saw the real Mason. His eyes disclosed how he knew that he had betrayed the love she had for him, he looked ashamed and defeated. Today Gemma has a fresh confidence with a sparkle in dry eyes.

Driving home she remembered that day in June when their lives changed forever, they were separated the moment the blood pulsed from his veins and flooded his brain, he was gone. His memories were erased of their short time together and only the long term memories survived after his two brain haemorrhages, they were memories of his ex-wife and two sons of times before he met her. She understood and forgave him. Life goes on for her now free to live in the knowledge and satisfaction that she had tried to save their marriage with animosity from Dwyane. Mason was destined to live in the past with no hope of a fulfilling future in a new world of Dwayne's heartless greed.

Chapter 16

We are all on this earth for a reason, she saved Mason's life those seven years ago when he would have died without quick medical intervention, she motivated him and encouraging him to stay positive following the brain surgery and she was prepared to give up everything to love and care for him. Gemma was satisfied that her job was done! She loved a man that maybe didn't deserve it but willingly did everything that was needed and now it was time for her to pursue a future meant for her.

Gemma's decision to file divorce papers was finalized, even though it was painful to leave Mason in the hands of someone that was never there when he wanted and needed them, she will stop worrying about him. Many people have told her she did a wonderful job providing him every opportunity to recover, she was satisfied that whether he remembers her or not, he once had that unconditional love in his life. Gemma had succeeded in loving Mason the best way humanly possible, risking life and giving all that could ever be expected of any human being. Whatever happened to him now was not down to her, she was moving away never to know.

Ultimately determined to use this year to gain financial security, inner peace and happiness, although sleep was occasionally difficult and sometimes she woke early, but it was not through worry anymore, it was because the sheepskin beside the bed was empty, she no longer had her beautiful dog Ombre' as he passed away aged 16 years. With the end of this era in her life so has he gone, he stood by her through her journey giving emotional support and friendship, it was time for him to go and he would be remembered always, always in her heart and soul.

Moving house was both exciting and significant because it was not only a move away from the past but a step forward alone with no ties.

The home that was once sanctuary for the two of them became a prison for Gemma and now she welcomed this new place the Lord has guided her to, so quiet with a magical beach, café and blue sea. Sitting beside the sea her one regret was that Ombre' wasn't there, he would have loved the beach, the only consolation being that he and Gemma had special times together at the pond and he spent his whole life on the one property which was fantastic.

Before leaving that place, her last duty of care was packing up Mason's belongings for him to collect, and she lovingly packed his clothes and personal effects into a bag feeling perplexed and unable to resist putting his soft woollen pullover to her cheek and smelling it for the last time, recognising that familiar scent of aftershave that will never embrace her again. A pre-arranged time has been agreed to for him to collect his things, she went out.

Having no interest in watching him leave with the remains of their marriage, not wanting the pain of seeing him leave his home for the last time. Sneakily resisting, she didn't pack his cosy black and white wind breaker jacket with its splashes of yellow and royal blue that used to look lovely with his eyes, a warm comforting zip up jacket reminiscent of Mason, she didn't really understand why she tucked it away to keep.

The picturesque white sandy beach was almost like a lost forgotten place, so beautiful and off to the side of the world, it was like an incredible dream come true. The peace was what she needed to further her ideas and creativity, to heal her heartache and lost love.

She felt blessed to be able to buy a home in the place she wanted to be, and it allowed the freedom of no longer working. In this magical place she would plant all the flowers she wanted and then get a little puppy when she was ready. Gemma enjoyed walking along the beach every day in the knowledge that no words could express her grief and loss as people could not hear what her heart felt, aware that this was the place she was meant to heal.

A remnant from her years of hell was the fear of commitment, and although she can not see herself with anyone else, her worst fear would be of falling in love and then they got sick! Selfish maybe, however she has learnt not to be magnanimous as life appeared to be significantly shortened and what life remains now needed to be hers to do whatever she wants with, she was content to live on her own, grateful for the sanctuary she had found.

Walking, and wanting to forget the lengthy five years that she persevered for a positive outcome that never came, she now impatiently awaits the arrival of divorce papers to confirm the end, before moving into her beautiful new home.

The day arrives and moving was made easy with the help of the wonderful new friends she had met through dancing and as the months disappeared like the tide, so do many memories of him. Sucking in a deep breath of cool sea breeze it filled her lungs and she was exhilarated with a newfound spiritual existence, at one with the sand scrunching between her toes, the wind blowing gently on bare arms and most of all, this new feeling of contentment and happiness she was able to smile.

How strange that life was somehow different, something wonderful was happening with every morning, feeling so thrilled and excited to walk to the sea, and watch the rippling water. How could she have been so happy with a pond of water that was constrained just as her life was? Compared to now, having a changing tide of sea with fish jumping up and wide open spaces, boats and people to watch and a lovely little café for a hot chocolate on a cold day. Gemma's new world was vast and her dance partner was now dating her. He had an attentive manner, listening, kind and understanding when she attempted to explain everything she had gone through. He was a sensible practical person which she valued more now than she would have before her years of hell, now stronger and resolute because of her life's experiences.

On a cold evening Gemma lit the fire and sat watching the smouldering ashes glowing in the bottom of the hearth, with its woodsy odour seeming to have a desire to flicker and burst into a live bright flame, such is the exciting aspirations that now fill her world, no more the fog that once had a hold.

The years spent wondering if her tragic marriage would affect her in a negative way she never suspected that it would work in reverse, and she is eternally grateful for the unwavering empathic person that she has become, after years of toxic emotional turmoil inflicted by her poor intellectually impaired husband.

Jonah Frederick is a fun loving hard worker who swept her away with his stunning two metre high stature of rugged weathered looks from years of outdoor farming, with muscled upper arms and strong shoulders. His black hair streaked with thick greying hair, and his suntanned skin giving him a permanent masculine appearance against his dark compassionate eyes. Gemma and Jonah have so much fun dancing and enjoying each other's company with the bonus of intelligent conversation as well. Having spent his life working hard at his farming he remained a bachelor all of his sixty-five years, and it worked well that they both enjoy their independence and space.

Peaceful but sad reflective moments sometimes try to encroach on Gemma's new life, intruding in her thoughts when she has quiet walks, the times spent sitting alone embracing the tranquillity of the sea's gentle waves breaking ashore brought time for memories. She pulls herself up before becoming melancholy and rejects them before any tears threaten. To Gemma it was as though Mason had died and that was as it should be, the man she married was gone forever. She would remember that he had condemned her to being alone in a new home, a strange place where she knew no one. She no longer loved Mason she had let him go when she saw him for who he now was and betrayed her, it was her right to take back her life. Gemma doesn't hold any anger, she forgave them as she enjoys a wonderful life she never dreamed was possible, times of abuse and family hostility have faded into oblivion as she moved forward. Moving house had been good because during the packing she went through photos of them taken in happier times and she burnt them all. The hollow emptiness had begun to dissipate and she was alive again as the devotion and responsibility that went with a great love she once felt long ago was no longer there, the man she married no longer existed.

Her cottage by the sea was charming, the tranquillity of sitting in the sun watching the birds in Camelia trees as she listened to their sweet song, alongside a huge silver birch weeping over the lawn it was both picturesque and idyllic. Just a two minute easy stroll to the sea was an inviting amble down the scraggy concrete path over a slight rise before the view hit her, with such a poetic breath taking surprise. The sea stretched out parallel along the shoreline continuous with no end in sight, it was magnificent and she took off his jacket, she no longer wanted or needed it. Walking past the café rubbish bin she dumped it into the bin beside the picnic table.

Positivity abounds within her and she trusts in Gods grand plan laid out for her, she perceives that she did the right thing letting go of someone who never deserved her and she was humbled to now understand that she can not save the world and was not expected to.

Gemma's time sitting at the seaside was sometimes spent strategically contemplating life, she understood that after the brain damage from the major stroke he incurred, their marriage began to slowly collapse, no amount of love could fix it because there wasn't any way to communicate to her husband, the fear, love and grief she felt, he couldn't comprehend the words since his lack of cognitive ability was compromised. Their world tumbled down like a stack of cards, no one could save it.

It was part of her history, there was no regret for the five lost years she willingly sacrificed, years off her life spent caring and providing some joy for her husband to motivate him to make the most of life after he lost his job, drivers license, his memory, ability to follow instructions, make friends or hold an intelligent conversation. They were just ordinary people and never destined to be indestructible, some things can not be repaired, and Gemma has an acceptance of her past devotion and welcomed the new enlightenment grown because of her unyielding love. She holds compassion for family members for their lack of wisdom about love and she hopes Dwayne can understand and discover it one day, love is worth experiencing.

Gemma believes people who do despicable things deserve pity. Dwayne now has his dad's money, but at what expense. What a shame he has not moved forward in a positive way, but backwards as his father disappears into a world of Dementia, and lastly pity him for the guilt that will remain with Dwayne forever, for destroying a marriage because of his desire for money, only to see the burdensome mistake later on.

The serenity and peace in Gemma's heart now was beyond her wildest dreams, and her one desire is for a puppy to share a bountiful love of nature and walks with. She continues to go on dates with Jonah, her dance partner and they laugh together. Whenever she needs a friend to help with heavy furniture he's there with his friend to move all the heavy stuff around her home, she never has to ask. Last Saturdays dance, Jonah invited her around to his home for afternoon tea and a walk around his farm on Sunday after church. She had never been to his home and had danced with him many times, so agreed to visit tomorrow.

It was only a twelve minute drive from the beach and parking the car in front of his house a surprised look spread across her face. She had never suspected it would be so beautiful. Knocking on the solid wooden front door he was quick to answer, looking very attractive with an air of confidence and a scent of aftershave on his cleanly shaven face. Stepping into an impressive open tiled entrance she removed her ankle boots. The home was gorgeous, she had imagined it would be an old farmers house, but no, as she glanced through glass folding doors to the open plan dining on the left and lounge on the right, quickly catching a glimpse through the ranch slider to the outside was a spa area all surrounded with lush green shrubs.

He guided her to a seat around the dark stained dining table in an expansive open plan room, she watched as he made them a cup of tea.

It was so strange because all the dancing and time they had spent together she never realized that he must be very wealthy. She listened attentively while he proudly chatted about his farm, glossing over the other business investments, in all sorts of enterprises he was involved with. He mostly talked about his cattle and deer, and she was certain by the way he spoke they were well looked after. Gemma wondered what she was doing here, this was a brave new self, after the life of domestic violence she had had. Caring for a dependant husband left her finding it difficult to socialize, in addition to a fear of new places and people. He offered up a choice of cream cakes, sausage rolls and a variety of plain biscuits or if that doesn't suit then she could try the platter of cheese and crackers.

He went on to explain that he didn't know what she liked so just got a selection from the home bakery. Gobsmacked Gemma was speechless, as there was no obvious concern over how much it all cost.

After a very pleasing time getting to know each other better she and Jonah walked around part of the farm, standing at the top of a hill he handed her binoculars and pointed out over to the far distance, explaining the paddocks that he owned, she nodded.

"Oh gosh that's a lot of land." Gemma was quite stunned that one person could own so much land that you couldn't see the end to it.

She stood, determined to become independent and managing to put her life back on track, she quietly, mentally praised herself about making good progress facing society again. Courageously going to dance lessons and to Jonah's house for tea, after a short walk back across one paddock to the house she thanked him for a lovely afternoon and picked up her well-worn handbag ready to leave. Opening the beautiful double front doors Jonah walked her to the car.

On the drive home she mused over the afternoon, her eyes had been opened to the wealthy lifestyle that some people have, she was astonished at this whole new world she had entered. Jonah phoned Gemma the following night and told her how much he enjoyed her company, asking would she like to watch a movie Saturday night as he has Sky TV.

"Oh Yes, that'll be great, shall I bring something to eat?" she enquired.

"No, don't worry I'll put some pizzas in the oven for us, it'll be healthier than snacks," he assured here with a laugh.

She felt impatient for Saturday to arrive and then when it did, she started to get a bit nervous. Nevertheless, ignoring it she staunchly headed off to settle down beside him on the couch to watch a movie.

After watching a while, he froze the picture and got up to put two pizzas into the oven for them to munch on. He returned and lifted up both of her bare feet resting them over his knee as he started to massage them. Jonah gently squeezed her toes and began to press the soles, it felt so good.

During the movie neither of them could really concentrate, aware that his arm had moved to rest on her shoulders and he was paying more attention to her than to the movie, fidgeting and talking. They ended up turning it off and gazing into each other's eyes as they chatted, enjoying each others company and discussing how they both love the Rock and Roll dances they go to. There was plenty for room for discussion on clothes people wore and the music that was played. Then he silenced and looked seriously at her, pausing before speaking nervously.

"I want to ask you something."

"Okay, what?" she probed.

"I'm wanting to go on holiday and I know that the school holidays will be coming up soon and you won't be working. How would you feel about coming on a cruise with me?" he spoke with a hint of apprehension in his voice.

"Oh, I don't know, I've never been on a ship before so I might get seasick."

"No, I have done a bit of traveling over time and the first time I thought that I would get seasick, but I found these sea sickness tablets that I take before I go, then one a day on board and I'm fine."

He continued on to say, "I can get some for you and the whole trip will be my shout, it won't cost you anything. I would enjoy your company and we can get a cabin with a balcony so you won't feel claustrophobic, it'll be a relaxing time. You deserve a holiday after what you've been through!" he said.

"Well, we can have a look at brochures and dates but it will have to be a short cruise just in case I can't manage on board," she warned amid a mixture of nervousness and excitement.

"Okay, we'll go to the travel agent one day next week and talk to them about where you would like to go, all right?"

"Sounds amazing." Her face lit up with a huge smile. (Was this really happening). Time to go home and just as she reached out her hand to pick up the car keys his warm hand rested on top of hers and said.

"Thank you for coming, it was great getting to know you better."

"That's okay, it's not far to go home and we'll see each other in a few days," Gemma replied with a smile before giving him a quick kiss on the cheek and a hug.

They walked in a strange silence to the car and he opened the door, she slipped slowly into the driver's seat. Leaning over he kissed her full on the lips, her face blushed at his touch as he reached his hand to softly brush back a lock of fly away hair from her face, Gemma's insides did a little flutter. Wow, she started the car and headed home.

Jonah's phone calls came every night, asking how her day had gone, and on Thursday they drove to the travel agent and arranged the holiday, flying to Sydney to get on the cruise ship that will travel around the islands, all of which she has never been to before.

While speaking with the travel agent Jonah was very particular about getting the best cabin on the deck level that had the least noise, or movement, and the travel agent advised them to be in the middle of the ship and not below the dance hall or near the engine.

They both needed to update their passports and now Gemma was feeling very excited, what an adventure for her, to be going on holiday with Jonah, on a lovely ship out in the middle of the ocean.

Chapter 17

Freedom and the universe was theirs to explore, she couldn't wait for school holidays to arrive as she looked forward to flying off to Sydney, how magical to be going on holiday. Jonah paid for everything, and organised that they receive the works on the flight. Gemma was delighted once aboard and settled, it was wonderful to try the food and have a glass of wine and thank goodness the plane landing was calm. They had a surprisingly short wait to collect the two suitcases off the conveyer belt before taking a taxi to the cruise ship, having previously been informed by the travel agent that they were able to drop off any luggage and then go to explore a little of the city.

The ship was due to depart after midnight, and everything was running smoothly, Gemma was totally over the moon with excitement.

After taking some really nice photos of the Sydney Opera House with Jonah's camera, he then set the timer, he put his arm around her back and captured them in some shots together. The Botanic Gardens were close by and they were able to sit on a little train as it toured around and they relaxed, his gaze followed her every move, and with a protective arm around her she felt safe and cherished which was all so new to her.

The weather turned on especially for them as the sun shone down and they walked around Sydney harbour eating ice-cream, watching the sea and chatting as they headed back to the ship, she was eager to see inside.

After passing through the quarantine and passport check-in, the ready crew directed them to their cabin. As the cabin door was swung open for them, they stepped into a brightly lit white room. Wandering around exploring Gemma was astonished that the bathroom, toilet and shower could be so spacious on a ship, and looking past onto the balcony were two comfortable armchairs outside, protected from the elements with an overhang from the deck above, the ocean looked an inviting beautiful deep blue and the ship was berthed beside the stunning Sydney Harbour Bridge. It was all so enchanting as she pictured having a wonderful view of the city lit up as the cruise ship left the harbour in the dark. They both felt weary from a long day of traveling and exploring.

"Let's go up to the dining deck and get a nice coffee and cake to bring back here eh?" he suggested smiling.

"Yes, that sounds lovely, do you think you know where to go?" she was a bit worried about getting lost.

"No problem, would you like to come and choose something to eat or shall I bring us back something?"

"I'm okay to go with you." With an adrenaline rush she leapt off the bed she had just had a bounce on.

It was exciting and she did not want to miss anything. Two frothy coffees were made for them, while they put together a variety of small cupcakes and slices to take back to the cabin. She just sat in awe for a few minutes, the ship was not moving yet so she relaxed with coffee and cake on the balcony, exploring the ship could wait as they have seven days on board, and as the evening settled so did they. Pulling their chairs close, it was nearly impossible to perceive that she was really here looking at the stunning Sydney Harbour bridge. They were on holiday relaxing, and they plan to go off to get some delicious food from one of the on board restaurants later on. Gemma was surprisingly relaxed with no seasickness while the ship was still moored.

The spacious cabin had a big TV screen on the wall that they could watch sitting on the bed later tonight after exploring, the room was warm and inviting just like a motel room. Not at all like a small cabin on a ship and Gemma was very impressed with the cleanliness. She laid her suitcase on the sofa so she could unpack a few things and freshen up before going to find something to eat, the booklet provided in the cabin described such a good choice of places to eat, with every kind of meal imaginable. They wondered around and the food was awesome and too tempting, so even though she intended to decide on one meal, temptation turned her to trying the buffet so she could have a little of everything. After eating at a nice table overlooking the Sydney Harbour Bridge they proceeded to walk around the various decks as Jonah pointed out how to find her way around, music was playing and they popped in to check out the bars and night club dance floors.

"We can come back to this bar for a drink later tonight, once our dinner has gone down if you like," Jonah suggested.

"It says there's a live band on tonight!" and she pointed to the sandwich board sitting on the floor.

"Yes, do you want to come back here later?" he smiled.

"Yes, let's go back to the cabin for a wee while, get dressed up and come back down at 8pm, it has a nice dance floor too." Gemma says peeking her head inside before continuing with their exploring.

After showering and a cuddle on the sofa, Jonah went to have his shower while she put on her makeup and got dressed up, the ship was so beautiful and it had a very impressive grand staircase that she insisted they must take the camera and get a photo of them both standing in front of.

The main central dance floor had a huge chandelier supported from a high ceiling and a circular dance floor beneath. Tables and chairs were positioned around the circular dance floor, it was all very ostentatious and for them they felt more comfortable going to the smaller more discreet bar on their first night for a drink. How wonderful that no one has to worry about drinking and driving, as long as she could maintain walking with rolling waves. Finding a lovely little round table for two, not too close to the band so they could talk to each other and look into each other's eyes. Jonah sat opposite her smiling and the ambiance in this luxuriously decorated room with curved chairs and small intimate tables was cosy with romantic subdued lighting creating a relaxing and inviting mood.

"What would you like to drink, shall I order you a pretty cocktail for a beautiful lady?" he asks.

"Yes please, but not too much alcohol as I want to dance," she giggled.

Gemma's life had changed so significantly, here she was with this gorgeous guy sitting before her looking like the cat that got the cream. He placed their order and they got up to have a dance to some lively music as the waiter went off to make their drinks. Both Gemma and Jonah loved Rock n Roll and she had bought a new long floaty dress especially for the cruise that she had been dying to wear.

Laughing and having a great time they try out some new moves, everything was fun. When the music stopped, she was reminded that it was not just them in the room, as their closeness was interrupted by loud cheering and clapping around the room, strangers cried out for them to keep dancing.

She gave a nervous little laugh and faced Jonah, "Maybe they think we're the floor show."

He laughed as they went to sit down and have the drinks that had arrived on their table. Gemma's was a pretty cocktail of three colours, pink, green and yellow with a miniature umbrella, a stick of pineapple and cherry on the side of a frosted sugar-rimmed champagne glass, and it was so chilled and welcoming after their vigorous dancing. Jonah had a bottle of Rose' in front of him with two glasses for them to enjoy the evening. Sitting together, his eyes twinkled in the dim lighting and he said how nice she looked, and that he was proud to have the prettiest lady in the room opposite him. Gemma's face warmed, she looked away as she thanked him.

Dancing the night away and finishing the entire bottle of Rose' together was something new for her. She figured with the amount of energy used up during dancing they probably burnt up the sugar content in the wine so she didn't care, she was on holiday. The beautiful evening was too much, with high energy, beautiful surroundings and a unique experience, exhausted but happy they decided to retreat back to the cabin before the ship set sail.

Jonah suggested that they collapse on the bed, the drapes had been closed for them so he swept them open both sides of the ranch slider, they lay on the bed in fluffy robes that were provided, and just looked out at the sea. This would be the first time she had been out in the middle of the ocean, let alone during the night which was even more spectacular with the stars sparkling on the water and the ships lights reflected on the waves. The cruise ship began to leave Sydney and the evening air became warmer as they headed northeast towards the islands which would take the next three days before disembarking at Mystery Island.

Lying in each other's arms propped up on numerous pillows, relaxed they talked for a long time about their lives and Gemma explained a little more about having a husband that got Dementia and having to divorce him through family pressure.

Jonah whispered gentle into her ear, "You don't have to live on your own you know, you can stay with me. I have a big house and we get on really well."

"I know we do and I enjoy being with you, but it seems that after everything I've been through I need time on my own to decide what I really want in life. I just need some peace and independence for now," she gently responded.

"Okay," he said in between long kisses and cuddles.

"Why have you never married?" she cautiously enquired feeling a need to understand if there was possibly a good reason why he hadn't, but he went on to explain in a quiet calm voice and without any hesitation.

"When I met my first girlfriend we were both very young and over time she longed to have children and I never wanted any. It was something we should have discussed before she moved in, anyway after a while she decided to move on. I was devastated so I through myself into working towards my goal of purchasing a farm and made starting a business my priority which put ladies off. I laboured long hours to increase numbers of cattle and growing them huge for the meat works, that allowed me to buy up more and more property and girlfriends weren't really in the picture."

"Oh, that's a shame."

"Most women that came to the farm hadn't any idea about the country and didn't appreciate the smelly farm life. Some just wanted a beautiful home and expensive holidays. Marriage just never happened, it is true what they say though, that money can't buy happiness, I have all the money and assets, I've meet you and it doesn't do the trick. That's what I want most now." Looking into her eyes. "The more time I spend with you, the more I want to settle down, I love you Gemma."

Lying comfortably on his arm, the gentle waves rocked the giant ship as they floated under a panoramic ocean sky of transparent blackness, the distinct bright stars reflected in the vast sea. She knew the memory of this moment would rule supreme, etched in her mind as she attempted to communicate her fears, insecurities and struggled to find the words that could express the warm burning desire within her.

"I love you too Jonah, but it would be a huge challenge for me to give up having the entire bed to myself now that's what I've become used to, six years of living alone would be difficult to change," laughing as she tried to make light of a serious situation and not have to talk about them being together. "We're both tired so let's get some sleep ready for an exciting day on board tomorrow," she said light heartedly.

"Yes, maybe leave talking for tomorrow, do you need a drink or anything?"

"No, I'm fine, I'm quite tired now." Making her way under the bedspread.

He gave her one of his stunning smiles and climbed into bed, happy chatter ensued for a little while longer, looking out at the ocean before pulling the drapes, removing robes and tucking down between the crisp white sheets for the night.

The next morning waking up to a rolling sea she was seasick.

"Oh no, I don't think I can make it up to the deck for breakfast, everything is moving!"

"What would you like sweetheart, I'll go and get it for you." Jonah offered.

"Maybe just some fruit juice and French toast please to settle my stomach, and then I might feel well enough to go up for a cup of tea with you later, after having another sea sickness pill."

While he was away getting her breakfast she made it to the bathroom, ran the shower water and just stood under the spray, letting the warm water run over her, hoping that would help to settle the nausea, she reflected on how lovely Jonah was and that she was out in the middle of the ocean, she would have never dreamed this wonderful trip could be happening to her!

The warm water had helped and she quickly sat on the edge of the bed to dry and dress herself without too much moving around. She still looked green. Jonah arrived back and hung the Do Not Disturb sign on the outside of the door.

"Are you feeling any better now that you're up and dressed?" genuine concern heard in his voice.

"Yes, I'm okay, just not sure about moving around the ship too much yet and I haven't tidied the bathroom after my shower."

"Don't worry about it, the cleaners will come around? You'll get used to the ship movement after a while, it's probably a good thing that we are at sea for a few days to help you get your balance. We can relax with breakfast on the balcony if you want, the sun is coming up over the water and it looks stunning."

With one hand he sweeps open the drapes creating a metallic sound of tiny hooks rolling and lets her look out at the amazing beauty of the open sea, she had only ever experienced from up high in a plane.

He was nice, and it was a convenient time to ask questions and get to know each other, even though she often dances with him and had been out on dates, this was a more intimate one to one, a closeness that couldn't be achieved on the dance floor in a public place. This was real she was actually here with him, and he was handsome!

The sickness subsided with the help of medication and breakfast, so they could spend the day up on the adult deck sitting in the soothing spa, eating and drinking. Gemma was tempted to try a tiny morsel of every delicious delicacy on offer as they strolled about in the sunshine enjoying each others company. Totally aware that her face was sore, not from the sun as she wore sunscreen, but from smiling and laughing so much, how could she stop smiling when this trip was such a fairy tale and so amazing.

Evening arrived, time to explore all of the night clubs on board, enjoying a romantic waltz in her new floaty dress at one of the clubs that had very low lighting, the dance floor was empty and as she moved around the floor to the dreamy music, a gentle hand on her back guided her closer in towards him, his face close enough to kiss her, but instead he just looked longingly into her eyes and her insides dissolved as she emotionally melted. Over the three days at sea they spend time trying out the huge array of tempting goodies in the food court, plus eating at one of the restaurants which looked beautiful, all in white tablecloths and gold embellishments, splendid gold and crystal chandeliers hung down from the centre of a massive arched ceiling. Of all the amazing things to do and see on board one of their favourite treats, was going to the sweet shop.

Gemma would pick and mix through the chocolate selection, and Jonah bagged up various mixes of Liquorice goodies insisting that she get whatever she wanted, he was paying. He didn't like chocolate! so she would not be sharing her bag crammed full of various flavours, colours and nuts all with white or brown chocolate. Gemma was saving most of it for later relaxing on the balcony watching the sea or lying on the bed in front of a movie, neither of them went to do the gym thing while on holiday, just hoped they don't put on too much weight and counteracting the bad stuff with lots of vegetables and salad at lunch times. There were live shows on board to watch, but they preferred each other's company, it was wonderful how compatible they were with each other, having similar likes, apart from the liquorice, chocolate thing.

Mystery Island was a welcome opportunity for a quiet walk back on land, it was possible to walk right around the island and then go back to the ship for lunch, so that was what they set out to do. The cruise ship berthed a little out to sea like it was relaxing, bobbing along on the waves created from the tenders, (small boats that travelled back and forth to the island) which were also a lot of fun, Gemma was hesitant about sea sickness at first but it seemed to be under control, she enjoyed being on the *tender* travelling quite fast.

Jonah managed to get the seat at the front where the boat bounced off the waves which then splashed up onto the windows, more laughing and shrieking from Gemma as she gripped tightly to the plastic seat. During their walk around the island his hand warmly entwined around her smaller one she knew what *happy* felt like, the serenity and isolation of this place was lovely and she was drawn to Jonah more and more in his peaceful presence. An abundance of time, going nowhere they sat on the beautiful white sand of the island and were entertained by the dancing and music of the islanders who travelled there especially to entertain and sell their wares to tourists from cruise ships, no one lived on the island. The water was warmly tropical as she ran her hand through it, warm and translucent blue with dozens of glass bottom boats dotted around for visitors to experience the fish, through crystal clear water. That didn't really appeal to them.

A few people from the ship took the opportunity to enjoy a refreshing swim without the limitation of being in a pool on board, the weather was hot but bearable surrounded by ocean breeze and they enjoyed being together, just lying in the sun with nothing to think about, no cooking tea, shopping or thinking about anything back in New Zealand. It had been such a momentous time just being together on an island, it was hard to comprehend how much she was enjoying the company of this charming man, the relaxing environment and being with him day and night hadn't scared her off.

Later back on board Jonah enjoyed spoiling her, wanting to look at jewellery, he bought her a very pretty bracelet, gold with sparkly crystals imbedded into it. There were all sorts of things for sale on board, and it was nice to have a keepsake for later, deciding to also get some professional photography done to take back to New Zealand as a memento of their trip together. Jonah insisted on buying her a pair of waterproof swimming shoes for the islands in case of sharp shells, they saw some on board, so rummaged through the bins to get the right size for Gemma, even simple things were fun with him.

Wednesday afternoon saw her go off to the women's pampering session while he played the poky machines in the casino, and when she came out his smile greeted her in the waiting area.

"I was a bit worried in case you got lost and couldn't find the cabin," he explained with a smile. "Would you like any of the makeup?"

"Well, I don't know, how do I look? She applied a translucent powder that gives a slight shimmer to the skin, does it look okay?" she queried.

"Yes, your skin does look nice. I'll get that for you so you can wear it dancing tonight."

"Thank you." Her excitement unrestrained, she radiated back at him, only just managing to refrain from jumping up and down.

Nothing was too much trouble for him, his constant caring and generosity making it an exceptional experience.

Once the cruise ship set sale for the next destination they decide to indulge in the adult's only area again, this time helping themselves to hamburgers where guests choose what sort of meat was cooked for them before adding their own choice of fillings. Sitting around on an outdoor lounger, with strings of tiny lights sparkling all the way around just like it was Christmas they ate chicken, and ham and pineapple burgers before relaxing for the evening in the soothing spa pool with a cold cocktail. Once the last flicker of evening light disappeared down into the sea they made their way back to the cabin to dress for an evening of dancing.

Tomorrow's plan was to go swimming in the outdoor pool and get some sun on the deck while Jonah ordered all sorts of lovely cocktails he wanted her to try. Looking around she saw people lounging in the beautiful bright yellow sun lounger made for two, some people fell asleep in them because they were so comfortable, and no-one had to move with attentive waiters on hand to take drink orders, it was luxurious.

Vanuatu was the next destination, the ship was able to pull alongside the wharf and their portside cabin looked down onto the market tents all set up, that convinced them to go ashore and share a taxi to the shops with another couple wanting to explore as well, walking past a women's clothing store Jonah asked if she would like to have a look. The window displayed all kinds of very elegant chemise and lacy underwear.

"I would love to but being a man you might not want to go in there."

"Yes, we can go in." Jonah says very self-assured and unfazed.

Everything was soft, feminine and pretty and he watched as she lifted a hanger off the rack and looked at a white lace blouse.

"I can get that for you," he said prompting her.

"No, I don't need it," she felt a bit overwhelmed.

"A lady like you should have pretty things, let me get it for you, choose your size and take it to the counter," his gentle touch on her arm prompting her to understand that he was happy to spoil her. He followed behind and paid for it.

The whole trip they got on so well, enjoying each other's company and it felt like they had been together for years, like an old married couple. At times she felt a little too shy to ask for things because she was not used to that sort of life, she provided for her husband and not the other way around, but he seemed to have picked up on that vibe and didn't take offence. When they toured around

New Caledonia he insisted on lavishing her with very expensive French perfume, she gasped at the price and he laughed, enjoying himself. He said it didn't matter about the price, tucking away the receipts for the duty free at the airport.

Awaking to the feel of arms draped across her waist in the morning felt nice and brought back memories of distant times, it wasn't the touch of another human being that kindled her comfort, although acutely aware of his presence and the warmth was enjoyable, it was not the physical feeling so much as the inner peace and contentment that consumed Gemma.

Lying quite still trying to perceive what this relationship was, what were his intentions as he portrayed a compassion and caring for her. It was difficult to comprehend the immensity of it after she had known great fear and disillusionment with life as a wife to a man that should have worshipped her as she had him. Soon the cruise would end and she would wait and see how things were in the real world.

Arriving back, they berthed alongside the magnificent Sydney Harbour Bridge with its concrete pillars standing stately at each end of the huge arch, they behold the Sydney Opera House towering out over the water with its many sail like rooves, sweeping across the vista with distinction. Standing on the balcony in awe, looking across the sea they contemplate the incredible creative diversity of its design, she marvelled at the designer's great imagination and achievement.

Time to leave the cruise ship taking with her fond memories of a special experience and companionship, they each pull one suitcase behind them, the wheels rattling along on the concrete path as they walk around the water's edge and take the last photos in front of the ship, before finding the kiosk to purchase train tickets.

It was an easy train ride from the cruise ship to the Sydney airport as they drew nearer to the end of a delightful journey they were both a little subdued and thoughtful.

Chapter 18

The two silent travellers endured a long two hour wait before able to settle into plane seats, ready for a comfortable two and half hour flight home to New Zealand, Jonah previously asked for them to have the works in flight again, so Gemma enjoyed a lovely meal and wine, it broke the monotony of sitting for so long before returning back to earth in more ways than one, it was difficult to clarify in her mind the regret, and the empty feeling in the pit of her stomach as her time with Jonah came to an end.

Jonah's car was waiting at the airport, so after collecting suitcases and with quiet mindfulness they made their way back to it with him holding on tightly to her hand, like he didn't want to let go. Gently bundling the suitcases into the car boot he began to drive towards home for their last night together. Looking across to Gemma he provided a strained smile, she caught a glimpse of the despondency portrayed in his eyes. It was getting late so they planned for Gemma to go home in the morning after a good night's sleep at his house. It was with mixed feelings as they proceeded along the familiar roads, happy to be home although melancholy also filled the car.

Peacefully falling asleep lying in the bend of his arm and waking up to another day with Jonah beside her, she still believed that everything happened for a reason, life would go back to normal with the promise of an outing to go on next week. There was an airy unspoken knowledge that she must go back to her own home. Jonah accepted that was what she wanted to do, fear of losing her freedom again and the risk of a broken heart was just unconscionable and left her no option but to not get involved.

A party invitation to go to next week was good going forward, he told Gemma it was someone's sixty-fifth birthday, apparently a long-time friend of Jonah's. Gemma leapt at the chance to see him again, she had been thinking about him a lot.

Living in her cottage by the sea was tranquil but secluded, the wide open sea and sand, rays of sunlight shining down to brighten her day and as the sunset she enjoyed being on her own. Time slowly healed the past and her evenings were filled with reading, writing and knitting, a few favourite television programmes to watch during the week, but mostly content for a winter of watching the glow of the fire, feel the warmth and tranquillity, enjoying a warm bed during a stormy winters night when the wind was howling and the rain pouring down, she did get cold feet and sometimes missed having someone to cuddle and a sense of security to fall asleep with. It must be time to get another puppy to keep her company and to have a little friend to walk with on the beach.

After many years spent staying home caring for her husband and not socializing except for the small stroke club support meetings she went to once a month, and a group of work colleagues she mingled with in the staff room at her workplace, Gemma was now finding that to get back into socializing and making conversation with strangers was more difficult than she had anticipated. She didn't want to appear different or inferior to all those women who had their lives sorted, so going to this party where she didn't know anyone would be challenging.

After feeling happy that she looked okay, setting off, Jonah parked the car and started to walk towards the hall where the party was being held. About twenty cars were already in the carpark and the closer she got the more nervous she became, finding it perplexing to face the unknown she tightly gripped onto Jonah's arm just below his elbow, he turned to face her.

"Are you okay?" he asked, as he sensed her hesitation, but then his best friend approached and welcomed them. An icebreaker which provided the strength she needed to face the crowd of strangers. The evening went well as Jonah stayed close, he was so supportive and they faced people together. She had to spend the night at his house after the party, and the next morning she woke with a new awareness that this man had come into her life at a time of transition!

Gemma went through a loveless time in her marriage and was still moving through issues and the weight of past promises weighed heavily, deceived by the man she loved who played cruel tricks, she had suffered harsh cruelty and betrayal. These fears from the past were still like ghosts hanging around in her new life, as she looked upon this person in front of her who has come into her life as a stranger, and yet was supportive and caring. His calming presence was accepted and she was confident of a listening ear, trusting, approachable and dependable, something that was alien to her.

Jonah filled her with a burning desire, like the heat of a sun ray warming the depth of her bones on a chilly day, it was an involuntary reaction. They had a slow breakfast together and as she got up to leave; he pulled her in close, his lips pressed down on hers sending a sensation shooting through her. His arms went around her waist pulling her in closer as he continued the long kiss, her hands slid down his back, inside the waist band of his jeans, with a short lived hesitance he continued to kiss as she tugged his neatly tucked in shirt and lifted it up allowing her to nuzzle into his chest, her hand beneath his silky shirt touching his bare skin. She was oblivious to his hands creeping up her back as she sucked in deep breaths of his spicy after shave. Feeling the smoothness of his shaven face on her cheek she knew she should stop now!

Two warm bodies so close together embracing as his fingers thread through her hair while holding her head close to him, kissing and promising she sighed as he pulled her closer, tilting her head sideways so he could kiss her neck. She was strong, but allowing and wanting, captured by his lips and the smell of his sweet fresh shampoo drifting from his newly showered hair, she continued to nuzzle up to his neck. He whispered into her ear about going into the bedroom and she told him that she needed to go now, reluctantly pulled away and reached for the door handle before she changed her mind.

Driving home she reflected on how love was a sharing between two people who care for each other and now that she was settled into her new home, the realization came to her that she was feeling the loss of that missing piece in her life, the sensation of touch and to love and care for someone or something undemanding, she misses her old dog Ombre' who passed away just before she moved there.

Gemma has been so busy getting sorted that she didn't have time to notice the loss. Now it hit her, going for walks to the beach without him. With this realization she decided to look for a puppy to cuddle and have that unconditional love and trust once again.

Walking on the beach at sunrise she settled at one of the solid wooden bar-b-que tables and reflected on her life, the startling realization that life had changed so dramatically, her whole being and existence had changed. She was compelled to forge ahead with renewed determination brought about through love and fear as she faced the question, *'Does she want to spend the rest of her life reliving what she had in the past.'* A renewed clarity of mind, body and soul, a spiritual awakening and a dramatic new understanding of how loneliness and hopelessness evolved into a feeling of defeat and powerlessness, which was her space before! But with courage, a new home and belief of a new positive future had grown, hoping for a better life gave her the strength to walk away, without hesitation believing that no one need endure more than we are capable of handling.

Come October Gemma rescued a Labrador cross puppy, Wilson! He will grow into a big boy and her intention is that he'll be a wonderful companion to go everywhere together, with the expectation he will love to go swimming in the sea. She now has company around the house and between her gardening and Wilson consuming a lot of her time the days are short, until Saturday comes around and she returns to dancing with Jonah.

Dancing rock n roll he attempted new moves he found on the internet and updated her.

"This next move is called the cuddle." Jonah was quite informative although unwittingly the information made her nervous.

"Oh, okay," she replied, while concentrating so as not to trip him up, as part of the move involved her walking backwards.

When his arm wrapped around her it had just the right pressure and enveloped her in a surge of security and comfort, Gemma's heart missed a beat as she held her breath and electricity surged.

They danced the night away and she was so pleased that she left her puppy at Jonah's house, because there was no way she wanted to go home tonight after the wonderful feelings he had aroused in her, she needed to stay close. Feeling self-conscious as he twirled her around the dance floor wondering if people would notice this heated passion, she consoled herself that of course it was only her that was aware of Jonah's magic.

Jonah continued to phone Gemma every night after the news had finished on television, he was encouraging and a welcome release from daily struggles and of training Wilson to walk on his lead. The goodnight whispers down the phone line were arousing with a closeness yet physically he was so far away. Scrutinizing the situation it was not so much the independence as the freedom that she relished. Sometimes after hanging up the phone she questioned if she was doing the right thing living alone, then at the same time she knew that she was afraid of being hurt again.

Fighting for control over her grief and with determination to find a way where Mason would never take any more of her life. Many days had been spent waking up and crying over what happened, never to know how he was and if he was being looked after, those mornings have long gone! Because after the tears, she dried her face and made a life after her lost love. Mason was gone, and she had her life back.

The following Friday there was a dance venue that had a live band Jonah and her were keen to try out, it should be good even though it would take about 45 minutes to get there, it was time well spent in Jonah's company. When Gemma arrived at Jonah's house he must have been watching and waiting as he swung open the door looking very smart. Gemma was dressed ready to go after settling

Wilson for the night in Jonah's spare bathroom, which was her good planning so she could spend the entire night with Jonah later on. He appeared to be just as excited to see her as she was to see him, as he reached for a hug, her face suddenly felt hot. They both smiled!

Dressed in a new cold shoulder v neckline dress with her little gold cross necklace showing, a respectable below knee length, light floaty blue fabric felt nice against bare legs. She was nervous and hoped that she looked nice, it was the latest European design so at least she was confident of not looking old fashioned. Chatting during the drive they discussed what they had been doing all week, before finding the hall.

They were both grateful to see ample parking and the weather was calm, so when she got out of the car there was no wind to mess up her brunette hair bouncing off her shoulders. Jonah assisted her out of the car and they could hear that the music sounded fantastic, he paid for them to go in and they proceeded to find a seat around a table, pulling out a chair for her and when seated he asked what she would like to drink from the bar.

There were a lot of people already, and the band was amazing, they danced the night away and it was fun. When it was time to leave, Gemma was joyously tired, standing up to put on her coat, he gently placed his hands on the top of her arms and planted a lovely kiss on the check.

"Have you enjoyed the band?" he asked.

"Yes," she replied unable to look into his eyes, too shy because of the way she was feeling inside, it had been an incredible evening in his arms and she could not wait to get back to his house (but she didn't want to let on). Yet another wonderful time had together, and again she will need to prise herself away from him in the morning.

After having a cup of tea and toast together and giving Wilson his breakfast Gemma put him into the car without lingering, saying she wanted to get home and take him for a walk on the beach and then be alone to enjoy a day of gardening, she loves time in the garden, there was so much new life to enjoy in a garden that was constantly changing.

Just finishing the stacking of the dishwasher after tea, the phone rang and it was him, Jonah. Her smile spread across her face, not wanting to let on that she had been thinking about him since the dance and was so glad he had phoned for a chat.

"Hi, how did your day go?" he inquired.

"Good, how are you?"

"Yeah good, I was wondered if we could go out for lunch one day?" he asked. Listening to him speak she could tell he was smiling.

"Yes that would be nice." She giggled with excitement and agreed on mid-week 1.00pm when it would be quiet down at her local beach café. It was so exciting that he wanted to see her as much as she wanted to see him.

Leaving Wilson playing in the back yard at home, she wandered down to wait on the pier. Carefully scanning the beach looking for Jonah she spent a few minutes watching a couple of fishing boats coming and going when he walked up behind her, put an arm around her waist, to turn her and gave a little kiss on the mouth. Being together seemed natural and comfortable, she loved that he greeted her like old friends, she pointed out the two little dogs enjoying a swim before they walked back to the café together hand in hand.

Trying to focus on the menu choice was difficult while mesmerised and unable to think straight, she was very conscious of him standing in close proximity. Luckily, it was her local and she had her favourites to fall back on. After placing an order they walked outside to find a comfy seat overlooking the water.

The cooling sea breeze gently brushed across her flushed face as she sat breathing in the fresh salty air and thinking wow! Is she still breathing or has it stopped completely with her heart pounding in her chest, her world had changed. Gemma focused on the moment, as he sat beside her. With a golden sunny sky above, it was looking to be a lovely day today, the tide was pulling back from the shore leaving behind a lot of sea birds standing on the wet sand searching for shellfish beneath their feet.

Lunch was really delicious, and she ate more than she should have, she was living life. After lunch, deciding to walk hand in hand and enjoy the bird life, only stopping when they arrived at a deserted stretch of grass at the far end of the beach, lying down he stretches out on it and as she sat down beside him he reached up and pulled her down as well. She lay her head on the grass and they laughed and kissed, contented to talk and enjoy each other's company again for a short time before he inevitably headed off home, it was a lovely finish to a wonderful day and she wouldn't need much for tea.

Sunshine radiated into her bedroom the next morning, while she looked forward to a quiet walk with Wilson to watch the birds sitting on the wet sand reminiscent of the receding tide of yesterday. Hundreds of very stately looking oyster catchers in their black and white are standing looking out to sea, as another swirling swarm of birds circle round and round before landing. Silence catches this incredible moment, leaving Gemma in awe and wishing she had brought her camera with her. Memories, she quickly prays that she will always retain her memories, forever in her mind, unlike her husband in the past, who suffered Dementia and tortuously lost his.

She and Jonah were going back to the same dance in a fortnight's time as they enjoyed it so much. Gemma was aware that she had another dress to wear that he hasn't seen yet. Captivated by the same band again, they were not disappointed and danced the night away until exhausted. Afterwards when walking to the car, he walked around to open the passenger door, but instead of doing so he turned and asked if he could kiss her (in a public carpark) with people going to their cars.

"Well, just a little one is okay," she whispered. Receiving a respectable quick brush across her lips she couldn't help but feel a missing out moment.

"That's no good," she laughed needing more.

"Is this better then?" his arms encircled her while he placed a full on beautiful open mouth kiss right there in the carpark. She laughed and staggered afterwards while managing to say.

"That's just like teenagers do standing in a carpark, everyone is going to be talking about us now."

"Well, that's okay, isn't it?" looking at her with large shadowy eyes straining through the darkness.

"Yeah, I suppose." An uncontrollable smile spread across her face.

Nearing the end of her first winter in her new home she had settled in well, sometimes winter cold can be miserable and depressing but not for Gemma this time, and she managed to maintain the property. One of the things on her wish list for finding the right home, was that it must have a wood burning fire, so she could enjoy the warm flicker of flames right through the cold winter months with her puppy, she was delighted with her decision to move here.

Morning outside brought green leaves glistening with droplets of last night's rain as she walked down to the beach, it was feeling warmer with the sun breaking through the clouds after yesterday's storm, and she started the day by seeing a rainbow stretching for miles across the foreshore, (like her life) the promise of better things to come. Gemma was content in a new appreciation of who she was, now having the freedom and power within her to create the life she wanted. Having a God given freedom of choice and a new awareness of peace, alertness and the quietness to push the limits of her mind.

Gemma wanted to push beyond the limit of existing reality and reach for the moon and stars.

Walking on the beach every day now that she had the luxury of retirement, gave her the chance to meet with the locals; one morning Betty was out in her front yard pulling out some weeds and Gemma stopped to admire her garden.

They both chatted about plants and she promised to visit Gemma on Wednesday to drop off a rose bush she had started from a cutting. She lives on her own as well, Betty looked a little nervous on Wednesday morning as Gemma watched from her kitchen window, sending a wave brought a smile. After greetings were exchanged they wandered around Gemma's newly formed garden she had spent a lot of time creating.

"Oh, it's spectacular," she says, and it's so peaceful and lovely here." Looking at Gemma with a surprised smile.

They sat down on the park bench overlooking the flowers and just admired how everything had taken off since being planted.

"Thanks, I'll get you some seeds from the plants." Gemma reached to collect some seeds from the end of spent flowers also pulling a small plant from the earth to give to her new friend.

This new world of kind people, sharing an interest together was nice and it felt like the sort of place where Gemma thought she would be happy to grow old.

Chapter 19

Continuing to go out dancing every week or two was fun and Gemma booked Wilson into the kennels occasionally, so he could socialize with other dogs and get used to having time away from her. That way she could travel or in the case of emergency if she got sick, he would be in familiar surroundings and know that he was safe. Wilson was her one responsibility now and she was so appreciative of his company, her gratitude was heartfelt as he had filled the empty void that was left after divorce, her old dog dying and moving house.

He was lovely with a gorgeous ginger and white coat and gentle qualities, now grown into an energetic and mischievous five month old, it was good to have a break from him when he went to the kennels. That also allowed her time for Jonah.

Going back to his house after a lovely dinner out followed by dancing, they returned tired and happy to climb into bed without even having a cuppa, they fell asleep, but with Wilson at the kennels overnight she would not rush to get up in the morning; Jonah appeared with a cup of tea, setting it down on the bedside table he sat on the bed and reached over. His strong arms embraced her as she sat up and his kisses took her away someplace else, goose bumps rose on her skin as he gently rubbed her back. Having someone who cared about her was new, and his slow gentle movements filled her with a sense of protection, she looked into his sparkling eyes and smiled. Goosebumps continued to break out tingling all over her body as if she were cold, an involuntary phenomenon as time stood still.

"Thanks, I better drink it while it's hot."

It was mind blowing being there, he had a completely different lifestyle and she was pulled between staying to enjoy lounging in the spa pool or heading home, it was almost lunch time before she arrived home. Gemma needed time to walk on the beach and process everything, she parked the car and had time before going to collect Wilson.

Time to think, she walked and sat at the beach, it came to her that maybe she felt a bit confused because Wilson relied on her, being just a puppy, subconsciously it was reminiscent of when she had a dependant husband, the feeling of confinement or prison-like, the memories every so often swept over her. She wanted to train Wilson, she already loved him so much, he was always on the move wanting to run and play, he was a lot of fun and made her laugh. Gemma wraps her arms around his tummy to hug him like she used to with Ombre'.

Walking towards home she counted all the things she was grateful for, the joy Wilson brought her, her amazing home, the lovely park to walk in and the sea views to lose herself in, she praised the Lord for the wonderful life she now had. She was grateful to have some time for herself, to not have demands on her after the ordeal of her marriage.

Perhaps the closeness with Jonah was pressure she wanted to avoid, even though they talked about how she felt and he understood she needed space, she was always glad to retreat back to her own home and that was no fault of his. Gemma wanted to take charge of her emotional and physical health. Having a puppy was time consuming and she longed to put him first at the moment, while he was growing and learning, so during her time walking she had decided to focus on Wilson as he was dependable, loyal and wouldn't let her down.

Walking him was challenging as he pulled a lot on the lead, he also liked to eat everything in sight and jump up on her, being at an age of needing lots of attention. He was hyperactive and demanding, but Gemma was confident he would grow out of it, becoming her protector and best friend. Sometimes sitting in the sun together in the front yard he played, running around the large lawn, grabbing his toys and running down the driveway, diving headfirst under the trees he would hide, and she could see two big brown eyes watching.

"Where's Wilson," Gemma called out laughing.

He leapt out of his hiding place, not wanting to worry her and she laughed, giving him lots of pats, he was a lovely dog and now he plays hide and seek.

Collecting him from the kennels he bolted from the doorway and jumped straight into his familiar car, he was happy to see her and looked happy like he had been enjoying a lot of play.

Gemma anticipated taking him once a month, but when it came time for Wilson to return to the kennels again she was reluctant to be without him, being separated was another thing to get used to, but he needed his independence as well. She dropped him into day stay on Wednesday just for a play, before heading off to do some shopping with Jonah.

Glancing at her watch, it was nearly 11.00 am, so she decided to stop at the bakery close to Jonah's house and buy some nice hot meat pies and cream cakes. By the time she drove to Jonah's house it would be lunch time and it would be good to have some lunch together over a cuppa. Her stomach was already growling because she missed morning tea.

Chatting over lunch Gemma mentioned how she wouldn't mind looking for a skirt, he had a few things to buy as well. Twenty minutes later arriving at the shopping mall, parking was easy to find and they decided to go off in separate directions, Gemma suggesting that he went to buy his jeans while she tried on skirts and then they catch up outside, she would probably take a while. Jonah's happy with that idea, a quick kiss and she headed for a lovely specialty store full of beautiful women's wear. The shop assistant helped to find what she wanted taking a load of items into the changing room to hang up.

After some serious thinking, Gemma decided on a layered skirt that had a shirred waist and would be fantastic for dancing. Leaving the store with great willpower her shopping bag only holding one gorgeous, three tired skirt, pink and white flowers on black fabric with a sparkly intricate gold thread running through, it was soft and feminine.

Jonah had no trouble doing his shopping as he was content with a pair of casual jeans and new printed tee shirt, leaving time to peruse several shops before they met up at the park bench not far from where the car was parked.

They wandered around a little before leaving, and on the way back to Jonah's they stopped to collect little Wilson and allowed him to run outside to Jonah's orchard, leaving them to climb into the spa clutching two goblets of a Rose', she was getting used to this! Climbing out, Jonah arrived back with the cordless phone and sunk back into the heated bubbles.

"What sort of pizza would you like?" he asked.

"I don't want a lot of Pizza, why don't we get a half capsicum, onion, pineapple, tomato and the other half chicken, pepperoni, beef and onion for you?" she suggested with a smile as she knew he wouldn't want all the vegetables that she wanted.

"Sounds like a plan." He happily ordered a 50/50 to be delivered along with garlic bread and chocolate pudding. When it arrived, she snuggled into a robe, fed Wilson, while Jonah saw to the delivery man. She again languished in the heat of the water until her fingers were waterlogged, there was no rush, lazily munching on pizza, relaxing as the evenings didn't get dark until later now for her drive home.

Gemma loved her solitary life; however she appreciated his companionship as well, it didn't matter what clubs she joined, having the chance to share ideas and personal beliefs with Jonah was very special. It was a quiet week just with his phone call each night before Saturday came around again, and they planned to spend the entire weekend together, Wilson was content sleeping in the spare bathroom at night and Gemma offered to cook a roast chicken dinner later on, after they returned from the garden centre. Jonah would be back in time to watch a game of sport he was following.

He settled in to watch sport in the lounge, she strolled past him to close the curtains, shutting in the warm air from the last of the days sun sinking behind the hills, they had enjoyed a wonderful time at the garden centre, buying six mandarin trees to plant one day soon. She had the chicken and vegetables roasting so jumped into the shower, spritzing herself with the perfume Jonah had bought on the cruise ship, she dressed in her new skirt and black shirt he hadn't seen yet before returning to the lounge.

As she brushed past the side of the sofa he looked up, she felt his eyes following her, she felt very flattered to be able to distract him from his sport and smiled.

"Wow is that your new skirt?" he asked.

"Yes, do you like it?" she looked at him.

"Yes." Somewhat distracted. "Have I got time for a shower before tea? I'm not watching sport anymore."

"Oh yes, that's about 90 minutes away. Plenty of time." Gemma exclaimed and went to collapse into a deep cushioned sofa with her magazine.

Sandalwood body soap fragrance drifted in the air and Gemma heard the suds gurgle down the drain, climbing out of the shower Jonah reached for a robe to wear. Gemma was still sitting on the sofa when he returned to plant a gentle kiss on her lips, his tongue pressing to enter her mouth she turned her head.

"I'll get us a drink and check out the tea in the oven, okay." Giving him a kiss on the cheek before heading to the kitchen.

"Hmmm, okay then, I'll find us a movie to watch." He couldn't suppress his startled smile.

A welcome escape to the kitchen as she questioned what she was doing! This was so out of character, but she considered there was only a certain length of time that one can fore go the desire to be with a man if you're a healthy woman. Pondering on it while she opened the oven door to check out the roast dinner. Gemma remembered the comfort she got as a child, when she had a cuddle that made her laugh, feel warm and safe, that's what attracted her to Jonah, whenever he smiled or cuddled her the ecstatic abundance of security and that was enough, for now!

Sunday morning arrived and it had been a wonderful weekend and over breakfast she was genuinely reluctant to tell him that she needed to go home soon. Jonah always allowed her to be liberated and free, he always told her she was welcome to come and go whenever she wanted, which was probably why she was able to continue seeing him. This weekend together had demonstrated to her how strong her feelings were for him, and now she felt fearful of losing control of her independence, with a desperate panic mounting inside and a growing determination not to be hurt again she could not wait to flee.

Tonight she would have her best friend Wilson, watching television together on the sofa at home. Whenever she picked him up from the kennels he recognised the sound of her little car, his excited bark could be heard the moment she opened the car door. He was so loyal and protective even at his young age and she loved him. Assured of a grand welcome after being apart, with slobbery kisses before he leapt into the back of the car. This weekend he had been no bother and had amused himself, they drove home in silence very happy to be just the two of them again.

"Wilson sit still." Gemma struggled to get him to sit while she put his lead on, he was so excited to be going for a walk. Proceeding down the hill the view stunned her, she never tired of the surprise, seeing the blue ocean before her. The tide had receded and Wilson would not be going for a paddle, so taking a seat in a corner sheltered by a wall of Pohutakawa trees he lay down at her feet while she recovered after the struggle with his lead. Seated at a solid wooden table with attached benches on either side, watching as approximately 115 oyster catcher birds waddled in the wet sand, now taking possession of the foreshore recently under water, pushing their long orange beaks into the sand in search of food in the shallow wet edge of the sea. With no swimmers around they strut with a self-assurance and confidence. She sat for a while observing before starting back through the reserve and offered the end of the lead into Wilson's mouth.

He held onto it as he ran around the trees and she attempted to hide, he was very observant and she couldn't hide without him seeing. Wilson was protective and kept watch on her, it was so nice to have his company and there was a strong bond building between them, she already loved him so much, even though he was a lot of work.

Tuesday brought the end of the nice weather as it turned dull and windy, she decided to pull on a warm jacket and get some exercise alone today, avoiding the trudging downhill to the beach and feeling unable to tolerate his pulling on the lead. Gemma was tired and her left leg was reluctant to move along with her, the leg she broke has always retained a stiffness about it but she hoped that it was not noticeable by people at the beach. She was aware that it didn't move as fast as her right leg, perhaps the cooler weather today could also be contributing to the stiffness. She slowly made it to the seaside bench, her little corner of the world that she enjoyed so much, tiny waves were rippling ashore as the tide pushed in, seabird shrills were heard loudly, excited at the promise of food and a new day they called to each other. One solo heron stood alone away from the commotion, his long red legs striding along the rising water line, ripples of gentle coolness not able to touch his sleek grey body he quietly strutted with majesty.

Perhaps her leg would still improve with time but it had been three years since surgery and she first started dancing in the hope that would also help, maybe it did, perhaps without the constant movement it would have been more of a problem. Gemma liked to watch the elderly couples who were still in each other's arms at dancing and envied them, but at the same time she was grateful that she could walk and was determined to keep dancing until she couldn't dance anymore.

The cool sea breeze blew the cobwebs away causing her to feel better physically and emotionally, she persisted, attempting an assault on the metaled path up to the reserve, it was beautiful once reaching the top, high above the sea with its old established trees rustling in the sea breeze.

The ground crunched underfoot while small flakes of white started to fall on her, thousands of tiny white petals showered down, surprised, she stopped to look up to heaven on this January morning to investigate, a multitude of Kanuka flowers all deciding to release their petals onto the gravel path made it look like it was snowing! Magnificent, beauty was all around, if only we took time to see it. Before moving to live by the beach, Gemma didn't have time, she would stare at others laughing and had forgotten what happiness was, now she knew! for her happiness was peace and time to not only see, but to be part of the bigger world around her.

On Wednesday, the weather was not much better than she was! And going down to the sea was always inspirational so decided on a morning's walk along the beach, it was a cool morning after rain the night before and crisp gusts of wind bit at her face like a grumpy old dog snapping at a child's unwelcome attention.

Even the sea was wild, the noise loud with waves crashing in a rhythm all of their own, it was not at all like a January day. Gemma spent time sitting at the usual park bench watching as the tide demanded space on the shore, rushing in taking as much shore as it wanted, unabated as any human would be powerless to stop it. Looking up at the clouds, observing a bright ray of morning sun shining through the gaps between the clouds, and scattering warmth on her legs only clad in a pair of denim shorts, she wore a bright yellow tea shirt with a long warm jacket over the top.

What a magical sight, watching as the sun's rays broke through, if only other people could enjoy it, but she was alone on the beach this morning, contented to sit and appreciate each fierce wave crashing ashore undaunted, Gemma was happy with her life now, quietly contented, mindful of all the magnificent creations to be seen everywhere. It seemed that when you are lost in the darkest moments, you pray explicit heartfelt cries to find the light at the end of the tunnel, she found it by reaching out, the Lord pulled her out of the depth of darkness. Faith and hope were the light in the dark, rays of light shone down to brighten her days beyond belief, warmth filled her heart and peace her soul, sometimes life was hard but she continued to believe everything happened for a reason.

Arriving back home she was not in the door long before the phone rang, it was Jonah and he invited her to meet him at the beach café for a hot chocolate and cake for morning tea, what a lovely thought, she didn't mind going back to the beach a second time. Then he sent a text message that he had arrived at the beach.

Pressing the buttons, "I'm on my way," she texted back.

He's still romantic after all three years of knowing him.

"You just order whatever you want," he said holding the door open for her.

"Just a hot chocolate please," she requested from the young girl.

Jonah turned to the shop assistant and ordered a carrot cake with cream and two forks along with his flat white coffee. Smiling they walked off to find a private table outside so they could be alone together, he divided the cake and pushed it over to her, how lovely it was to sit enjoying morning tea together. He wanted to talk, stressing how he really longed to see more of Gemma, and invited her back to his place to stay on the weekend.

"Okay, but it looks like a stay at home weekend with a movie instead of going out dancing, the forecast is for bad weather." Gemma said with a smile.

"Okay, I'm happy with that," he says.

Friday came around and he ordered their favourite pizza, Gemma set about packing a weekend bag and some food for Wilson. Pulling up outside Jonah's house she was excited as he swung open the front door and quickly came to greet her at the car, she let Wilson jump out of the back and he leapt up on Jonah for a pat before running off through the house, and out the ranch slider to the orchard.

Gemma followed and Jonah's long strides sounded behind her, he gently tugged on her hand so that he stood directly in front of her, pulling her into his arms, his mouth searched with a heated urgency. Melting into him she didn't resist his exploring tongue slide between her lips, her hands went around his neck with fingers pushing through his hair in a heated moment. Their breathing was louder as they both staggered through the doorway and she shock off her shoes.

She just stood stunned in the middle of the room and again he cuddled her in his arms and she felt his body warmth through his clothes, he let go. He felt good to cuddle into while his beautiful blue eyes and intense gaze met hers rendering her oblivious to Wilson running around outside. With arms still wrapped around each other they collapsed onto the sofa and shared serious kisses, whispering how much they have been missing each other and it was good to know that they were both passionate about spending more time together. They have the whole wet weekend to watch movies, sit in the spa, talk and eat pizza.

What an amazing weekend it was, gone so quickly but with a lot of shared thoughts, concerns and wishes for the future. As she drove home with Wilson on Sunday morning her mind considered back over what had been discussed. Spending Saturday with Jonah was amazing, and as she drove she hoped the car behind her couldn't see her smiling to herself, perhaps he would know she has someone significant in her life.

Chapter 20

Gemma was pleased that her darling little puppy also had a lovely weekend away. They drove home to the sound of her chatting away to Wilson in an attempt to show him how much she appreciated having him in her life. The first thing he did on arriving home was head for his rug, he was tired out after all the attention and playing, plus chasing leaves in the orchard when wind swept them along. They were both happy to be home.

Gemma decided to get some fresh air and unwind at the beach while he slept. The council were doing some improvement work on the beach now that summer was nearing an end. Last week they finished laying a new concrete path making it safer to walk on instead of using the top of the sea wall, which she used to walk along in preference to walking on wet grass. She was secretly hopeful not too many people hear about the improvements as she was partial to the seclusion.

Strolling down the newly laid path she came across a sweeping bend in the concrete where masses of oyster catchers with their smooth black backs and bright orange beaks accumulated, they had found refuge in the high tide ridge of sand and shells left behind when the tide receded, they all stood facing the same way as solders in training. But these birds were looking into the wind ready for take-off, she continued to walk slowly past admiring their beauty, a few took flight followed by more and more until the entire flock relocated further out towards the sea. Before landing they soared round and round over head in a truly wondrous display, but no doubt a bit disturbing for the fishers on the jetty who were underneath the sea birds with full croups of food. It was a brisk lively start to the day with the fresh promise of good weather. What a wondrous gift this place was, wild birds flying free and white top waves lashing the shoreline, the horizon showing a bright line of glistening water where the clouds above had parted to allow rays of light to infiltrate through and shine down on the sea. The other side of the harbour had dark ominous clouds threatening the unknown, so she hastened her walk home with uninterrupted gratitude.

Her life, before she was grateful to have a pond at the bottom of the property, now she had an infinite ocean a few doors along from her home, she regularly visited and enjoyed a wonderful new life. The beauty of this environment healed her from the unintentional cruelty of her ex-husband and the injustices of life. The ocean, sea birds and weather was forever changing and continually inspirational in its variety, some days she sat watching sparkles as the sun rays reflected off the clear blue water looking like billions of diamonds were bouncing off the sea, it was just a spectacular sight. She had the time to comprehend the beauty now.

Jonah never failed to ring Gemma every evening, asking how her day had gone and they always had plenty to talk about. Friday arrived cold but fine, so she and Wilson headed off to help Jonah continue to plant the orchard as the mandarin trees needed to be in the ground, and be well staked ready for spring growth, if they can get their roots established Jonah could possibly get some spring blossoms and a few fruit. They worked quite hard on the land planting all day with woollen hats, rubber gloves and warm sweatshirts on. Wilson had a good time running around the fenced orchard and picking up the stakes lying on the ground, he tried to entice someone to play with him but they were too shattered after planting rows of lush lime green citrus bushes, tall plums and straggly berry vines.

Going back to the garden shed to pack spades and stakes away for the night, Jonah suggested that she stay over.

"Don't go home, you don't need to!" he pleaded.

"Well, I suppose there's nothing stopping me from staying as I did bring a clean set of clothes for after the planting."

"Great, I'll leave the ranch slider open for Wilson to go inside to his blanket if he's tired and I'll get us a glass of wine, you hop into the spa to warm up if you want." Jonah suggested as he took off his gumboots and commenced to drop his gardening clothes onto the floor of the garage next to the washing machine.

"Sounds good, can you manage with the wine?" she asked, while washing her hands in the tub.

"Yes, I'll be there in a minute." And he headed towards the warm kitchen.

Peeling off the soil clad jeans and grubby sweatshirt she dropped them into the corner of the bedroom, thinking that she would do all of the washing for Jonah tomorrow. Planning to leave her clothes here for next time as they still have more trees to buy and plant to fill the orchard.

The spa pool was just through the bedroom ranch slider, climbing in while Jonah was still in the kitchen. The water was just superb, a welcoming and unpretentious temperature for her to just sit and let the bubbles fizz around, it was bliss. Jonah returned with two glasses of white wine and two enormous towels, which he draped over a deck chair after handing her the drink.

"Thanks, don't get cold." She reached for a crystal flute of bubbles.

He rushed to climb into the hot water to warm up, they both felt an amount of self-satisfaction with the number of fruit trees they had planted, and just sat in silence for a moment letting the bubbles smooth over tired limbs and revive sore muscles.

The evening was closing in on them, along with hundreds of string lights turning on automatically with the departing light of the day, carefully threaded around the pipes on the protective sunroof overhead, no matter what the weather, soaking exhausted bodies in the spa was always possible.

"Oh, how beautiful," she exclaimed in surprise.

“I thought you’d like them,” he laughed. “I rushed to put them up on Thursday for you, hoping that we could have tonight together.”

Here she was sitting in a lovely bubbly spa pool, a glass of wine in her hand watching the twinkling of hundreds of tiny lights with a wonderful guy looking after her, Wow! Closing her eyes and relaxing they talked a little, while both contentedly soaking in the warmth of the spa bubbles as the evening air cooled and darkened around them.

“I’m going to get out soon and feed Wilson, what shall we have for tea? I’m not really hungry,” she exclaimed.

Jonah beat her to it as he climbed out of the warm spa, reaching for one of the fluffy towels he left on the deck chair.

“Cheese on toast, after a cuddle and kisses,” he joked, the dusk now shining a glow on his muscular arms, he wrapped a towel around his lower half and like a gentleman handed the other towel to her.

Standing, she wrapped the towel around herself, his arms encircled her, snuggling into his chest it was warm with the thirsty towels between them and she felt really cosy.

“Shall I get us another drink?” he asked.

“No thanks, I’m fine.” She proceeded to quickly pour some dog biscuits into Wilson’s dish in the spare bathroom, threw on her dry night clothes, said good night to Wilson with a full body hug and patted his soft little head before shutting the bathroom door for the night, he was happy. Returning to the bedroom Jonah turned towards her and brushed a stray wet hair off her check. As they stood in the dark of the room she could see the sparkly lights he had strung outside the ranch slider, and because they hadn’t pulled the curtains it was all very romantic looking with the sky adding the final touch, now filled with stars, he gently kissed her.

“I love you,” he said still huddled together, both standing in the dark.

Gemma gazed into his darkening eyes, speechless, smiling and helplessly happy as his lips again sent shock waves through her entire body, arousing every nerve ending and creating small shivers across her skin.

"I love you to." She paused to soak in the blissful moment before they both dawdled into the kitchen to get something to eat.

Jonah sliced the cheese and onions while Gemma arranged them onto the bread under the grill, they were both in a strange state of euphoria. It seemed like there was so much to explain and yet they were both silent, not wanting to break the spell of their friendship, just experiencing not being alone. When morning broke she had decided to rush home as soon as she had hung out the washing. After last evening she now felt quite strained as she feared a relationship, her past had left an indelible impression. No one had the right to possess a person and she didn't know what love meant to Jonah, Gemma valued her newfound freedom in her own home and she worried if her diffidence would become a problem.

Arriving home she headed straight down to the sea with Wilson, sitting on the park bench with an open mind she watched as the water was rough, with thunderous waves crashing ashore, sea birds were squawking and on shore two birds were fighting over a fish skeleton emitting a fishy aroma, able to be smelt from where she sat contemplating life. She was sure of being strong and very capable of sorting out her emotions, nonetheless she needed to decide what she wanted in a relationship as she didn't want to hurt Jonah.

Evening came and he phoned her again, they chatted about the day and she glossed over her feelings a little, everything was good between them as he understood her reluctance to lose any independence and he was good with that. They would be off dancing again this coming Friday night. Wilson's going back to the kennels for a play and because they needed to spend time together after the dance.

Gemma decided to wear a short floral skirt with black stockings thinking Jonah would like it. So they danced, laughed, and were close during the romantic songs, consumed a drink together and had fun twirling around enjoying Rock n Roll. When the dance was over, no time was wasted by the many couples who made their way into their cars and quickly disappeared back to their homes.

When Gemma arrived back with Jonah they were both alive with adrenaline and desire, she knew he adored her and there was a strong emotional attachment between them. He respected her views on remaining independent but she couldn't deny how appealing it was to fall asleep in his arms.

Every day was different, some days were lonely at home with her dog, especially on a really wet day when she couldn't go to the beach, when he jumped up on the back door with wet paws and left his paw prints on the glass, which made for an annoying day, but mostly she couldn't believe how happy and stress-free her life was now.

Gemma headed to the beach every chance she got, preferring to watch the morning light breaking through the clouds overlooking the sea, it was so magical and inspirational every time she saw that happen. Listening to the sound of the sea gurgling and crashing, created its own kind of music, each wave making a different sound to combine to make a united melody. Gemma perceived how she was part of not just this world but of the whole universe and became more aware of the magnitude and of the changing seasons and tides. Small waves each running in their own time, appearing to be dark green waves further out but changing to opaque as they floated ashore to expose glass like translucent water over the many broken cockles, scattered everywhere beneath her feet. Watching as one lone seagull bobbing over the constant ripples, with a topaz sky above where a layer of mid grey clouds sat hanging low over the water, no sign of rain yet but it was imminent.

Across the horizon was an island of tree clad land, dark green, displaying a stretch of well used sandy beach on its edge. Sitting alone in her little place in the world the beach elevated calm and she was appreciative of the undisturbed time to herself, restful and without any conflict, just unified with the world around her and connected with the universe.

Three years had flown rapidly since moving into her new home at the beach and Wilson had become a huge part of her every day. When she bought the house she straight away started planting flowers and roses along the front rectangular garden, aware that everything took so long to grow and become established. They have now grown so well that it is a welcoming sight every time she drove toward the garage, her flowers blooming and she too had become established in this her new home.

Waking to a beautiful morning, Wilson had his routine, he expected either a play or a walk after sitting quietly by her feet, she watched a lot of miserable morning news on the television. Anyway, he couldn't go for a walk at present because she found toadstools had sprouting up everywhere, ugly slimy beige coloured ones popped up overnight in the park and under trees where he would want to forage. Gemma was unsure if they were poisonous or not but Wilson couldn't be trusted not to eat them, even though he had grown tall with long legs he was still only an eighteen month old puppy. When he stood on his hind legs and jumped up he reached Gemma's shoulders. It was amazing how much he had grown in just a short time. After enjoying toast and the mandatory morning cup of tea he looked longingly up at her. Praising him on how good he was Gemma patted his head as he waited patiently, he accepted her routine and left her to have breakfast before requesting a play, he wanted her to chase him and attempt to grab his tatty rope from him, he also liked to fetch the ball which he had mastered really well.

Wilson tires after running to fetch back and forth for half an hour, then he was ready for a puppy nap, the perfect chance for her to use this time to her advantage. Making a hasty retreat down to the beach with just a pleasant breeze blowing up from the sea, and it was so tranquil, she didn't meet anyone on her walk today and there was no sign of traffic on a Wednesday.

Her long brunette hair blew out behind her and away from her face, and she was grateful for the sunscreen she had applied with the bright morning sun now warming her face.

Walking and musing over things she decided this was the best place for her and Wilson, she had been satisfied with a lifestyle block, (her thoughts regressing back to the past) in that specific time but thank goodness she moved to this beautiful beach where she could enjoy her new life, believing it will be even better when Wilson is older and he and Gemma could swim together. The sand was again lined with hundreds of oyster catchers all sunbathing and only two large black backed gulls standing majestically amidst them.

Carefully scanning the beach, she sighted a fluffy young grey bird standing in line with a small fish in its bill, the other birds around it didn't appear to be interested in picking or pulling bits off the dead fish the young bird held, maybe they were too well fed. Continuing to walk along another fifty metres to her usual picnic table, next to the water's edge a revolting fishy smell hit her nostrils, before she spotted a huge, stinking stingray washed up last night, the birds have probably had a hearty breakfast on it as the flesh had been torn and the odour was putrid.

What amazing wondrous things there must be under the ocean, Gemma could only try to imagine how big fish might grow, and marvel at the incredible secret treasures the ocean must hold. Many wondrous creations and mysteries on how the moon works with the ebbing of the tides are all incomprehensible, helping her to realize that there was more to life than she ever knew existed. Gemma was convinced she had found the right path for her life and while she kept enjoying her walk, a cheerful retired couple came along and chatted, acknowledging that she didn't have her dog today! After explaining that he just had to play at home today because of the number of toadstools appearing, they laughed, nodded and told her they once had a Labrador and knew really well how they ate everything. Smiling back at them, it warmed her that she was starting to be known and accepted around the neighbourhood.

Jonah was invited to have a meal at Gemma's Wednesday night, she had advised him to only expect a salad and cold meat, as she still needed to put a new kitchen in her home, she didn't like using the low under-bench oven because of the bending and would get around to ordering a completely new kitchen with an eye level oven, then she would enjoy cooking for him. After mowing the lawn she stood to admire it just before he arrived with the onset of a beautiful clear evening.

It was perfect for a stroll around the block before they sat outside on her new three seater colonial bench seat, beautifully crafted and stained a crisp white, they watched Wilson run around the entire yard. Tea didn't take long and Jonah helped take the dishes back inside to stack the dishwasher, before returning outside to relax in the refreshing evening air together. Jonah sat peacefully listening to the many birds nestling in the trees which edged the lawn, the pungent smell of cut grass and shrubbery filled their nostrils as she placed her legs over his lap, making it easier to face him. The heartened look on his face reflected how well they got on together, he was still, silent and all seemed right with the world as they both sat back comfortably against the lime coloured cushions. Pushing off her shoes he gently picked up one of her legs and began to gently massage her foot, she smiled back at him, contented together.

Gemma knew she needed to get over the past by forgetting it ever happened and go back to being the romantic she used to be before she was disillusioned with love. Jonah was calm and tolerant, and Gemma was more motivated these days, she was settled and it seemed like the right time to cope with getting the new kitchen sorted out. She set about making a list of must haves and decided this week armed with her list she would go around the kitchen consultants to get things started. The list contained eye level oven set into an oven tower that would also house her stainless steel microwave plus it would provide her with two pot drawers and two cupboards for the microwave cookware. Also a 'must have' was a pull out tall unit beside the fridge-freezer to store a supply of numerous cans and dried foods.

By the time she had the wish list fulfilled everything would be out of sight, clean, new and bright white cabinets with lovely charcoal grey bench tops and brushed stainless steel splash back. Going around the consultants was easy with her list now knowing what she needed, it was just a matter of measurements, colour choice and quotes for cabinets and installation, it seemed a bit daunting at first when she moved into the house and that was why she had dallied, now things were underway she was very excited and moving forward.

On her way home she text messaged Jonah that she was popping in to show him the colours and ideas for cabinetry. He opened the door looking gorgeous as usual, his hair slightly wet from just jumping out of the shower was starting to curl at the bottom, he needed a haircut, and when he reached to kiss her sweetly on the lips her senses were ignited to him smelling gorgeous.

"Would you like a cup of tea?" he asked.

"No thanks, I had a hot chocolate while I was at the shops." The fire was on and it was getting a bit warm in his lounge so he started to unbutton his shirt, her eyes followed his every movement, attention captured by his smooth tanned body, slim and still with arm muscles flexing from his farm work. With them both being in their sixties he still looked and felt great, she hoped she did as well. Again he put his arms around her pulling her in to nuzzle against his warm bare skin, his body so close and familiar her senses were alive to how attractive and immensely masculine he was. She was becoming nervous, then interested with a mixture of excitement and a small amount of mental conflict, about going down the couples track, reluctantly enthused around her brain. After past betrayal, hurt and loss, she had settled for love of a dog and was rather content now after many years of craziness and selflessness, she now had control of her own life. Dare she contemplate letting someone else into that world?

On some level all the local groups and socializing she did was adequate, she had made a new life for herself getting involved and meeting people, sometimes admitting that could not replace the natural instinct to be with that special person.

Chapter 21

Gemma admitted to enjoying the sharing of ideas, hopes, outings and fun with Jonah and maybe one day she would want love in her life again. It would mean accepting vulnerability, opening herself up to hurt again if one of them got sick. Maybe it was worth it, to have good times together and to make memories, it was like feeling stuck in an emotional avalanche, the risk taking to quench personal desires, to share the deepest thoughts with that one person, to open her heart to an unknown future was a return to those innocent years before all of the emotional scars.

While standing entwined in his arms, breathing in his erotic aftershave she contemplated. Gemma's fears sabotage her, but then their eyes meet, she melted and they shared a long kiss, they were connected, strangely victorious and yet vulnerable.

They needed time, *she needed time*! Wrestling with an overwhelming longing to head for the safety of the beach she proceeded home with her dog. She surveyed the calm blue sea, and gazed up at the cloudless sky, Gemma slowly sat down on the grass and contemplated the spark of a startling new bliss she had for Jonah, she never expected that to happen to her again. With her puppy beside her there was little time to sit, he was very active and mindful that the reserve was just up ahead, he longed to run around the reserve with his lead off, he started to leap up and down resting wet sandy feet on her jeans, he tried to coax her to do what he was eager to do.

Standing up, she brushed off the gritty sand and they continued up to the reserve, he ran around like he had never felt freedom before, while Gemma stood watching. She smiled, pleased that he loved to run like the wind as it came so naturally to Wilson, he was built for streaking along with ease, his long golden legs taking in every stride was a delightful sight and his coat shone radiantly in the light of the day that managed to penetrate through the canopy of the overhanging Pohutakawa.

"Come on, let's go home Wilson," she called out after seeing his little chest puffing away.

Walking home slower now, he had worn himself out so didn't pull on his lead as much. Opening the front door she then took off the lead, and they sat together on his rug she spread out on the sitting room floor, picking up his paw and holding it. Gemma calmly talked to him and her mind was taken back to memories of nursing her husband Mason after brain surgery, memories that made her restless. Remembering how she sat with Mason for nine hours every day, praying for him to get well. A loving sense of duty that continued when he returned home, day after day for five years she prayed and cared for her husband to get well, only to watch as he deteriorated further.

Now a changed person, with a new life she was unable to endure sickness for any length of time. Gemma wondered if those memories would always plague her or would fade with time. Holding Wilson's soft little paw she ran her hand down and remained optimistic, everything about her life was positive now with no room for doubt or gloom, she was bright and cheerful and loved Wilson.

Every day brought her pleasure, observing the morning dew on the lawn with a flock of beautiful goldfinches, all happy to peck around the lawn that needed mowing. She sat on the patio watching them as she relished sipping on a morning cup of hot tea, Wilson was in the back yard behind the tall metal gates so couldn't chase them, taking time to see and enjoy all the beautiful things in her life, she was, strong, resilient and grateful to the Lord.

Jonah phoned, asking if she were keen to go dancing again this weekend, she leapt at the chance and would take Wilson to zoom around in Jonah's big back yard, he loved running around the tree covered orchard. Accepting the invite, she couldn't wait for Saturday to arrive and decided to get dressed at home before going to Jonah's.

She had applied her makeup so he saw her looking nice, also remembering to throw a t-shirt and jeans into the car for Sunday, along with Wilson's food. As soon as she arrived at Jonah's house, he advised her he wanted to take her to dinner and had made a reservation already for them.

"Oh, that's nice," she said smiling, "I thought we were just having toast together before going dancing."

"You look lovely so I'm glad I'm taking you out for tea." He grinned.

They didn't have far to travel, it was a newly opened restaurant only a half hour down the road, arriving to plenty of parking spaces they settled in. Placing their order with a slim, blonde waitress.

Jonah sat opposite Gemma, he reached out across the table to hold her petite hand and gaze into her eyes. Oh my goodness thought Gemma, his sensitive touch and eye contact sent gentle shivers running along her skin and the evening had only just begun, she still had dancing in his arms to romantic music to come, how would she cope. Looking away and trying to chat about everything and nothing, she requested a cup of coffee while they waited for their meal to arrive.

Gemma's steak was succulent and delicious and Jonah's seafood basket looked full of delicious crispy battered mussels, oysters, calamari and various fish. Munching away on a separate order of aromatic roast vegetables, she was happy while Jonah had spicy fries. It was a delicious meal and quite a treat, she felt like she needed to exercise after, pleased to be heading off to dance the night away just a half an hour further down the road.

"I don't think I've seen that dress before."

"No, it's new," Gemma countered smiling.

She had bought the dress to impress him, a low cut soft floral fabric to float around the dance floor in his arms, as they looked into each others eyes all night laughing and having fun. They had a wonderful evening; she was intoxicated by his aftershave wanting to breath it in all night long. They managed to stay until just a few stragglers remained and they were both weary.

Starting the next day together was overwhelmingly wonderful and she leapt out of bed with excitement, pulled on the tee shirt and jeans and rushed off to make two frothy mugs of coffee for that lovely guy who she was very much warming to, saying good morning and giving Wilson a cuddle, she let him outside to play before returning with piping hot drinks, she carefully set one on his side table whispering into his ear as she bent down to kiss his cheek.

"Do you want coffee darling?"

"Aw yeah," Jonah groaned as he stretched and opened his eyes. An appreciative smile spread across his face and warmed her heart, how lovely to have a man that appreciated her!

"What are we planning to do today?" Gemma asked him as she gently sat on the edge of the bed staring into his twinkling eyes, wanting to bounce on the edge of the bed but not wanting to spill the coffee she sat still.

"Aren't you feeling like you want to run back to your beach after being with me since yesterday?" he asked with kind concern in his voice.

"I've had such a wonderful time and we get on really well, so I think I can stand another day together if you're up to it." Gemma was unable to hold back a shy chuckle.

"Sounds good."

They drank coffee, chatted about what was happening in the orchard, and what still needed to be done. Gemma jumped into the guest shower while Jonah got himself up for the day. Arriving back in the kitchen about the same time to make banana on toast together.

"I'm starving," she cried out loudly.

"You're always starving!" he replied, with a chuckle. "The meal last night was good wasn't it."

Laughing and nodding in agreement, as he gathered her into his arms, kissing her until she protested that she was still starving.

"Where would you like to go today?" he queried.

"I love gardens, do you think the weather is good enough to go to the city gardens and look through the glass houses, I haven't done that for years." Gemma said bubbly and full of life.

"Okay, it'll be a good ride out and if we see any markets on the way we'll stop and have a look, we need to just have a slow day after all that dancing, I'm actually feeling quite shattered," he admitted.

"We don't have to go anywhere if you don't want, we can stay here."

A big grin spread across his face, "Better to go out than me having to keep looking at this beautiful woman, I'm not strong enough to resist you all day," he said joking, "and the boundaries you've set are quite high."

Gemma didn't reply, just walked away. After scoffing down her toast they both went outside to play with Wilson and let him zoom around the orchard for a while as they strolled around looking at how rapidly everything was growing, picking some raspberries and a couple of boysenberries they were feeling really happy with the orchard progress, walking amongst the young citrus trees that would take a bit longer.

Once Wilson was willingly settled back into the house they got into Jonah's lovely new Kia car and headed off for the day, like they had been together forever. Slowly perusing around the hot house holding hands, he squeezed one making her senses constantly aware of his presence, she was drawn to him like a moth was to a flame, and at the same time trying to shrug off her sense of foreboding of *what if the moth gets too close to the flame*. He instinctively knew, and without speaking they finished looking around and headed for home, there was an unspoken anxiety in the air, a growing urgency to make her escape again, giving him a big cuddle and a sincere kiss and thank you for a lovely couple of days, she was confused and sorry as she fled his beautiful home and wonderful company, it was getting too serious, too comfortable and she couldn't face it.

The next day, back to her usual routine with walking, playing with the dog and gardening, the phone rang.

"Hi, it's just me, are you okay?" asked Jonah.

"Yeah, sometimes I just feel a need to run away, it's nothing you've done because it would be like that with anyone. Everything is great between us and I just need some time to get used to a relationship again." She tried to explain and he invited her around for a relaxing spa later in the evening.

"Oh, that sounds like a good idea, I'll see you later after I've finished some weeding in the garden."

"Okay." They both hung up the phone feeling like the ice had been broken.

Gemma thought she had better pack a few things into an overnight bag just in case it got too late to return home. Grabbing some macaroni pasta and readymade sauce as she knew he always had plenty of cheese, she put Wilson's food in the car. He loved going to see Jonah as he got spoiled with new toys. She parked in the driveway and the front door flung open without her needing to knock, he welcomed her into the house with a warm cuddle and kiss.

Gemma let Wilson outside while they prepared to climb into the spa, he already had a bottle of wine and glasses waiting on the round table beside it. A good chance to just chat and relax while bubbles swirled around them, with his arm around her neck she lay her head back and enjoyed the tingling on her skin, turning her head they kissed, a combination of warm spa bubbles, wine and kissing made her face a rosy pink. His eyes showed genuine concern.

"Are you okey, it's not too hot in here is it?"

"No, its good I'm fine," Gemma said wrapping her arms around his neck not knowing what to say.

Sitting mesmerised they watched as Wilson came running around the spa and back out to the orchard again. They laughed.

"He's just checking on me." Gemma smiled.

Jonah held her hand tightly beneath the bubbly water until it was time for her to get out.

"I'll just have a quick rinse off in the shower, won't be long." Gemma said, with a hurried desperation and longing for everything to work out.

She grabbed one of the fluffy towels waiting, wrapped it around herself while heading for the bathroom. Getting out of the shower she was freezing so wrapped the towel around herself again and went in search of a warmer room. Returning to the lounge she found him dressed, standing in front of the fire he had lit, and she rushed over to get warm in front of the roaring flames and crackling logs. Her rugged farmer had lit the fire knowing she would need to get warm after the spa, she was gobsmacked at how thoughtful that was.

"Ooh, that's good." She huddled close beside him in front of the warm fire with her towel wrapped firmly around her and an arm load of clothes ready to put on.

"I'm making macaroni cheese for tea tonight," she began to call out as he headed for the kitchen. She quickly dried herself, without dropping the towel and modestly got dressed.

"Great, I like that and it's something I can't make for myself," he called out as he walked back into the room with a broad smile.

It had been a few years since Gemma felt such a passion and desire for someone, although it would take a special person to cause her to give up her newfound freedom and independence, at the same time she didn't want to lose him, he meant too much to her. He reached across to the stool she sat on beside the fire and held her arms, planting a warm kiss on her lips, he was sweet but he had an urgency that did not need any encouragement.

Whatever happened in any future relationship she was resolute about keeping her lovely home to always go back to. Gemma had grown to love her cottage by the sea and life with Wilson, and her past had driven her to prepare for the unknown. That's what her mind and emotions were telling her, although physically her body had natural desires and feelings, it was so nice to be spoilt and looked after and she attempted to convince herself that maybe there was no physical dilemma, that Jonah understood and accepted what they had was enough or was that just a romantic illusion and too much to ask of a man. They enjoyed the macaroni cheese and had a nice teatime together, then she was content to go home in time to settle with her furry friend, to watch a movie.

Back home settled back into her routine, Gemma understood that at times relationships could be vexing, but actively deciding to avoid any emotional connection could also inhibit the chance to find love. Allowing some vulnerability and sharing with others who matter, even if it was the love of a dog, brought with it duty, trust and respect and in turn it reinvigorated people. Gemma believed what people needed was either platonic, romantic or just love for a pet as it gave life energy, purpose and enhanced wellbeing. Standing on the sandy seashore with Wilson beside her, looking up at the parting in the clouds, a ray of light shone down, and she had an awareness of being at one with the tide, moon and the universe.

Upon reaching the reserve with its beautifully aged trees, Wilson gently took his lead from her hand and with it in his mouth took off for a free range run, as always it was exhilarating just to watch his enthusiasm as he rocketed with long strides, slim legs gliding gracefully like he had wings, he appeared to float and not touch the ground. It was beautiful to watch, and he was also an affectionate pet, with Gemma finding that if she even just coughed or sneezed around him he instantly appeared. Responding in his own protective way, two big feet flop onto her shoulders and his inquisitive brown eyes stare with concern into hers.

She knew he was an amazing dog and she has never encountered one like him before, possibly it was a result of acquiring him as a puppy, and with it being just the two of them he had picked up very human like qualities and caring for his master.

The weather forecast came on the television after listening to the news, and it predicted a fantastically beautiful week, so Gemma decided she and Jonah should do something together. When he phoned at 7.30pm he was thinking the same thing.

"The weathers going to be nice tomorrow, would you like to go and explore a different beach; I'll buy us some lunch at a bakery and we could go hiking if you want?" he suggested.

"It's a Wednesday so I'm not really doing anything important, so that sounds like a good idea. I won't bring Wilson though in case it's 'No dogs allowed.' Shall I drive to your place or do you want to pick me up?"

"Let's leave early, I'll pick you up around 9.30am so we can drive a distance and allow plenty of time to hike," he suggested.

"Okay, see you tomorrow darling," Gemma agreed before hanging up.

Waking up to a very hot day was a surprise, she put on a pair of good walking sneakers and found an over shoulder bag to pack with a large water bottle, towel, sunscreen and sunglasses. Putting on a nice pair of cotton shorts and her favourite bright yellow tee shirt, she would be easily seen, also squishing a fabric sunhat into the bag for later. Just enough room for a few mandarins, some serviettes and the camera, she was looking forward to a pleasant day. Driving along they came across a nice bakery on the way, popping in and out quickly to not waste any time before heading on their way again, feeling so pleased that spring had arrived for today.

They walked up and down glades, beside paddocks and always stayed on the well-worn public track that trekked alongside the seashore. High on a hilltop she stopped and put her bag down as she got out her old camera, to take what she hoped would be scenic photos of looking down to the sea. Setting off again they passed cattle that stood menacingly staring at them over the fence.

"I'm not stopping to photograph them, they're a little scary."

The cattle stood quite still and calm, trampling through decaying dung letting off a pungent aroma, and Jonah suggested they must be used to watching people walking the track and were perhaps quite well behaved. Further on they looked down over a step cliff, beyond yonder pasture to the bottom of the hill and they could make out a lush green patch of grass right beside the sea, there was not a soul in sight.

"Shall we make our way down there; it looks quite easy to get down to the water?" observed Jonah.

Gemma nodded her approval and her sunhat fell off, picking it up and carrying it she carefully started to follow him downhill, hopeful to not end up on her bottom.

Proceeding slowly was the way to go, and they arrived safely off the slope to a charming spot of secluded short grass to spread their towels out. Looking around, it appeared to be an inlet with banks of paddocks surrounding it, people must use it or the grass would be longer, she surmised that towels and bodies had stunted its growth. It was quiet and cool where the sun had moved around, the calm blue water looked very inviting. They both stood at the edge staring in, it was shallow and clear enough to see the bottom.

"Go for a shallow dip if you want to," he said.

"I might have a paddle; it looks safe enough eh? Are you going in?" She was a bit nervous of the unknown.

"I didn't bring my swim shorts but it would be nice to cool off." he replied and proceeded to remove his shirt. Gemma watched him dump the shirt on top of the towel, her mouth dropped open sounding a gasp of surprise as he continued to drop his shorts as well.

"Your shorts will get wet if you're coming in, just take them off, no one's around," he said as he started to step into the clear water.

"Oh, what if someone comes," she shrieked, this was difficult!

"It's Wednesday, no one is coming here today, come and cool off before we eat, we'll dry out on our towels."

Stripping down to her underwear she carefully entered the water up to her panties, trying not to get them wet, with gentle waves lapping to the top of her legs. The water was cool and refreshing after hiking and she was appreciative of it, although uneasy. What an impromptu act this was; but how exciting that they acted impulsively. Standing in the water she convinced herself it wasn't illegal because they still had clothes on. Gemma was aware of Jonah's eyes looking her up and down and she was pleased to have a solid fabric sports bra and briefs on today.

"I don't want to get my underwear wet," she announced tottering on her toes. "Anyway the sea feels quite cool in contrast to me being so hot from walking for a couple of hours." A nervous giggle escaped; she was a little self-conscience.

Gemma didn't linger too long in the water, just had a quick paddle to cool off. Tip toeing out cautiously avoiding sharp shells she carefully sat down on her towel she had spread out, trying not to get sand on it as she lay down to get her legs dry and her circulation flowing again. Thank goodness her clothes were still dry with just a few splashes that wouldn't matter. Jonah came running over shivering and wrapped himself in his towel looking frozen. Gemma proceeded to spread out the goodies to eat, she focused on tearing open the brown paper bags, they were faced with inviting asparagus rolls and tempting apricot pies with a circle of mock cream around them, Yum!

Smiles spread across their faces and they were both ravenous after their hike followed by the thrill of the refreshing dip, wide open spaces and a lovely day together, things couldn't be any nicer. After eating, Jonah lay down in his underwear to dry in the sun, she was a little shocked and just averted her eyes and talked directly to his face, he appeared to just feel very comfortable around her. She warmed quickly after drying her legs, pulled a tee shirt over her head, slipping goose-bumpy arms through the sleeves to cover up, she would blush profusely if anyone walked passed.

Now she was more comfortable to relax, Jonah watched on with a smile, the sun was glorious, sea sparkling, a deserted track, nice food and companionship, life was good. They sat and talked about life and enjoyed each others company, the friendship was lovely and the tranquil place was beautiful, just them alone in the world. After their rest they later clambered back up the hill, with Jonah offering a hand to pull her up and they again walked past the menacing cows.

It wasn't long before she offered the juicy mandarins still rolling around in the bottom of her bag, their water bottles were nearly empty which made the packs lighter on their shoulders, and Jonah still had the two cans of coke in his backpack if they became thirsty.

Chapter 22

Returning to drop Gemma back at her house, a pink sky was radiant with the sun setting over her front lawn, they sat watching it change to a hot red before disappearing behind the hills, a brilliant finish to a lovely day together. They were both deep in thought, silently contemplating while finished the plate of toasted cheese sandwiches, Gemma had made for a quick tea. After a perfect day out like the one they just had, an unspoken question hung in the air, were they at ease to simply slip back into their usual routines and separate homes.

Gemma woke to a heavy spring dew on the lawn and found herself strangely cold, but after breakfast the air blossomed into a gorgeous warm day. She decided to spend some time sitting outside in her private, paved patio area surrounded by camellia trees, they were no longer in flower and only had shades of green leaves to lift her emotionally. When she moved here she under planted the trees with spring flowering Iris, freesias and daffodil bulbs which had now started blooming, she looked on, valuing her effort with a sense of pride as the sweet spring perfume pervaded the air. With Wilson beside her, she examined the majestic bare silver birch, with its first showing of leaves yearning to burst forth on a silvery skeleton of shiny branches that wept over the lawn, she wondered how old it was.

To the side of the cottage was a young clematis climber that she planted, it had now intertwined with a dainty apricot scented rose set to climb the black steel fence, they were pretty and worked well together, lending a serenity to the setting. Indoors she had decorated, keeping with a theme of pretty pastel flowers on the cushion covers that were comfortably scattered around the sofas. The main bedroom brushed pastel peach on the walls with a floral and frilly bed set. Very expensive heritage looking lace curtains hung at the window of her bedroom. She had splashed out to create that oldie world look, and everything was feminine and pretty which she could do now because there was no man about.

Feeling relaxed, with Wilson asleep in the sun, she began to read her book and again paused to remind herself how much life had changed from just a few years ago. Then her body and mind were completely racked with sorrow, but now here she sat, absorbing the last bit of heat from the fading sunlight soaking deep into her entire presence, with the certainty that everything happened for a reason, just like thunder clouds moving across the sky, life moved on and the world kept on spinning. The phone rang interrupting her thoughts, it was her usual 7.30pm phone call made a bit earlier.

"Hi, I have a few mates coming to stay next Friday night and we're planning to go hunting on Saturday. So I'm sorry we can't go dancing, but I was wondering if you want to come around and meet them?" Jonah asked.

"Oh yes, I could cook a roast dinner at your place for everyone, for after you get back from the hunt on Saturday, if you want." She made the offer resisting the urge to feel a bit challenged and nervous about entertaining, she was no longer used to socializing. Her heart was open to it, she wanted to return to being that confident person she was twenty years ago, once upon a time she loved having people around.

"That would be great, I can leave a key in the usual place for you to let yourself in, to start preparation. We want to be back before dark, so maybe try to have tea about 6.30pm," Jonah suggested.

"Okay." She made a mental note of that and suppressed her fear of inadequacy.

"Well, can I take you out sometime before then, to buy you a nice cocktail dress?" he enquired and she could imagine him smiling, he loves to buy her things.

"Oh, if you want to buy me a dress I won't complain, how about we go on Tuesday?"

"Sounds good, talk later, bye." Jonah was thrilled.

Well, filled with anticipation her week couldn't go fast enough, Jonah was taking her shopping to buy a new dress! Something elegant for her to wear while entertaining his mates, a string of wealthy farmers all interested in talking about their deer and cattle, or the horticulture profit and losses. It all seemed a bit boring to Gemma who was mostly looking forward to getting a pretty cocktail dress. They travelled into Auckland city, which was just over an hour away, spent time browsing through the boutique clothes shops, admiring a lot of dresses, but it had to be the right knee length she decided, a party dress not too evening like. She had in her mind exactly what she was looking for and tried a few on before she spotted the one, royal blue with tiny flowers, a nicely cut neckline, perfect for showing off one of her good features but still very demure, pulled in at the waist with a flared skirt in a stiff satin like fabric, shiny and elegant with slinky lining. Gemma popped her head out of the changing room and with arms waving wildly, summoned Jonah over to the draped doorway.

"How's this?" she asked smiling, hoping he would like it as much as she did.

"Wow! That fits you well, you look amazing, do you want it?" he asked stunned, knowing that he will be proudly showing Gemma off to his mates.

"Yes please." Gemma was hesitant as she had already looked at the price tag $250, but he was not concerned with the price, just zapped his card when the shop assistant told him the price before she carefully folded it between sheets of soft white tissue paper and prudently slipped it into a bag.

It felt nice to not have to look at how much something cost. Remarking to Jonah on how expensive it was as they walked to the car, he looked at her with a smile and kissed her gently on the check as they stood, he opened her door.

"If it looks right on you, don't worry about the money, just buy it, I have enough money to provide for you," he explained. "Plus, I'm proud to show you off, I've been talking about you so much, it's time you met some of my friends," he said.

A cocktail blend of anticipation and anxiety about what they would think of her made it difficult to sleep on Thursday night, with her mind continually fixated on meeting his friends, she had to make a conscious effort to focus her thoughts only on Jonah and that finally helped her to drift off to pleasant dreams.

Friday arrived and she stayed home to relax in the hope that she would look her best. On Saturday afternoon she took her new dress and makeup to Jonah's house, decided to leave Wilson at home to return later that night, leaving the guys to talk and have a few drinks without her around. Jonah probably expected her to spend all night with him, but she preferred to return home as she thinks the stress will have been enough for her by then, she could see him later on his own.

After letting herself into his house and making her way to the large cream and stainless steel kitchen, discovering the cream coloured marble bench top with its huge breakfast bar piled high with bags of grapes, packets of strawberries and various fruit ready for her to cut up and plate as snacks, along with boxes of various crackers and cheese in the fridge. Opening the brushed steel fridge door, she was confronted with a good supply of assorted wines and other bottles of alcohol which she was not familiar with, she found a large leg of lamb thawed out ready for her to cook. Jonah had already cut up the hard skinned pumpkin because he knew even with a sharp knife she would find that difficult to do, all she had left to do was to peel a few potatoes, kumara, carrots and prepare the roast by pushing slices of garlic cloves just under the skin, putting it all in the roasting dish and back into the fridge for a while, it was big so would take about 2 -3 hours to cook.

Once everything was finished it gave her time to formally set the table with cutlery and scrunch caramel coloured serviettes into each wine glass. The fruit and cheese platter she created looked amazing as she covered and popped that back into the fridge for later.

Preparation was so easy in his kitchen, it had plenty of bench space and after peeling and chopping she pushed the rubbish into the bin drawer just below the bench, it had taken a little while to find everything, but it was convenient and easier to use than hers. She busied herself getting everything ready then placed some small tea lights onto a decorative glass tray in the centre of the table ready to be lit later. She stood back to view the table, wow! It all looked nice with Jonah's beautiful sparkly glassware and trays.

Jumping into the shower, before dressing and meticulously applying makeup, she spritzed with his favourite perfume, dried her hair, carefully plaited it down her back, securing it with a royal blue tie. Gemma headed back to the kitchen to turn the oven on to heat, while making her coffee. Time to sit down in the lounge and chill out, looking through the floor to ceiling glass sliding doors to view the undulating acres of paddocks Jonah owned. Gemma secretly hoped that the men did not manage to shoot any animals.

The light went off on the oven so she put the meat and vegetables into roast, searched the cupboard to find a sleek white porcelain gravy boat, she was ready to subsequently prepare gravy, placing a pot of green peas on the stove. It was easy to be organised and able to concentrate while she was on her own, she knew that meeting and entertaining his friends could be more challenging. As she enjoyed the fussing around his kitchen she gradually gained back her self-confidence, if she spent more time with Jonah she felt positive that maybe one day she would be able to move on from her past to this new glamorous world of entertaining.

Through faith she rebuilt her life, and now she faces the fact that she lives a solitary life with her dog. Since meeting Jonah she has come to question herself about advancing further, to emerge from the protective cocoon that she has spun around herself and turn into a beautiful butterfly, should she allow herself to soar, carefree, beyond self-imposed limits.

The sound of the garage roller-door opening with a rattling and squeaking and excited chatter could be heard, many feet were overheard travelled up the hallway, and she was introduced to Jonah's three friends; all relatively rugged, good looking and dirty after trekking through the forest, they shot two deer was the first thing called out as they bubbled over with excitement, (after a short introduction) the animals were left in the back of the Ute.

"I'll just go and put them into the cool room outside and look after them tomorrow," Jonah explained as he gave her a quick kiss while holding her by the shoulders. "You guys make use of the showers and I'll be back in a moment."

"Shall I make a coffee or would you like a cold drink," Gemma asked, hoping that if she kept smiling they wouldn't see how tense she was.

Jonah yelled from the garage, "Open the wine Peter I'll be back in a minute."

Peter appeared to be familiar with things around the kitchen and offered Gemma the first glass he poured.

"Oh, thanks." She took it from him and had a small sip before putting it down on the corner of the dining table, which was the closest thing to hand.

There was only a half hour left on the timer before dinner was cooked and it gave her a good excuse to escape back into the kitchen to turn the roast vegetables and check on how it was going. Jonah rushed back through the garage door and down the hallway towards the ensuite, so Gemma snuck into the bedroom to talk to him while he was under the water.

"They're staying overnight," Jonah informed her, "and plan to leave after breakfast tomorrow. You look nice," he says.

She smiled before she quickly returned to the lounge where the three were gradually returning, wearing clean clothes that they brought with them, all laughing and chatting over a glass of wine.

When Jonah arrived back in the kitchen, his familiar musky scent made her heart miss a beat, and she felt a shortness of breath, he picked up one of the open bottles of wine proceeding to top up the other glasses before helping Gemma serve in the kitchen. The roast was sliced and piled high on white platters with the vegetables and serving tools along the breakfast bar and everyone helped themselves, before taking a seat around the beautiful dark wooden dining table. Jonah was the perfect host and a welcome presence, reassuring and assisting her in the kitchen, she noticed his wonderful manners and was proud of him.

Everyone relaxed, there was laughter and talking about the shoot as she focused down on her plate rather a lot, between sipping on wine to gain some courage, her face flushed warm as she seldom drank alcohol. Sensibly deciding not to have any more, but to just look on and listen, a good time was had by all and Gemma was happy for Jonah. The large dinner was welcomed as they were all ravenous after their adventure. Afterwards everyone moved into the lounge for a platter of multi coloured cheeses and various crackers with more wine and fruit platter for desert.

Smiling and helping with offering food around she started to long for home, tired but glad to be included, it all seemed to be going well with the three guys saying that they were happy to have met Gemma after hearing so much about her from Jonah.

Jonah caught up with her alone in the kitchen, and gave her a big kiss and hug, she explained that he should stay and spend time with his mates and she would go home, returning to see him tomorrow to help clean up, while he dealt with the butchering of the animals. Gemma returned to the lounge to say goodbye, with *'hope to see you all again soon'* she fled for home.

Arriving home to a sleepy puppy, she let him out to the toilet for the night before making herself a welcome cup of tea and then headed for bed. Sleep came easily as she was confident that the dinner went well although she was tired and had found it quite taxing.

She woke feeling refreshed and relieved, pleased she had gotten through entertaining Jonah's friends albeit that she retreated home afterwards, it was a new chapter in her life and she was happy it went well. Heading outside to feed and pat Wilson she then returned to open the drapes to bright sunlight streaming through the windows, the promise of a beautiful day as she prepared a nice cup of tea and toast to have in front of the morning news.

The sweet smell of cut grass from two days ago filled the air, after the light covering of rain that had fallen through the night, refreshed with the sweet promise of spring bursting forth it was synonymous with new life. After a quiet breakfast, Wilson and she strolled around the garden scanning for new buds appearing on the plants, the rose bushes bursting with strong new red branches ready to hold flowers a little later on.

Gemma loved life, her garden, home and her independence but she had definitely become more in tune with Jonah now, he was so kind, considerate and seeing him aroused her senses, finding him more attractive every time she saw him. The universe kept changing, could he be the one in her future?

"Oh my dear Wilson, it all seems to be escalating so quickly, even though I've known him for over three years now, perhaps I've let my guard down. Opening my heart without realizing it." She bent to pat him while contemplating how she had trudged through the grieving process, anger and despair and finally reached an acceptance.

Gemma stood in her garden and said a short prayer, asking for clarity, she trusted that various people came into our lives for a reason. Accepting that sometimes opportunities for us, were far greater than our own expectations for ourselves. She continued her way around the garden and planned to head back to Jonah's before noon.

It was perfect timing, she arrived in time to wave the guys off together. Jonah looked content, and once alone he reached out, his arms encircled her waist and she stretched her arms around his neck, it was nice to be alone with him again.

"Did you have a nice time?" she whispered in his ear.

"Yes, and now I'm going to have a better time." He reached down gathering her into his arms and carried her to the bed while she protested laughingly.

"Let me down, you'll hurt yourself," she giggled and they ended up both falling onto the bed with Jonah snuggling into her neck.

"I'm very proud of you, and loved showing you off to my friends, I hope you didn't mind," he whispered while snuggling into her hair.

"No, it was okay, I enjoyed it and now I have a new dress for you to take me dancing again," she teased.

"Come for tea next Friday night, stay over and I'll take you on my boat early on Saturday, we can stop off to have lunch at Kamara Island and spend the day there if you want. Wilson is happy to stay here all day playing in the orchard."

"Do you have a boat?" she shrieked in surprise.

"Yes, it's not huge, but the weather is forecast to be perfect, would you like to spend the weekend doing that?" Jonah smiled proudly.

"Yes!" Gemma replied with a broad smile, silently hoping she wouldn't get seasick.

There was not much to clean up in the kitchen, she just throw everything into the dishwasher and scrubbed the bulky roasting dish and large platters, then made her way around with a wet cloth to wipe any areas where the wine glasses had been placed after she had left last night. Jonah got busy outside chopping up meat for the freezer, he had a proper stainless steel sink bench in a cool room outside away from the house, specially set up for butchering animals he shot, storing the meat in a huge chest freezer to give his mates later on.

When he returned, they kissed and spent a few hours together walking around his vast property, the orchard was her favourite place, before it was time to say goodbye. Heading home happy and looking forward to next weekend, Gemma settled back into her routine of time at the beach and looking after Wilson. She had a boat trip to look forward to now, her life was full of surprises.

The weather improved every day and as she sat at the beach with Wilson, looking out over the expansive sea she understood that she has learnt to be mindful of small things people take for granted, she was appreciative, whether in need of love and affection, kindness, wealth or better food, she was gratified being able to enjoy whatever she does have, she needs very little. Through her acceptance and gratitude she can now understand and have empathy for the many tragic situations people endure, through no fault of their own.

Gemma was grateful for the caring man that has come into her life, the peace and tranquillity, and very thankful for her good health and renewed self-confidence to go on with her life. Walking out onto the pier while still contemplating, she looked down into the deep dark sea water, reminiscent of the days when she was in the depth of darkness, she struggled with sorrow and for survival to regain what she had lost, only to become a stronger person gaining insight into what wisdom really was! Not regaining but discovering a layer within her that she didn't know she had, finding an entirely new life after experiencing tragedy, she was very privileged.

Full of excitement, looking forward to going out on Jonah's boat she planned what to wear, and what food to pack for nibbles on the way, (she felt she needed to take something.) The day arrived and Gemma was pleasantly surprised, stepping onto a very generously sized boat, not that she knew much about boats. With a delighted smile, Jonah explained he bought it about three years ago but had hardly used it, he lent it out to friends and paid to have it moored safely, but today it had been left ready for them, by his friend at one of the gorgeous bays just up from Waterworth.

Chapter 23

Stepping carefully onto the deck looking out to the front, it had a nice big, blue tinted glass window that stopped the wind while they sat hunched looking through it from two sunny yellow, plastic chairs fixed behind the main seat where the steering wheel was. Exploring downstairs she found a small galley, an open plan room with a blue leather sofa and small dining table, with the far end looking through to a bedroom with a queen sized bed, a small desk and a bathroom with a shower. It was all very jaw droppingly surprising and she was stunned speechless.

The polished brass shone and the aged timber was elegant and quite beautiful. Going back upstairs to the bridge, she sunk into the seat behind Jonah to watch as he started up the motor with just a push of a button. Holding onto the steering wheel, traveling slowly and carefully with a look of concentration shadowing his face, then appearing to gain confidence he sped up. Bouncing over waves it was exhilarating, Gemma still hoping it wouldn't upset her stomach, but not wanting to spoil the day she never mentioned it.

While cruising along, the further out to sea they voyaged the calmer it became and he suggested they lower the anchor for a little while and have a snack. Jonah started to strip down to his briefs as she busied herself finding the sunscreen. He was relaxed, utterly in his element as she handed it to him, he was obviously very comfortable on the water, while she concentrated on arranging cheese, crackers and putting some fruit on a platter in the centre of the small table downstairs. Struggling to put all her focus on what she was doing, instead of the fact that she was afloat in the ocean and feeling a little nervous, the aroma of saltwater hung heavy in the air and the breeze stung her nostrils.

"Do you want to come and have something to snack on before sunbathing?" she called to him.

"Yes, I better had after getting up quite early this morning, and I need a drink. Are you going to put your swimsuit on or stay in your shorts?" he queried.

"After I eat something, I have my swimsuit already under my shorts."

Sitting closely together out of the sun, they enjoyed a healthy snack and Jonah had already stashed a bottle of red wine in the small on-board fridge.

"Would you like a wine or a fruit juice?" he asked, quite the host.

"I might save the wine for lunch time later, and just have some water for now thanks, I packed my water bottle in my backpack," Gemma replied, a little cautious about risking wine while surrounded by ocean.

After eating they climb back up the narrow stairway, suddenly struck by the glare of sunshine bouncing off the water, they spread out to relax with sunglasses on and Jonah applied sunscreen on her back for protection. Lying around and getting to know a little more about each other, they talked as if they had all the time in the world, bobbing in a boat, tranquillity and not a soul in sight, it was impossible to be concerned about life's problems, on board nothing else existed, just the two of them drifting. Then after a while, the glare from the sun shining down and reflecting off the sea, dazzled Gemma and it became quite sickening, so she had to go downstairs to have a lie in the cabin and read a magazine for a while. Jonah raised the anchor and set sail again, the journey was going well and then he called out.

"You can see Kamara Island up ahead."

Gemma quickly dumped the magazine and headed back on deck, again taking the yellow seat behind Jonah, she watched as they pulled alongside the wharf. The water around the island was a shade lighter blue than what was out in the dark ocean, and Gemma delighted in how calm it was. He softly cruised into the jetty like an expert to allow her to climb off before he motored along the beach a little further to anchor, and wade ashore to meet up with Gemma.

On the island they searched for shade under a tall tree and spread out the rug Jonah brought ashore. They lay down and time escaped them as Jonah talked for ages. He set about explaining how he has been wanting to talk with her about looking for a house, somewhere that he could launch his boat into the water from his own property, then he would sail more often.

"I don't want to keep working, I don't need to. Besides, now that I've met you I want to downsize and move to somewhere that has water," he explained as she listened intently, this was news to Gemma and it would be a big move for him.

"I've found a few places that I'd like you to have a look at with me next weekend, if you wouldn't mind?"

"Okay, where are they?" Gemma asked.

"Not far from Waterworth, do you think that's a long way from what you're used to?"

"I like Waterworth, it's not that far really on State Highway 1, I could still come and stay with you for the weekend or maybe longer if Wilson was safely fenced in. We could have a look." Gemma studied his solemn face.

"There are a few places backing onto the sea up around Marangi Harbour, it's still in the Auckland region and there is a ferry to Kamara Island. I'd be able to give up farming and just enjoy fishing whenever I wanted." There was a thoughtful silence as they headed towards the café.

After ordering lunch Gemma was fascinated by the wallabies hopping around the outdoor table. There were signs everywhere telling people not to feed them, so they resisted the temptation to do so. After devouring a delicious lunch of seafood salad, green salad with crispy bacon bits scattered through and freshly baked bread rolls they finished with delicious cheesecake and both stood up energised and ready to explore.

"I've been looking forward to going through the historic mansion house, I love old architecture and the craftsmanship that went into them, these days it's all about speed to get the houses built." She said smiling and excited that they were there.

Jonah acted like he was interested in the building as well, but his mind did seem to be a bit distracted since the chat about him moving. Afterwards, they started to hike up the hill which gave a stunning expansive view from the top. Still carrying the rug they deciding to spread it out and sit to enjoy more time there. Jonah looked very serious as he moved closer to kiss her.

With a solemn voice he spoke quietly, "I love how you're so appreciative and not expecting of what I can give you, other women have wanted more and more in the past, I never found someone satisfied with everything until you."

"It's exciting that you are financially secure, and I'm constantly amazed as it's a new world to me, but it's not for me to interfere or ask. You should be very proud of yourself to get this far; I think you're very clever." Gemma smiled.

"I hope it will become our world, you and me together enjoying what I can provide for you, I get pleasure from treating you with lovely things, because you don't expect anything." He leant in to drop a gentle kiss her on her cheek.

Hot from embarrassment Gemma's face flushed, she was not used to complements, she smiled and said nothing about his hopes and plans.

"It's a wonderful day out, and I'm glad we came. Thank you for today." Turning to let him see her happy glow.

Gemma turned away from looking into his eyes, she was mesmerized with the kind things he was saying, the solitude of the natural surroundings and it was all very surreal, he was sweeping her off her feet while she was on dry land. It was time to go back to the boat.

Rolling up his trouser legs Jonah waded out, offering to carry her if she wanted. Laughing hysterically she was very hesitant and told him no! she would meet him at the wharf. Back on his boat, they only went a little way out and he put the anchor down.

"What's up?" anxiety rife in her voice.

"Don't ask, just follow me," he kindly requested.

Gemma followed Jonah carefully down the narrow stairs and sat on the bed. He was finding it too difficult to go any further out to sea, after enjoying a lovely day just the two of them together he explained he was overwhelmed with emotion, and the both of them started to kiss gripped by intense passion, embracing and hastily exploring while whispering how they felt about each other, Jonah saying he needed to know. Not much was said later on the way back, they both cruised in a world of ecstasy where knowing how they both felt inside was better than anything they could talk about. There were decisions to be made and Jonah knew what he wanted, but how does he go about getting it.

Back at Jonah's beautiful home she stayed another night, and after having had a long emotionally charged dreamy day, they both sought a peaceful sleep in each other's arms. Wilson was pleased to see them both arrive back safely, and the following morning he was exuberant wanting to return home, leaping out of the car he ran into his backyard, returning with a favourite toy in his mouth. Gemma was not in the mood for playing so made a cup of tea, Wilson enjoyed a biscuit while she pondered on how Jonah had said to her about his future hopes in a kind of obscure way, she wondered if he was hinting that what they had could turn into a committed relationship. She was unsure of how she felt about that.

Joyful sun rays streamed through the kitchen window, it was the onset of another beautiful day and Wilson was all set for a walk to the beach. Now nine months old he knew all about the beach, so he was very excited about getting there as fast as he could and pulled hard on his lead.

"Go slow," Gemma growled at him to no avail, as he could only think of the park and the beach and did not have the maturity of restraint just yet.

Never mind, she told herself to be patient as he would grow up one day and until then she might have to get a longer lead to keep up with him. It was a time of puppy mischief as well, sometimes he ran into the kitchen, snatched the mat and ran off around the house with it hanging out of his mouth, knowing full well that Gemma would chase him to rescue her mat before he took it outside and got it dirty. She had to smile!

"What are you doing Wilson, that's not a toy?" she growled at him as his tail wagged.

Wilson stood his ground with gorgeous big brown eyes pleading for a play, he looked like he was smiling and knew how to get Gemma's attention, so to confuse him she headed outside, he was fast and it would be pointless to chase him, that was what he wanted so she had to outsmart him. He followed her with it still flapping from his mouth.

"Can I play? Find a toy," she suggested to him.

Off he went, tearing around to find a blue rubber ball to play fetch with, she picked it up, throw it and quickly grabbed the mat he dropped on the path, he had succeeded. Gemma was playing with him whether she wanted to or not, but the mat was safe.

For her, thoughts of wanting someone to go out with or travel overseas with was nice, to have that special person to share the happy and sad times with would be lovely. She could hear herself laughing out loud with Wilson and was content for it to be just her and the dog for now. How could she explain her feelings to Jonah? He was ruled by his heart and full of hope, he shouldn't be burdened with the baggage left from her past, but then again, how does someone prevent falling in love!

Sitting at the beach watching someone else's dog run into the water to fetch a stick, she realized that worrying too much about Jonah's feelings was weighing her down.

After some deliberation and a glass of wine with her dinner she decided to just cruise along and not go to his house so often. She would continue to have faith that everything would work out for the best, she did not want to hurt Jonah and there was no urgency.

It was so strange that even the chance to be with a multi-millionaire could not tempt Gemma to give up the newly found independence she valued more than any amount of wealth, she felt safe that she did not have to rely on anyone, maybe it was still early days after moving house, she couldn't tell, and perhaps she would change her mind one day.

Gemma arrived at Jonah's on Saturday morning instead of staying over Friday night, they set off to look at the property's he had talked about, a quarter acre property with a jetty, not too far from shops, it was a lovely section, then when he asked her what she thought about the house, she told him honestly that it was too small and the kitchen was horrible. Getting back into the car, he didn't speak, just drove to the next one with a look on his face, maybe it was important to Jonah that she liked the house, even though he said he was looking for somewhere to retire.

Gemma patiently spent several weekends looking at properties around the Northern Bays and the many bays near to Waterworth. She was becoming bored, so politely told Jonah he should just wait until something really good appeared, either in the paper or an agent contacting him, give it to the Lord to guide him. Jonah looked a bit dejected, but it was a mystery as to what he actually wanted, he needed to be honest with her. Teatime hunger meant sending for a pizza and relaxing on the soft leather sofa, but after a spa and wine they ended up relaxing on the bed instead of the sofa. He ran kisses down her neck sending a stream of warmth through her and she giggled.

"I love your innocence with everything, you're so trusting, you're honest and I truly believe you're not interested in my money, which I find very refreshing," he said.

“No amount of wealth can buy my friendship, it’s the person that matters to me.”

“That’s exactly what I mean,” he laughed too loudly, making her suspicious, intuition told her he hoped that she would be happy to give up her life because of what he could offer, or maybe he felt he could not offer her enough.

“I am who I am, and what you see, I dislike fake people or deceit, those people that don’t see the beautiful life around them are materialistic, they need things to make them happy,” Gemma tried to explain as she lay on his arm and he had his head resting on the top of her hair.

He lifted her face towards him and kissed, the room was thick with emotion which enveloped her like a thick fluffy towel and a little tear ran down her check, maybe he was upset because he couldn’t impress her with money. Gemma trusted him and she was fearful that her feelings were opening her heart to vulnerability. A strained silence and aura of unspoken words floated in the air for a few moments before subsiding, still wrapped in each others’ arms, time helped to make the tense moments pass, and the joy of just being together returned.

“I think we should go on holiday, what do you think of a break away in a campervan?” Jonah asked.

“I loved traveling in a campervan around New Zealand, it’s a beautiful place and we have so much here to see. Waterfalls, mountains, snow, sun, sea and countryside, we have it all.” Gemma started to rise from the bed and straighten her clothes.

“Where would you like to go?” he pushed weathered fingers through his unruly hair to try to smooth it down.

“I would like to travel down the West Coast from Auckland as I’ve always gone down the centre on State Highway 1 or gone over to the East Coast. Let’s have a look at the map and decide what we want to see. I wonder if there are any Home and Garden shows or Festivals to look at. Let's plan it later, do you want a coffee?" she asked, not really interested in a heavy discussion right now.

"Yes, I'll get up and have it in the lounge, we can go anytime you want, and so we'll get a pen and a map one day next week and do some research online," he said thinking out loud, as he started to put his shirt back on and looked thoughtful again.

"You won't have to cook; we'll buy and eat out the whole time, with not having to worry about booking accommodation we will have the opportunity to enjoy everything along the way."

"Sounds good!" Gemma smiled, making her way to the kitchen to prepare coffee so they could watch the Saturday night movie.

Snuggling up together was nice and with her feet nestled into his lap she lay back on the end of the sofa while he massaged her feet, then when she stayed over she could put her cold feet on him instead of having to wear bed socks. In the morning, nothing more was said about the campervan trip before Wilson and Gemma headed for home.

Even after having a lovely time together, it never ceased to amaze her how nice it was returning home to the beach with Wilson. Walking down the hill to the sea, her senses were heightened by the cool refreshing breeze blowing gently on her skin, and the smell of fresh crisp sea air stinging her nostrils while walking along the seashore. The dim buttery light piercing through lumpy white clouds was so spiritual and welcoming to Gemma, she could come here any time she wanted. What a privilege to have an endless sea view blending with the sky, a beautiful beach to tread sand and earths ocean that was forever changing, the sound of birds in the trees and a park to stroll through, it was like a dream, she viewed herself to be so lucky. Everything happened for a reason, and the culmination of her husband's demented cruelty resulted in her freedom to be part of not only this place but taught her to be at one with the earth, sky and ocean, the whole universe had opened up to her.

Jonah was excited as they started to plan their trip away, deciding to take Wilson for security as he was already a great watch dog. He could mind the van for them while they slept and when it was empty. With pen and paper they set about making a rough plan for their trip, promising to stop and see anything of interest along the way. Even though neither of them wanted to spend a lot of time traveling the main state highway as it had been driven many times before, in the end decided it was the most practical way to reach the first destination.

The Hamilton Gardens which neither of them had seen before, even though they had both been to specialty days that were held off to the side of Hamilton every year. After appreciating the gardens, roughly speaking they planned to turn off and head for Te Kuiti on the way across to the West Coast of New Zealand by taking the main highway that lead to Mt Taranaki, they were both exciting about seeing the mountain, making it an absolute must for their trip.

During the drive they plan to warm up along the way by staying at a Holiday Park, making use of showers and recreation then head back up to Taumarunui.

The goal was to head away towards the end of September, subconsciously Gemma began planning what to take, it was very exciting and also wonderful that they could include Wilson.

Jonah booked a really nice self-contained campervan and Gemma started to get quite impatient to set off. Jonah was adamant that it would be beneficial for them to get to know each other more and to make memorable fun times together.

The day finally arrived and she had already said her goodbye to Bridget, who was pleased for her to be having this trip away. Gemma's enthusiasm had been escalating and she had found it difficult to sleep last night with her mind going over everything. She carefully parked her car in Jonah's garage alongside his, he had already picked up the grand looking campervan which was parked out the front of his house.

Chapter 24

Gemma took Wilson's bed and laid it in the van which had the door open, so he would know where to sleep tonight, also finding a place for his long lead and tucked her small suitcase in the bedroom.

The three set off! first stop would probably be after leaving the motorway traffic and they would have travelled for at least two hours, both of them enthusiastic to put some distance in when starting out, then it would be time for a much needed stretching of legs and a morning tea comfort stop. Gemma was appreciative that she got to sit and look out of the window, fresh green paddocks flew past the van window and she could walk between the front seats to go back and make another hot drink from the flask of boiled water they prepared before leaving. While Jonah continued to drive she brought back a slice of cake from the tin of snacks she had organized for them. No need to turn the gas on until they stop to settle for the night. The van came furnished with plenty of cups and dishes so she was able to leave the used ones in the sink for later. Everything was going well; Jonah was happy, commenting on how easy the van was to drive. Once seeing the waterfront they spend a little time stretching their legs and then headed off for Gemma's preferred destination, Hamilton gardens, at which they intended to spend an entire day, eating at the cafe' and getting plenty of exercise while taking countless photos of gorgeous gardens.

Both Gemma and Jonah were familiar with the area and the gardens were of particular interest to her, so as they walked around the elaborate Italian garden designed with huge white lion statues and admired the perfectly trimmed box hedges which surrounded the humanmade ponds, Jonah watched her and smiled. It was all very tidy, impeccably laid out and interesting but not all of it appealed to her, she loved colour. Wilson was content to have a long walk and sniff at everything as they searched for the English flower garden which she found to be magnificent with all the flowers, colour and floral perfume floating in the air, it looked very natural and even had an old building to sit under. Sitting there holding hands, tranquilly resting with what seemed like all the time in the world, Jonah couldn't stop smiling and turned to face her.

"It was worth traveling here just to see how relaxed you are in a garden," he laughed contentedly.

"Yes, I do find smelling the perfume, seeing the myriad of colour and growing things is food for the soul, I love flowers," she replied joyously smiling back at him.

"Would you like to go on the paddle boat river cruise? we can do whatever you want. It doesn't matter how long it takes before we head off again," he reminded her.

"I would love that, going along the river would be great." A sweeping smile soared across her face excitedly. "I'm enjoying every minute and the calm day couldn't be more perfect."

Driving across the Hamilton Bridge they parked carefully on the other side for Gemma to take a photo of the old arched concrete structure, before finding a parking spot close to where the boat was moored and Wilson could have an hours sleep.

The old paddle boat was a replica of a boat from 1876 and they climbed aboard to enjoy coffee and fresh scones with jam and cream for afternoon tea, due to depart at 3pm and return in an hour. Sitting on the boat which moved very slowly in the stream of flowing water the movement was relaxing and they were able to look at the backyards of beautiful homes that overlooked the river, that wouldn't be visible from the road, they were stunning homes with stairs that lead down to the water's edge, some had balconies build on the second floor, overlooking this wondrous sight of slow flowing water or for the lady of the house to sit and sunbathe, how wonderfully civilized!

Arriving back on shore happy and in awe of the river trip they then headed for the van, Jonah opened the passenger door for her and instead of getting in she turned towards him and flung her arms around his neck.

"Thanks for a lovely day," she cried out.

"You're welcome sweetheart, I'm glad you're having a nice time."

Well, the first day had been a full day, after traveling down from Auckland and seeing the sights, the air was beginning to cool and Gemma was tiring, ready for a quiet tea in the van, it felt like quite a lot of travelling when not used to being in a big van. The happy couple had not gone far but she supposed it was a bit more stressful than being in a car so she was happy to settle for the night somewhere.

Jonah wanted to keep driving saying that it will only take about an hour to get to the next destination, which was Te Kuiti, he assured her that there was still plenty of daylight left to view everything on the way so she agreed with the driver. No more than half an hour later they came across a lovely fish and chip shop on the side of the road, looking at each other and smiling they decided to pull over to buy hot food to have in the van for tea. With the warm paper-wrapped bundle on her lap they set off to find a place to park, a few minutes further down the road coming across a rest area with running water to wash their hands, praise the Lord.

There was also a large picnic table to spread out the takeaways so no need to have the fishy smell in the van, it was nice there and sitting restfully watching her dog run around it was meant to be that they stay for the night. Under the native trees and with the glow of a streetlight they had privacy, room for Wilson to enjoy the grassed area and everything they needed in the campervan.

As nighttime darkness fell, they settled in, had a good play and chase with Wilson, before moving into the van to shower and relax for the night. Wilson was happy to curl up on his rug in the corner of the van while she poured two glasses of wine for them. The bed was already made up, propping pillars up against the side of the van they prepared to get comfortable for watching television. Jonah looked serious as his eyes meet hers putting his arm around her shoulders he gently guided her in to lie on his chest.

"Are you okey? you seem a bit quiet," she asked.

"Yes, I'm fine, do you want to watch anything or just sit and talk?" he asked respectfully.

"We can talk, what do you want to talk about?" Gemma enquired sipping on sparkly white wine.

Jonah's face stilled as he looked directly into her eyes.

"Talk to me about your life and why you moved to the cottage," he requested gently and with genuine concern in his voice. "It's just that I wonder how you can be so happy and content to be on your own, aren't you lonely?" Bending his head down and gently planting a kiss on her check.

"Well it's a long story, but I only had one good year with my husband before he sustained a serious head injury and his character changed, he got more and more difficult to live with as he grew moody and unpredictable," Gemma calmly explained. "He went on to have a major stroke and years later he was diagnosed with Dementia. I've told you some of that before, but I haven't explained to you how it affected me, I sought a quiet place near the sea after years of sleepless nights and living in fear of my violent husband. I loved him dearly, but he wasn't the same person I'd married.

I became a prisoner in my own home because of my devotion to help him, believing that I married in sickness and in health and not wanting to give up on him. He gradually declined over our 18 years of marriage, leaving me in need of emotional and physical healing. The cottage by the sea has been perfect for healing and putting myself back together without the pressures of life, I found a refuge which was both comforting and enlightening, I'm part of the world again." She hoped that he understood.

Her hand received a gentle squeeze as he listened intently, an outwardly display of caring not sympathy, as she continued quietly explaining what he needed to understand.

"Listening to the gentle waves on the shore helped me forget and heal from the lost love and hurt, it is probably hard for anyone to fully comprehend what it was like to live in fear day and night, unless you have walked in my shoes. I found a sanctuary and appreciation of my peace, freedom and security."

"What do you want now, is there room for some form of us?" he asked, again very gently.

"Well, I have copious amounts of determination to keep moving on, I'm shaking free of those memories that haunted me. The days of praying alone in my bedroom with desperate heart wrenching tears running down my face and my chest heaving in pain have gone. He is gone! And I feel happy again." Gemma looked up at him, she saw sadness and concern spread across his face, he wasn't cross or disappointed and her heart melted, in his arms they started to kiss.

"Let's not talk anymore tonight I just want to cuddle up with you, hold you and make everything alright. I wonder what I need to do to make you mine," he murmured while sweeping a hair away from her eyes.

"Everything is alright! I'm okay." She tried to reassure him as she cuddled close and accepted his welcoming embrace.

His face felt prickly, overdue for a shave and she felt his masculine strength against her, he pulled his shirt up over his head, then started to climb into the makeshift bed.

She was grateful that he didn't want to dismiss her fears as unimportant, he didn't dismiss any of her emotions, everything was listened to, and he seemed to be searching in an attempt to understand why Gemma was content to be on her own with just her dog. The fact that he was so caring and interested, was more than Gemma had with her husband and she was finding Jonah very alluring and attractive as they snuggled down together as best friends, she felt security and love.

The morning started earlier than preferred as they were woken with brilliant sunshine shining right through the front windscreen and into their eyes while still in bed, something to learn, they had not thought about which direction was east and how the van should be parked, not that it really mattered anyway because they don't want to miss any of this day together, his arm was resting over Gemma's waist, like he didn't want to let her get away.

"Good morning, you stay there and I'll get us a coffee in bed, there's no rush, we're on holiday." He popped a kiss on her cheek.

"I'll just let Wilson out the door, there's no one around and then I'll get us some toast while you make me a cup of tea if you like."

"Okay." Jumping out of bed he headed for the gas stove.

Pouring water into a pot to boil before he pulled on a pair of jeans and a tee shirt, she couldn't help but watch him, not only because of the close proximity, but he was attractive and she noticed how the jeans showed off his tight butt, pulling herself up she stopped her imagination from working overtime. Finding the bread she popped two slices into the toaster as a distraction. Standing next to him she could sense his eyes watching, so she looked up to see him glancing down at her braless breasts through the stretch fabric of the top she had slept in, the toast was cooking so she turned away to get dressed.

Wilson returned from under the trees, drawn in by the aroma of toast cooking, he enjoyed a slice of toast outside after having his dog biscuits, while they sat on top of the bed to have their breakfast. The closeness of warm bodies next to each other very evident as they endeavoured to abstain from human desires.

"Let's get going again on our adventure, I'm really enjoying this time with you." She smiled harmlessly at him.

"Me too darling," said with a lovely smile.

"Not far to go to Te Kuiti, do you want to go to the glow-worm caves or take Wilson to the beautiful big reserve there?" he inquired.

"I think the caves might be a bit cool inside so let's see that first then come out into the warmth of the sunshine the rest of the day, what do you think?"

"Sounds good, and we can find somewhere nice to buy lunch to have in the sunshine."

A quick tidy up around the van, wash and pulling her hair into a ponytail, Wilson's back in the campervan on his rug all set to head off, and she clips on the seat belt while Jonah jumped into the driver's seat, ready for more exploring. Just a pleasant drive, gazing out of the window now in the north of the King Country region so the scenery was picturesque and there were a few newborn lambs in the paddocks. Gemma was in charge of navigating the way to the glow worm caves, it was a nice day but being early they were sure it would be cold inside the caves. Tugging on warm hats, they grab at jackets before leaving the van with Wilson happy to sleep.

At the entrance they were greeted with a good solid wooden handrail, thank goodness because she was a bit concerned about slipping over. The narrow track into the cave also looked manageable, sometimes narrowing to single file and she went first behind the guide but always felt the reassuring weight of Jonah's hand on her shoulder, letting her know of his presence behind her. The cave had a reverence about it with its beauty, and seeing the fossils imbedded into the rocks made her want to whisper, the glow worms created a string of pretty lights along the way, it was creepy to know they were actually alive and the thought made her afraid to touch the wall of the cave in case she touched worms. It was damp and musty with green algae growing where the water ran down the wall and further in had turned into frozen stalactites, it was amazing and quite unique. Although in awe of the cave, Gemma started to feel a bit claustrophobic, because of the overhanging rocks and the narrow spaces to push through, the air was stuffy and she felt alarmed so she concentrated on Jonah's presence pressing on her shoulder, it was a memorable experience for them.

Strangely enough coming out into the light, they stopped, stunned and in awe for a moment while pulling themselves together, appreciative of seeing such an amazing beauty under ground but also pleased to breathe in the open air again, as they made their way back to the campervan for a warm drink and a sit in the sunlight to warm up.

An odd silence reigned for a few minutes as they sat and watched Wilson rummage around in the trees, before Jonah offered to make the drinks and Gemma entered the campervan to take off her hat, jacket and to wash up, she felt quiet grubby after climbing around in the semi-dark. Returning to sit in the sun Jonah had drinks and a packet of biscuits sitting on the picnic table, he stood up and reached out, putting his arms around her waist and pulling her into him, his lips pressing on hers sent an erotic rush through her body.

"Argh, you better have the drink now that you've made it," she laughed.

"I suppose, but somethings are more important." Smiling back.

After a warmup, cupping the warm drinks in their hands, she had put her cup down as he tried again, moving in closer to start kissing her, she was not averse to his attention. A happy couple as their lips met under the grip of longing, gentle and desperately seeking his warm hands were felt under her shirt, as they wrapped around her waist, she allowed her lips to invite his tongue into her mouth. Her friend was chipping away at the wall she had built around herself and all emotional resistance was crumbling.

It didn't matter if this relationship was different from the normal, as long as they were together and yet still apart on her journey, sharing and individual at the same time, maybe it could work, she assumed he understood her.

"Do you understand that I don't know if I can risk heartache all over again, that's why when you get too close, I run back home. And I can't promise that it will ever change, I don't want to hurt you if this relationship can not go as far as you would like it to."

"I understand, it'll be fine, you'll see. Let's just take things slowly, I'm not going to rush you into anything okay," he whispered sensually in her ear.

Her dubious response was one of concern, and she endeavoured not to get his hopes up.

"Life isn't always how you want it to be, I love you and we'll work it out together," he murmured encouragingly.

"Let's continue on our way to the township and maybe see the magnificent scenic reserve on our way home if we're up to it, what do you think?" he asked.

"Yes lets," she smiled back, not wanting anything to spoil there trip together.

The small country looking township was rustic and charming, with a very nice bakery full of delicious goodies, she chose a bulky homemade steak pie full of meat, and he chose ham toasted sandwiches as well as assorted cream cakes to put into the van fridge for the evening. They walked, taking apple short cake and carrot cake with cream cheese icing with them. Yum.

Later the scenic reserve was well worth visiting, surrounded by native bush and well laid out walking tracks for those that chose to do that. On the other hand Gemma was delighted to just sit in the shelter of the wooden gazebo and have lunch overlooking the riverside with its beautiful planting of spring flowering purple irises around the waters edge. Afterwards after a walk around, they decided to try the 30 minutes return trip to view the falls after reading that they were supposed to be spectacular! With approximately a thirty metre drop they were stunning and roared with the rushing of falling water. They stood hand in hand marvelling at the natural wonder, unquestionably delighted to have the camera for a photo, they were having the most amazing trip and making loads of memories, Gemma's face displayed a heartfelt continuous smile so much so her face hurt from smiling so much.

Returning back to the van they let Wilson out for a short run and then decided to keep on going to New Plymouth, which should take about another two hours in pursuit of viewing the mighty Mt Taranaki which could be seen from all areas of New Plymouth. Of course it was breath-taking as well and more photos were taken as

Gemma stood shivering with the piercing cold wind managing to force its way through her merino clothing, even the sturdy farmer was looking pale and frozen.

They rushed back into the warmth of the van and continued on for another 35 minutes to reach the advertised, popular holiday park campground in a brochure they had collected somewhere on their travels. This was the perfect opportunity to collect themselves and relax from all the sight seeing adventures and spend some time out of the van, walking around doing nothing, enjoying longer showers and going to a lovely restaurant for tea. Jonah had a restaurant pin-pointed on his map, Gemma navigated the way to a parking space for the campervan, she wanted to dine before settling into the holiday park.

Chapter 25

Gemma's treat was enjoying a really nice corn fritter stack with spinach, yoghurt, lashings of grilled bacon, avocado and feta cheese which she loved and Jonah's Turkish bread with sirloin steak, onion, tomato, salad and fries looked mouth-watering too. Now they were satisfied to book into the holiday park and take advantage of unlimited time in the indoor heated swimming pool and warm lounge, it was still bitterly cold below the mountain. As they just sat soaking up the gloriously warm water, her wet hair hanging in long tendrils it seemed to her that this was a vital part of just chilling out after travelling.

"Hmmm, that's lovely," she murmured to herself.

"Warming you up and relaxing the mind and body," he calmly whispered.

No matter how good it was, everything comes to an end eventually, and soon her fingers were wrinkled like an old lady, both content to dry off and return to the van. Wilson gave his usual grand welcome leaping up and down, because he wanted his tea before they settled to sleep. Tomorrow morning the plan was to go on the nine hundred metre walk through the Goblin Forest, which sounded interesting.

Gemma turned to say good night to Jonah before she snuggled down to spend a second night of blissful sleep cuddled into the back of him, her arm slung over his hips and her head nuzzled into his neck felt comforting, she started to fall asleep under the perfectly familiar smell of his deodorant.

"It's hard for me to concentrate on sleeping with you so close you know," he said as he rolled over to face her.

"I'm sorry but I like it," she giggled unsympathetically.

Without speaking his lips pressed hers and his wet tongue probed inside her mouth, her body was in growing arousal as his lips moved down her neck, the duvet was thrown aside finding herself lying in just a tee shirt and panties, feeling a little self-conscious but her skin shivered up and down her body with anticipation and welcoming of what was to come, Jonah was aware of how far he could go and what was out of bounds as she gripped tightly to his muscled arms. Both of them were breathing heavily, they kept on kissing and cuddling neither of them hesitating as they had talked about boundaries and both had so much trust in each other, they were absorbed in the heat of the moment and the joy of a wonderful day spent with each other. Jonah whispered into her ear about being together one day, and murmurs went back and forth about her concerns, until the heavy weight of tiredness following their day out, they could not help but succumb to falling asleep in each other's arms.

That's what the trip was all about, spending time to discover more about each other and to understand if they could be together. Their nights were close and wonderful, but the fear was still there for Gemma, she couldn't commit and didn't want to lose her independence again.

Morning light gradually lit up the interior of the van and she awoke with an awareness of Jonah's presence feeling quite normal beside her, gradually getting up and making her way to the shower block, followed by tea and toast together in the van, Wilson lay at her feet. Looking into Jonah's sparkling blue eyes, her stomach was all a flutter with excitement, she was really looking forward to another day together.

Driving through a small community it was only a short drive before quickly finding the entrance to the Goblin Forest Walk, they headed off on an imagination stimulating stroll through the strangely gnarled trees, discovering that it was quite unique. Full of dampness, lush and wild looking greenery very conducive to triggering anyone's imagination, to believe that Goblins, hobbits and elves could all live there. This was a fantastic place for children and adults, to walk and talk about the possibilities of fairies in the forest. Jonah then drove to Pukekura Park, an absolute must see place for everyone to enjoy, fifty-two hectares of botanical gardens and birdlife. Walking around this lovely garden Gemma adored the various vistas and flowery scents, she could not resist taking a lot of photos, one outstanding sight was looking over the lake with not only the elegant teahouse to the side of her photo but also a view of Mt Taranaki towering about the scene, it was an absolute wonder and Jonah squeezed Gemma's hand as he turned to look at her.

"You look happy, it's beautiful here isn't it?" and his smile was a giveaway of how much pleasure he got from making Gemma happy, he really cared and wanted to show her the world.

"Oh yes, it's outstanding, I'd love to see it in the summer as well." Only just managing to respond while feeling so breathlessly excited and astounded by the water fountains and the magnificent waterfall, words could not express how beautiful Gemma found it.

Jonah laughed at her and suggested taking a photo of her on the arched redwood bridge that crossed the lake, overlooked by the charming white teahouse she was standing and admiring. Then they enjoyed a delicious lunch of smoked salmon and various meats and cheeses with an array of crispbread and crackers finished off with dainty squares of slices decorated with angelica and cream. It was amazing and for Gemma, this place had to be the most unforgettable and best adventure of everything she had seen on the trip so far, because to her, with her love of gardens it was insurmountable, something Jonah understood and treasured about her.

"It's starting to get a bit cold so if you have seen enough shall we go back to the van?" he asked with those lovely big eyes looking at her with genuine caring.

"Yes, it's been lovely and I'm quiet tired now, it's time to go back and see Wilson, and settle with a nice glass of wine to end a wonderful day." They walked hand in hand out of the park, she secretly trusted that they would return again one day when it's all lit up in the evening.

Stepping up into the van, thud! Wilson greeted her with two paws in the middle of her chest, it hurt a bit but she was used to it luckily, so she managed to keep her balance, but his manners still needed some work.

"Hi, it's nice to see you too," she said grinning widely but with a stern voice, "Stay down!" His tail automatically wagging he bounded off to find a toy to share while Jonah set out drinks.

"Well, this is our last night in New Plymouth, we'll head off home in the morning," she sighed into her glass of wine as she sat resting on the small but comfy sofa.

"I was wondering if you're still up to travelling inland, we could go off to look at Cambridge as our last stop on our way home. We thought about maybe doing that or have you had enough?" he inquired.

"That would be splendid, if you're not sick of driving."

"It's not far out of our way, we could detour off to view Cambridge it has a scenic reserve and beautiful lakes. I was thinking that you would enjoy the natural beauty of the countryside."

"Yes, let's do that and look at the scenic reserve on the map."

Nodding his head, if we find a nice bakery on the way you can choose something nice for lunch and we'll take the insulated backpack with us to lunch in the park, what do you think?" and he gave her hand a gentle little squeeze.

"Yes lets," smiling back at him, "That sounds like a lovely idea."

"Okay than." Secretly he was trying to extend the trip, not wanting to let go of Gemma.

"After we've had a sit, why don't we leave the park and head off to the shops, get whatever supplies we need and pop into a supermarket for some salad and roast chicken, to have over at the beach tonight?" he hinted.

“Okay.” She agreed, wondering what he had up his sleeve, it sounded like a romantic gesture.

Being a small community it was easy to park the campervan in the supermarket carpark with plenty of empty spaces, while they stocked up on fresh milk, biscuits, fruit and dog food for the trip home tomorrow.

Gemma was enjoying spending time wondering around together in an everyday place with shoppers, meandering around the isles as he pushed the shopping trolley with an air of confidence, appearing like an old married couple, it was so natural and she sensed how compatible they were together. They both agreed that neither of them really wanted to wonder around to look at any other shops, and she just wanted to return to the van she suspected he felt the same, his twinkly eyes watching every time she bend to put something into the trolley, she was wearing tight fitting jeans and a lose flowing tee shirt.

Returning to the van he drove the short distance to the West Coast were they spent time searching for a nice spot with a patch of grass beside the sea. Coming across an area where it looked safe enough to stay for the entire night, they had all the facilities needed in the van so decided to park up. The roast chicken was okay left in its foil packaging for a wee while, as they wanted to let her much loved Wilson run along the beach, he had been perfectly well behaved throughout the entire trip and she was so proud of him.

Wilson had grown up knowing the beach the whole of his short life, and he absolutely enjoyed beaches. He even braved the cold to go in for a paddle and then ran madly around the sand afterward to dry off, there were no people around for him to bother at dusk, so they let him have an off lead run.

Walking quietly along the white sand, hand in hand, to the gentle sound of water ripples rushing in and out on the sand with the familiar smell of salt water. Life was good, Jonah held her hand and there hadn’t been an ill word spoken the whole trip, it was such a new experience for her, she would remember this time with him forever. There was no need to speak, both contented she let her thoughts wander, she couldn't pinpoint when it happened but along the way during the years at her beach cottage her past was slowly disintegrating into bits of distant memory.

There was nothing stopping her from falling in love and feeling comfortable with this man that made no demands, he gave of himself to make her happy and walked beside her. Gemma was free to live, love and share her life. Having faith that just as the worn indent on her wedding ring finger had faded and was no longer apparent, so were the many bad memories of her past almost gone. It was only the fear of losing her freedom that still haunted her. Gemma had needed time, and God had been kind leading her to meet someone completely different, a man who loves, understands, was persevering and respected her idiosyncrasies.

They strolled happily back to the van for a nice chicken and coleslaw dinner and settle Wilson into his corner, they ate eagerly and chatted about Jonah's farm, he explained how he didn't want to work forever and talked about his hopes of finding the perfect place on the sea boundary, he wanted a jetty to moor his boat and go fishing whenever he felt like it. After eating they got up to move away from the table and sit on the sofa, it was easy to dispose of the paper plates and made very little work for themselves. Gemma reassured him that he only needed to trust that when the time was right, he would find the right place.

On the sofa with his arm around her the desire was building, she ran her fingers through his hair feeling breathless under his kisses and once again reminded him that they couldn't!

"I know, we won't." He squeezed her shoulder in reassurance as he kissed her unadorned lips, a growing moan of pleasure escaped her.

"We have too many clothes on," she whispered, feeling uncomfortable.

"Come to bed," he said, as he gentle moved her aside so he could stand to remove his outer clothes.

"Don't wear much please," he pleaded quietly.

She acknowledged his request starting to remove the layers, he would abide by her rules, she was sure of that and it was wonderfully natural to slip into the warm bed snuggling up to him for emotional comfort. The night disappeared too fast and when sunlight eased its way through the windows it changed dark to light. Gemma couldn't wait to push aside the thin curtain on the small window, looking out onto the cool blue sea they parked beside last evening. Just a sprinkling of sun was glistening on top of the waves, but it looked cold and angry, pushing its way ashore. The waves much fiercer than they were before and the sky held angry dark grey clouds overhead.

Suddenly aware that they have been lucky to have had such good weather so far, now it was time to move back up the North Island to greet warmer weather.

Jonah's out of bed and standing behind her. "What's the weather like sweetheart?"

"It looks terrible, we better get moving soon I think, before the rain starts." She turned to face him and he put his arms around her waist. Looking into her eyes.

"Did you sleep okay?" he asked, pulling her in for a hug.

"Yes, sound asleep, I only woke up because it was getting light through the curtains. I'm dying for a cup of tea, it seems like ages since I've had a nice cuppa, because we had wine last night."

"You jump in the shower first and I'll put the jug on, do you want some toast too," he asks.

"Yes please, I'll be quick." When she came out she decided to pull on a long sleeve merino top and a warm pink jumper. She could always take it off later after warming up on their travels, which was one of the benefits of having the camper van, she had been able to bring a varied choice of clothes to cater for all temperatures during the trip from north to south.

"Come on Wilson, go for a run and have your breakfast outside on the grass." Opening the door, she sat at the fold down table to enjoy her breakfast while Jonah quickly got showered and dressed.

He came out looking sexy with his tight butt jeans on and a warm check shirt, smelling divine. Packing away the breakfast dishes and settling Wilson, they then headed on their way, a quick kiss and a big smile on both faces. The drive back up the North Island and heading inland to Cambridge was very straight forward, and fortunately the weather kept improving the further up the island they travelled, leaving the forecast of horrendous rain behind them and traveling away from the coastal winds. After about three hours driving they were due for a stretch and welcomed a rest stop at Maungakawa scenic reserve, arriving to the glorious sight of thousands of daffodils nestled in the reserve grasslands, many of which were still flowering.

Brewing up hot coffee and opening a packet of biscuits in the cosy van, they stretched and relaxed before changing into cooler clothes and venturing out, Gemma took full advantage of having her camera handy to take some lovely photos.

"Let's go and get some lunch at the river café before heading off towards home," Jonah suggested, Gemma picked up on a hesitant sound in his voice.

She knew what he was feeling, as she was also a bit hesitant about the conclusion of their trip, separate homes will be a sad contrast after having such a lovely time together.

"I'm glad we took the time to see the reserve, and we were especially lucky to see the drifts of sweeping, golden flowers," she said quietly to him.

"Everything we do together is lovely," he murmured, a little reservedly.

The remaining trip was sombre as they both had private thoughts running around in their heads, and it was difficult for Gemma to speak, afraid of the lump in her throat turning into tears, so she didn't say anything as they drove along all the familiar roads leading to

Jonah's farm. They were both tired, and Gemma planned to spend the night there before going home tomorrow morning.

Jonah called from the bedroom, "Come and watch the sun going down over the orchard with me!"

"Okay, I'll grab a rug out of the cupboard to sit on," she called back down the hallway, in her attempt to sound chirpy.

Wilson was already in bed.

"I'll just get us a couple of glasses of fruit juice." Smiling and sounding a little bit more cheerful he headed for the kitchen.

Jonah and Gemma were trying to cope with the inevitable separation.

"It's always good to be home eh." Staring up at him in smiley trepidation.

"Yes and no," came the reply, looking a bit preoccupied as he spread the rug out on a nice soft tufted grassed area, he dumped a spare blanket to one side, placing the tray with two glasses of juice within easy reach.

Standing in front of Gemma, the last of the evening sunshine felt warm on her skin, she watched as his body cast a tall shadow across the ground, he walked forward stretching his strong arms around her waist, gently pulling Gemma into him, his kisses were long and inviting as his tongue encircled hers and they were both desperately lost to rising passion.

A confused mixture of thanks for the trip, close companionship and expressing her feelings for him, they had confided their innermost feelings to each other and each one knew the other a little better now as she tugged at his shirt. Gemma longed to brush her face against his bare chest and it was all happening very quickly, the desperation of knowing that tomorrow she would go home. He helped to undo the button she was fumbling with and dropped his shirt to the ground while she stood searching for another hot wet kiss, she was now aware that his hand was under her tee-shirt. Gemma lifted the cotton tee-shirt over her head and it fell to the ground. Jonah stood in the dusk with just his briefs on. Modesty took over as she became self-conscience, taking hold of the blanket she pulled it up around herself.

"You're beautiful," he said, adding, "That won't work." Jonah laughed kindly as he gave the corner of the blanket a gentle tug.

Laughing, she tried to hold onto the crisp cotton fabric of his discarded shirt on the ground and pulled it over her.

Giggling she nuzzled into his neck and when he rolled on top of her, all her nervous play ceased as it became full on sensual and sincere.

The sound of loud breathing filled the silence of dusk around them, while her senses picked up the scent of this morning's aftershave pervading the now darkening evening, running her fingers down his hairless chest, touching his smooth tanned skin his body heat warming the tips of her fingers. This was no easy dance, both of them aware of forbidden limits, but touching and loving whispers, happy lying outside under the stars, like they were the only two people in the world, and content to go to bed knowing that tomorrow was another day. Believing that everything happened for a reason and they would find their way.

Chapter 26

Gemma lay still as morning arrived and neither of them really wanted to move, but she had to get up to see to Wilson. Duty called, she quickly pulled on some clean clothes to go and let him outside before making the breakfast, they sat smiling at each other as Jonah stayed in bed and she sat on the top of the luxurious silver coloured duvet.

"Well, back to normal today, holiday over! Thanks for a lovely time away," she said cheerfully.

"My pleasure, it looked like you were having a nice time," came the sombre reply.

"After I finish this toast, I'll head off and leave you to your shower, we'll talk later tonight okay darling. I think I've collected all of my belonging from the van, ready to go." She was feeling anxious saying goodbye.

"Okey, see you later then," Jonah said as he reached over to kiss her goodbye.

"Come on Wilson, jump in the car." The little car burst into life straight away, like it had been waiting to go home. Wilson was happy and Gemma although euphoric, the 15 minutes it took from Jonah's house to hers also held a sadness about it.

Pressing the automatic garage door opener and waiting, the car slowly inched into the garage and the door closed behind them, she had mixed feelings, but it was nice to be home. Wilson jumped down from the car seat all excited the instant she opened his door, heading for his back yard full speed ahead. She smiled, following on behind, they had only been gone a week but considerable had happened between her and Jonah.

Gemma's much loved garden was bursting with spring flowers and the glossy white picket fence she had put up on moving there still cried out vintage cottage, she might go over it again during the summer with another coat of white just to keep it looking fresh. Tall spires of white, pastel pink and dark pink flowers that she planted from seeds given to her (unfortunately she can't remember the name of them) competed for every space, complimenting bushes of yellow daisies and three shrubby white flowering daisy bushes now two foot high. Beneath the bushes the ground was filled with blue lobelia, and brightly coloured freesias with their delightful flowery scent to enjoy as you walk along the cobblestone path. Gladioli had all burst through the ground with tall spikes of leaves ready to send up spires of orange over the summer months. Nowhere compared to this, her sanctuary.

The following morning now that she was back home, meant giving herself the goal of planting the tomato and lettuce seeds into tubs and covering them with chicken mesh, she had everything waiting since before going on holiday. Walking along the cobblestone path to sit on the comfortable old park bench brought back memories, (one of the few possessions that she had brought to her new home). She was relaxed, thoughtfully surveying the scene, noting how the purple lavender bush that was trimmed just over two weeks ago was already bursting into upright stems of lavender and attracting many bees, beside it was a small Michaela tree newly planted a year ago, it stood proudly holding onto its first cream coloured flowers, her heart and soul derived so much pleasure to see it thriving and promising to be a beautiful tree in years to come, she loves her garden with its aura of serenity and beauty.

Accepting that she had something else in her everyday now that she did not want to do without, his phone call! Longing to hear his voice every evening, understanding the fact that she enjoyed their conversations, showed how important Jonah had become to her. Gemma ensured the kitchen was tidied and everything done, as she watched the clock for his call every evening, then they caught up on the day's events; like teenagers infatuated and interested in each other's day, neither of them wanting to end the call.

Jonah always respected her right to privacy at home and to have independence and freedom to come and go, to do what she wanted, if it be placing furniture wherever she wanted or planting the fruit trees she liked best, it sounded trivial and selfish, but it was difficult to consider another person in her life now after regaining her freedom and he understood that.

Not today, but first thing tomorrow morning she was venturing down to watch the sunrise over the sea, she found it so inspirational to start the day watching the buttery ray of light push through the nighttime clouds, insistent on the day beginning. The short walk down the footpath and around the corner, the expansive sea view opened up before reaching the beach, and that was always inspirational and stunning. Today she was treated with a high tide gently lapping the sea wall, and further along the footpath she found the blue water was calm with no wind to ruffle it, as though everything was still asleep! With the rays of light brightly pushing their yellow between the clouds, insistent on shining and bouncing into a million sparkling diamonds. The sight enlivened her whole being and inspired her to also start the day, looking into the distance she knew that she wanted to make her time here count, she didn't want to waste another minute of it.

Deciding that she wanted to leave an imprint behind, just like the sea on the sand, it was time.

Wilson continued to pull on his lead oblivious of anything amazing he just wanted to get to the park, so to stop the pulling she sat at the aptly placed park bench. Snatching some time for herself to reflect, speak to the Lord and soak in this wondrous sight, while in the background still listening to the sound of sea gulls happily crying out their morning songs to each other. The colour of the sea turned from deep blue to a turquoise green as she looked out across to the far shore and saw the long strip of gleaming white sand just down from the grasslands, she could catch a glimpse of the winding road that she used to travel north. She sat and patted Wilson's smooth head deep in contemplation over the trip and time spent with Jonah.

His concerns and their friendship, she had become torn between her comfortable existing life and a promising new one. Gemma praised the Lord for giving her this quiet place and time to contemplate, to clarify her thoughts, speak out loud with no one around except her furry friend, as she began to walk toward the park, so grateful to have her lovely little Wilson, thankful for having Jonah in her life and soul searching for help to know what to do with their relationship.

Letting out more of his lead they continued to walk towards Wilson's favourite place, knocking all thoughts of Jonah out of her mind she wanted to fully enjoy her dog, as they walk along the overgrown gravel path up from the beach. The ground was already dry and cracked before the summer had even arrived. This was nature at its best; the universe opening up every morning, waking the birds in the trees and the people in their homes, life began with a fresh new day that everyone ought to be mindful and appreciative of.

A smile spread into a full on belly-shaking laugh out loud, while playing chase with Wilson off his lead, free in the park. Life was slowly becoming routine again, plus Gemma was pleased at her progress with painting the inside of her house, a very pale grey on the walls and a darker grey on the doors, slowly room by room she had plenty to keep her body and mind occupied.

Since buying her home, her bedroom had remained the pastel colour it was when she moved in. It seemed too daunting and strenuous, strength she didn't have then and now everything has changed. She was driven as she pulled the king sized bed into the centre of the room; it was challenging but she let out a sigh of satisfaction when persistence paid off. No longer afraid, the task of painting the inside of her home by herself was rewarding. She bought a ladder with a holding bar at the top for her to feel safe when descending down the steps. Every time she dragged out the paint Wilson had to play in the backyard alone and sometimes he got restless about that, so she painted in short bursts and when he went of for a sleep.

Gradually over a fine weekend her bedroom received a second coat and after sleeping with the bed in the middle of the room, she finally pushed and puffed until the bed was back in place, throwing the sheets and duvet on she stood exhausted to admire how fresh, clean and nice it all looked. Relief flowed through every vein as her choice of colour proved successful, a suitable colour was always ambiguous until finished and after all that work she was ecstatic she didn't have to change it.

The phone sounded, a bit earlier than usual tonight, Jonah sounded anxious, he wanted to invite her to go dancing on Saturday night, informing her there was a good band playing at the East Coast RSA. Maybe he was a little worried about her inclination to avoid socializing now she had returned home.

"Oh yes, I'd love to go," she shrieked, excited to be putting her paint brushes away for awhile.

She agreed to arrive at his house dressed ready, and with dog in tow, she would leave Wilson at his house all night, he didn't want her to drive home in the dark when tired after the dance, which she admitted seemed sensible.

"We can only have a short chat tonight because I've been in the garden, in between painting my bedroom. Now with day light saving and the evenings not getting dark until later, I haven't eaten yet and I'm starving," she rattled off quickly.

"Okay that's fine, you get something to eat. If you want a new dress sweetheart I'd like to buy that for you, is that okay?" he carefully offered, and his voice sent pleasant shivers through Gemma.

"Oh that's nice, I'd love to go looking and if I find something special I'll save the receipt for you," she giggled.

"That's my pleasure love, now go and eat and have a good sleep."

"Night, see you on Saturday," replying cheerfully before hanging up and proceeding to pull the fry pan out of the cupboard, she never bothered too much about recipes anymore, and just cooked basic food for one. Which usually meant having meat and three vegetables or tonight it would be a quick stir fry.

A cool crisp feeling of waking to a spring day, it was Friday and everything was right with the world, as Wilson and Gemma set off for a casual walk past the half dozen old houses on the left, and on her right a high cliff bank of solid clay, with just a few shrubs managing to cling to the rock beneath. She never really looked at that before, but today she stopped as activity captured her attention; a dozen or so round entrances had appeared in the bank. Ingenious birds were very busy coming and going making cooing sounds, as they started nesting safely on the side of a sheer drop cliff, no predator could access their entrance ways. How lovely, they had a home at the beach as well! It was a great place for their food supply, happy and safe they wake each day to this wondrous sight and their homes overlook both road and sea. When the road was constructed someone had the insight to plough through the middle of clay and rock, creating this breath-taking sight of the beach access, a striking view as soon as you turned the corner.

Wilson and Gemma continued on, arriving at the strategically placed park bench to sit and ponder, taking in the bird life and breathing in the crisp morning sea air, early feeble sunshine warmed her back and saturated her tired joints as she sat side on to the sea and marvelled at the turquoise blue. It was too early for cars, boats and trailers to arrive as the tide was still a long way out, she sat quietly with Wilson and watched as it gradually made its way ashore, when at high tide the local community would amass in the hope of a good catch for the day under a cloudless soft-blue sky.

Ready to receive more arm wrenching on the lead, they head off again, continuing on past the Pohutakawa trees which were sparsely scattered along the shoreline grassed area to provide shade for swimmers in the summer. Pausing for a quick look at them, they now had a sprinkling of early deep red flowers. She was suddenly forced to continue on to the park. Gemma often met the local people going for a brisk stroll along the newly laid path in the mornings, as she meandered around the water's edge, stopping to chat about the weather or what was happening in their garden at the moment. What a joyous location, greeting locals with smiles while walking along with the revitalising sea breeze gently wafting her face.

The incredible sea environment was forever changing, refreshing and consistently interesting, it allowed her peaceful moments. Gemma found the beach was mentally relaxing, and a release from many of life's stresses of things needing to be done. As she attentively observed what was happening around her, thoughts of bills to pay and household chores that need doing were prohibited, she allowed herself total immersion of peace and tranquillity, exploring all of her senses. Gemma has found the time and place to acknowledge living, and to be mindful and appreciative as she moved forward on her journey.

Wilson and she walked up a short rise to reach the park, passing an area of rampant honeysuckle, the sweet perfume was a welcome contrast as were the lemon and cream flowers which the bees noisily buzzed around, the honeysuckle plant enjoying its freedom to meander unattended. Upon reaching the top of the hill, and looking down towards the beach, the sea view spread far and wide with just the sound of gentle fuzzy white ripples rushing ashore, breathing in the unlimited fresh air was sublime.

In the distance a group of people had arrived and were setting out their rugs waiting for high tide. Colourful buckets and spades were strewn around for the children to play in the sand. With the expectation of warmer days to come, more people were impatient to walk on the beach, strangers drift in on the weekends, and the locals are out with their dogs all going for a run in the park. It was glorious to see the contrast of seasons as people swap their dull jackets and winter jumpers, to brighter colours and more cheerful styles.

Walks to the beach and park are just one of the many things that Gemma enjoyed about her home, and although Wilson was still a puppy and demanded a lot of her time, the fact that he loves going to the kennels to have a play with other dogs provided the chance to follow her interest in gardening and travel. Gemma had the reassurance that although Wilson completely relied on her, the kennels were a great backup plan, a familiar place to go. Wilson being a fantastic watch dog looked out for her, and she did the same for him, in the 10 months that they have been together he had become a caring companion and an important part of Gemma's existence.

Wilson came bounding over and she bent down to cuddle and whisper that she loved him, receiving a big slurp in return before he ran off around the stately old Pohutukawa trees.

"Come Wilson, time to go home," she called out loudly, he looked up and responded, rapidly running back across the lush green grass of the park to be with her.

Wilson was terrific at returning when called and a great dog in many ways, although the occasional time when he dug holes in the lawn did not impress Gemma. Rides to the shop were always a favourite treat with him, he didn't like to be left behind, and because the weather forecast was for drizzle on Wednesday it was the perfect time to take him to the shops, letting him sleep in the car without the worry of overheating. He can go when she has a look for something beautiful to wear for Jonah on their Saturday night out.

The shopping day arrived and the whole shopping spree turned out to be such fun, because she was not paying. Gemma enjoyed looking for that special something without looking at the price tag, usually the first thing she looked at. Unfortunately, the dresses were a disappointment, then a silver crinkly top with a shimmer to it caught her eye, and she purchased it. It was unique and special, so even though she will need to wear black trousers again, the top was elegant and exceptional so she thought Jonah would like it.

Gemma drove around the carpark to the drive-through at Burger Bar, Wilson sat up watching! he loved the drive-through because they pass food through the car window, the smells drift into his nostrils and his mouth waters. She ordered a small cheeseburger, and a yummy ice-cream sundae without any topping for Wilson, a large burger and delicious strawberry sundae for herself. Thanking the girl Gemma began to drive out to find a quiet place to park, it was an overcast day with only a few people around while they sat eating burgers in the car. Wilson was familiar with drive-through takeaways and displayed good table manners, he had a doggie dish on the back seat and never made any mess.

After a week of reflective pondering over everything, Saturday arrived and she looked forward to seeing Jonah again. Wilson and Gemma enjoyed a laid back Saturday while she worked in her garden and he watched with intent, various bits of weeds ended up in his mouth as she threw them into a pile on the lawn. She didn't mind if he wanted to play with them, creating a bit more work before it went into the compost. The lawn ended up resembling a war zone but Gemma laughed and took him inside the house as she prepared tea, going back out later to pick up. Early evening also gave her time to get the ride-on lawn mower out and quickly cut the lawn shorter, now that new spring growth was making it grow faster. Returning back inside she jumped into the shower while Wilson enjoyed a run around the tidy freshly mown lawn.

Full of excitement Gemma decided to just pop some toast into the toaster to quickly have with a tin of baked beans, she was impatient to see Jonah. Wilson sat on the mat outside watching through the glass door and inhaling the wonderful aroma coming from the toaster, her heart melted and she spread a slice of toast for him, he loved it really crunchy and then she poured a tin of puppy food into his dish outside, while she ate her dinner. Her heart was all a flutter to see Jonah and she was excited to get dressed in her best pair of black trousers, pulling on her new silver top, she hoped he would like it. Being very feminine and a bit transparent she had first slipped on a silver chemise underneath making it look even more pretty.

Gemma was thrilled and looking forward to going dancing again, although in the back of her mind she was a bit concerned that they were spending a lot of time together, she didn't want to lead him on, still unsure of how far she wanted to commit.

After eating, dressing, and a quick glance into the mirror, she was confident that her makeup looked good and her hair was smoothed down with styling spray. There were no sticky up bits, a mist of the lovely perfume Jonah had purchased for her and she was ready.

Opening the car door Wilson was used to jumping into the back of the car without any help, he could smell the perfume and knew that she was going out. Gemma was pleased as she didn't get covered in dog hair. Staying focused on driving down the deserted road to Jonah's house, Gemma was conscious of how excited her insides felt, all in a flutter to be seeing him again. It was also a stark contrast between her old restrictive life and the fun dancing times she now had, how wonderful and so exciting to be going out with new clothes and makeup after years of going without.

Arriving at Jonah's home, the lawns had been mown and the grounds were perfectly manicured. The drivers side, car window was down a little as she drove up to the house and the sweet smell of citrus flowers permeated the air. Jonah looked after the place well and the only thing she did not approve of was his streaky glass shower. She used the guest room bathroom anyway so said nothing as she cleaned it herself, he did well for a bachelor.

It was no coincidence that the front door swung open immediately her Fiat pulled up to park, he had been watching and waiting, anxious to see her as well. No sooner had she parked and turned the key off, he was instantly there to open the car door for her, gently pulling her into his arms with a sexy smile on his face, he was happy. Holding Gemma close to his body, she willingly absorbed the emotional comfort and sense of security having someone that cared and valued her.

"Umm," she giggled as their lips touched, it took her by surprise.

"Do you need a hand with anything?" he asked.

"No thanks, I only brought one change of clothes with me."

Chapter 27

Jonah opened the car door and received a big slurp from Wilson before he zoomed off, running through the house and out the ranch slider, he was headed for the orchard because he loved running in the wide open spaces and around all the fruit trees.

"Leave him to have a run before he goes to bed. I brought some supper for him to have. We can head off whenever you're ready." Gemma explained and he nodded in agreement.

Setting her overnight bag on the tall boy in his bedroom she noticed a nicely wrapped present on the bed.

"What's that?" Gemma queried.

"It's for you, I hope you like it. You look lovely tonight," he said very quietly.

"Oh thanks, I bought the new top because I couldn't find a dress that was anything special, so I hope it's okay." She sat down on the side of the bed and looked at the present.

"Don't forget to get the money off me before you go home, I probably have enough in the house for that." He nodded.

"Okay thanks, we'll sort it on Sunday," she said with a grateful heart, he's so kind.

Slumped on the bed, she started to unwrap the soft pink tissue paper to reveal a pretty silver photo frame and a photo of the two of them taken on board the cruise ship.

"Oh it's lovely!" she exclaimed loudly. "I haven't seen that photo, but I remember us standing on the spiral staircase while the photographer took it. What a nice photo of us, thank you so much."

Her face was beaming with delight while her insides burned hot with pleasure that he had gone to the trouble of getting this lovely gift made up. Also showing that he was proud that there was a photo of *the two of them* together. He was such a romantic and was fast melting her resolve to never risk a broken heart again.

"Well, I love you." He says unreservedly.

"I love you too Jonah." Smiling back at him, Jonah reached out to cup her soft face between his hands, he planted a kiss on her reddish lips.

He sat on the bed beside her and she felt compelled to explain, completely unprepared for the intensity of emotions surging through her, it was difficult as her eyes threatened to well up, she blinked and found her voice was shaky.

"We need to talk about where this is heading as I'm afraid, I don't want to be vulnerable, and I don't want to hurt you."

"Yes, I know you've been through some tough times, we'll work it out," he picked up one of her hands, stroking it as he spoke in a serious tone.

Gemma must make him understand, "I feel like I'm on the edge of a cliff and I don't know if I would survive another fall." She struggled to make him see it wasn't his fault.

"You're not on the edge of a cliff with me sweetheart, you're on a footpath and you just need to decide which road to take. You're a strong lady, you survived losing your husband, home, friends and almost your life. You will always survive and this time I will be walking beside you," he paused as his voice crackled and he wore his heart on his sleeve. Jonah continued holding tightly to her hand.

"You know that heartbreak shows you are alive, and the ache in your chest shows the depth that you enjoyed life with that person, no matter what happens to one of us, we will have made good memories."

"What if they're not good," she reflected on her bad times.

Jonah turned to face her, "Your husband was sick, I'm not. When we use all of our senses, during our times together they become lasting memories, that's what I want in my life with you, to make you so happy, you will remember the love in the air. Do you want to miss out on that?" Jonah looked sincerely at Gemma.

She listened closely to his seriously sad voice.

"I'm reluctant to give up my home, even though yours is much bigger and better, it's not the value of the house, it's the fact that it's my security and no matter what happens to you, my life won't be turned upside down again, leaving me to start over." She struggled to express the extent of seriousness, her love, compassion and caring for this man, it caused her to choke up with tears and she couldn't put words to it.

"I won't let that happen, we can see a lawyer and I'll get everything signed that we don't sell your home, it will always be there for you." He fought to explain but Gemma's fear was so ingrained that she couldn't think clearly enough to talk about it.

"I'm scared of you getting sick," she blurted out, "My heart would break all over again." He reached for her other hand while still sitting closely on the bed together. Grasping her hands firmly, she found his very protective nature.

"Think about letting go of your fear, remember the bible tells us, *'Fear not, I am with you.' Isaiah 41:10*

The ice has broken and she started to laugh, "You're quoting the bible at me now eh!" says Gemma looking up from the bed quilt.

"Thanks for the beautiful photo of us, let's go out and have a nice night, I do love you and there must be a way. I don't want to lose you, can we talk about it tomorrow?" speaking quietly to him while she returned the squeeze to both of his hands in her lap.

Wilson came running in with a stick in his mouth, they both decided it was time for him to go to bed. He had lightened the serious nature of the situation and now it was important for them to be alone together.

"I had tea before leaving home, do you want anything before we go?" Gemma asked.

"No, I'm good, I just have to shave and put on a good shirt as I didn't want Wilson jumping on it," Jonah stood up to go and finish getting ready, while Gemma showed Wilson to bed with supper.

She walked on the plush beige carpet through to the lounge and sat in the lazy boy chair with her feet up, deep in thought.

Jonah's musky aroma reached the room ahead of him, as he appeared in the lounge, he had so much charisma and looked gorgeous. Settling into the car and heading off, they have put further discussion on hold and everything was good.

On the way to the dance they chatted light heartedly about how they had spent Saturday and on arriving at the venue they found easy parking available, and a lot of empty tables, maybe because they have arrived quite early. They wandered around the edge of the dance floor, holding hands and headed towards the bar to get drinks before settling on one table, not too close to the loudspeakers, although with easy access to the dance floor.

Jonah sat beside her as they sipped on their ice cold drinks, a beer and a white wine. The lounge was pleasantly warm as they watched the band start up, the lighting was dimmed and the atmosphere relaxing as he leaned in closely to her at the table, they smiled adoringly into each other's eyes and anyone watching would know.

Gradually the room filled with people, and before you knew it, all of the tables had someone at them with no spare chairs available, they were glad they arrived early or they may have missed out on getting a seat. Jonah was right, it was an amazing band! And that's why so many people had turned up, she was pleased that he had suggested the dance. As she twirled round and round it was such a lot of fun, and so much high energy that it was a relief when the band took a break, forcing them to.

After 30 minutes of sitting, it started up again playing a slow waltz, and Jonah stood with a slightly bent waist he offered his hand out to Gemma with old fashioned courtesy.

"Would you like to dance?" he asked.

She didn't reply, leapt up to take his hand with a slightly demure smile, they walked onto the dance floor joining many other happy couples. Dancing around oblivious of what her feet were doing, he swept her around the floor. Jonah was just the right height to be able to look deeply into her eyes as she was being held intimately in his arms. A small gasp for air escaped from her lips, being so close made her pulse rapid and as his beautiful azure eyes seduced her, they were guaranteed to make any woman blush. He was really pulling out all the stops tonight, with the photo gift, erotic scent, fantastic music and dancing to all their favourite tunes, plus he looked hot, add in a bit of alcohol and her pulsating heart was being overcome with passion.

As the night continued, the music changed to more romantic favourites for the remaining couples on the floor, with their arms firmly entwined, some woman seen to be dancing with their eyes closed, moving as if drifting on air. What a magical night this was, and it was not finished yet, just because the music had. As they made their way out to the car she was mindful of being cuddled up to him tonight, they travelled home in surprising quietness, maybe he was thinking the same thing.

It transpired to be an expressive time of self-awareness and surprise for Gemma, to be aware that she wanted his arms around her and his lips on hers, she looked forward to his phone calls and time spent together. She was suddenly discovering that it was nice to have that special someone, that he made her life more complete. She couldn't deny that they got on well, and it seemed like they had known each other for many years, not just the four. The more time she spent with him the more focused she became, wanting to find out more about him. Although she was never tempted to let caution fly to the wind, there may come a time in the future when she has to listen to her heart, have faith and follow the light in front of her.

Once home, safely tucked up in bed they were both tired but joyous, the heat of excitement still fuelling their bodies from the romantic evening in each others' arms. Lying on her side, he turned towards her and his lips planted little kisses moving down her neck, just very gently, and she craved his pyjama shirt off. Longing to get as close as possible with skin to skin contact, enjoying each other's warmth and companionship. When the morning offered up a new day she embarked on a whole new perspective on life. Granted they could not spend the day together as he had farm work to do, and she again felt the draw of her home to consider where she was at, she knew what she wanted. Saying their goodbyes with tender kisses, she drove home in cloudy weather which didn't help her vague psyche.

Once home, she deciding to leave Wilson warm in the house while she rugged up and braved a walk down to the beach. The weather was even more cold and windy at the seaside but she needed to blow away the cobwebs of her past. With her warm knitted grey hat, matching gloves and a windbreaking jacket she walked on. There were no other people around as the sea was too rough for any boats to go out, and it was impossible to sit and ponder anything with the wind so bitterly strong. She just kept walking up the hill, on the damp cold lose metal path, the sound of scrunching heard under her feet and everything was wet and miserable. Her relationship with Jonah weighed heavily on her heart and she prayed for guidance as she walked alone in this beautiful world, through the park trying to understand where to go with her life and what path to take.

An epiphany, the realization that 'Storms in life will come, but she can be sure that they will also go, she must understand that they will pass, and the sun will shine again on her path.'

Gemma's eighteen year marriage with her husband was controlling and abusive, he took advantage of a kind soul and the belief that she would stand by him no matter what. Her constant wishing that he would one day be normal again, like the one year she spent with him before the accident, before he was changed forever. Now that he was gone, she no longer lived in darkness and fear.

Gemma's walk has never been alone, she walked home with clarity, an open mind, heart and soul and an understanding of what she needed to do. She will return to the beach again tomorrow for inspiration, and the unyielding strength of mind to discuss everything with Jonah.

Yesterday, walking along the seawall, huge waves crashed ashore, claiming the sandy beach and sounding loud and wild, each wave blackened and appearing with such force that it lead her to believe there was a deep hole behind each foaming white top. The sea was angry, unable to be tamed and warning all not to enter. That being the force of nature which was just a part of the bigger picture.

For today in stark reality, as she sat on the sculptured surface of the seawall with her feet dangling over the edge, the sea was beautifully calm, and in complete contrast tempting her down to the water's edge, how she longed to enter the cool transparent sea. Sea birds were happily bopping up and down searching for food and the tranquillity of the scene was so breath-taking, Gemma was drawn to bend and touch the crystal clear water longing to connect with this unique picture. Her jeans and sneakers prevented her from entering for a paddle, but the desire to go for a swim was strong and the temptation to unite with the sea was there, although it was not practical today.

Gemma returned home to have lunch with Wilson and have a play with the ball, later in the day she decided to make a second trip back to the water's edge *'the call of the sea'* was strong with its changing mood, she had witnessed its angry waves and forbidding to something quite stunning today. Just as yesterday's stormy sea was a distant memory so was the trauma of Gemma's life, she sat and reflected on the similarity of that untamed storm claiming everything in its path, and realized in comparison she was stronger, the storm had passed in her life.

Watching as a fishing boat finished for the day, arriving back to the jetty, it berthed a little out in the sea and they started to gut fish and throw innards into the water, there was a noisy commotion from the sea gulls who circled for the scraps, and the sound awoke distant memories of Gemma's childhood. A Christchurch beach with her mum and the same cry could be heard from the sea gulls as she threw left over sandwiches to them. It was strange how something like sound brought back memories of by-gone years, a pleasant sound for her reminiscent of happy times. However, it was the fisherman's folly as he should have cleaned the fish further out to sea before heading back, because now he battled to come ashore with gulls souring around his head wanting more food and harassing him, he waved with his hat to shoo them away. She smiled at that memory he will hold in the future.

Looking out over the sea the expansive arch of a beautiful rainbow had now spread across the clear blue sky in the distance, it was a delight to behold and created an assurance, like a promise that she was going forward into a new calm world full of love and happiness, not only does the world constantly change but so do our lives. She must trust, have faith and welcome it, she had found that ray of sunshine in herself, feeling rejuvenated and unified with something beautiful, bringing peace and tranquillity into her very existence.

In this world and in our lives, light symbolizes goodness, knowledge and wisdom, grace and hope, whereas we address darkness as symbolising evil, sin and despair. Light being a fundamental symbol and being a vital part of our daily lives for health and wellbeing it was an essential element. Gemma decided that happiness lay silently within the human mind and heart awaiting the chance of solitude for us to rouse, we should be alert enough to connect and recognise it independently without interference.

Strolling back to the house Gemma decided to bake some biscuits ready for the next time she sees that man who has won her heart, instead of feeling reluctant to risk heart break she now misses him and will move forward. There was no pressure to move things on to further their relationship, but with love there was always the expectation of continuing to the next step whatever that maybe.

Relaxing outside her home, she was lounging under the clear roofing when a little warming sunshine filtered into her heart, Wilson had woken up and sat at her feet, she patted his smooth little head and his big brown eyes looked up at her with adoration, he pushed his velvety nose into her leg. It was more difficult being human, it's easy to be afraid of heart break and that painful hunger, aching inside especially after experiencing the loss of someone you love through unexpected causes. The lost years were valuable experiences that taught her the need to be strong for her husband, courageous in the fight to protect him and endurance to maintain mental wellness during her struggle to do the right thing, now there was the reality of no longer dwelling in dark memories while she had a ray of light guiding her.

When Jonah phoned at 7.30pm Gemma tried to remain composed, restraining her excitement welling up inside as she explained to him that things have changed, she was anxious to live a full life, explaining that she had rested and healed. Gemma believes that everything happens for a reason, and she was meant to meet and fall in love with Jonah.

"I can't wait to take you in my arms," he manages to get out amidst the crackle Gemma could hear in his voice, as though he were choking up. "Can you come around so we can sort out where to go from here?" It was the news he had longed for.

"Yes," she managed to affirm breathlessly. "I'll be there in half an hour."

"Come on Wilson, lets go and see Jonah," calling out to him as she opened the car door and he jumped in.

A massive smile covered her face, as she drove frantically towards the man she longed to be with, remembering the times she watched others, and wondered what it would feel like to be as happy as them, now she knew!

Pulling up in his driveway alongside his house, the front door was flung open and he sprinted over to the car in bare feet, opening the driver's door he scooped Gemma into his arms. The joy was too much as they kissed, and like a balloon full of energy about to burst, she was so grateful for everything that had happened to bring her to this place in her life.

"Put the jug on, and I'll let Wilson out into the orchard for a run," she managed to utter in between kissing and snatching a breath of air.

"Okay," he gasped, reluctantly releasing his hold and half running towards the house.

Laughing, she called after him to stay calm or he'll have a heart attack.

"I love you!" he called back to her with a heart-warming huge smile.

"Yeah me too," she replied as she walked through the front door and headed for the ranch slider.

Wilson was happy to play outside and Jonah had managed to make a cup of calming tea for them both while he was still floating on air, it was nice to see him so happy as he waited in anticipation to hear what she had to say. They each took a comfy armchair in the lounge across the room from each other, so they could discuss their lives over a cup of tea.

"Well, just let me explain how I'd prefer not to have gone through some of the misery I've endured in my life. But looking back I understand now that it was all meant to happen, because it has made me the strong resilient person I am today and helped me to appreciate the wonderful life I now have. I'm so grateful that you have been patient and really tolerant while I've been going through stuff, and I'm so grateful we found each other. The time on my own has helped me have clear vision to see what I was oblivious to and getting through the anguish of losing what seemed like everything at the time." She happily explained between sips of much needed tea.

Looking across the room into Jonahs eyes, she saw the pain and compassion he felt for the suffering she had endured, it was unmistakable as his eyes filled with tears when she explained it to him. Jonah walked silently across the room towards Gemma, offering his hand and pulled her to her feet. With his strong arm around her waist, his other hand squeezed gently into her palm and he started to speak.

"You've kept me waiting long enough, I can provide you with everything you ever want, and that would make me very happy. Will you marry me?" he asked with such warmth in his voice.

"Yes! Oh yes," she shouted out, "But we must sort out the legal stuff first." She pointed out.

He lifted Gemma off her feet as he swirled her around.

"Hey, take it easy!" she giggled. "We're in our sixties remember." His tight grip on her demonstrating his reluctance to ever let her go.

Holding Gemma in his arms, he pulled her closer into his chest for another kiss and she realized that he was scantily clad with an old tee shirt and shorts on from the farm work today. After she phoned him, he had been so preoccupied he hadn't taken time to dress properly after work.

"Don't get cold. Do you need to put some jeans on?"

"Oh maybe, I didn't have time for that," he whispered, "You're beautiful and you won't regret marrying me, I'll always be here for you. You've made me so happy," he said.

"Can I stay with you tonight, I put some dog biscuits in the car for Wilson so he'll be okay?" she asked, feeling a little bit overwhelmed and shaky from all the excitement.

Gemma couldn't possibly leave to go home, there was no urgency or panic propelling her back to the beach now, her place was with Jonah.

"Of course, and I'll order us some take aways to celebrate with, I didn't have time to shower and change after your phone call, my mind was just all over the place," Jonah apologized.

"You shower, I had my tea before you called, so I'll hop into the spa to relax, until you join me. Are you okay darling?" lying her head on his chest.

"Yes, I am now that you're here, I'll be quick. If you don't want anything I'll just have some toast and we can both have ice-cream later if you like," he called back on his way to the bathroom, looking a bit flustered.

"That sounds good, just you get in and out of the shower as fast as you can as I can't stand to be away from you. I'll just have some ice-cream later on when you have some," she called.

Climbing into the spa she ducked down up to her neck in the water and was more relaxed than she could ever remember being. The bubbles tickled and fizzed on her skin, lying her head back she pondered how she came to be living this life, not in her wildest dreams could she have hoped for such contentment and with an anticipation of a splendid future ahead. Gemma's journey had moulded her to be more understanding, humble and have immeasurable compassion now towards others who were going through terrible injustices in life.

Celebrating Christmas in a month's time with their families together, followed by a new year, for Gemma that was synonymous with the closing of one chapter of her book of life, to go forward with a profound knowledge of her strengths and weaknesses which will elevate her to even higher achievements and spiritual awareness.

Promising herself to take the wisdom she had gained and the lessons learned to grow in strength and prosperity, always knowing that the light at the end of the tunnel was not an ending, but just a beginning, this was her life and now she was living it!

Have you followed L.J. Bernard

on Facebook?

Keep up to date on Lynette's latest books,

stay in touch

with news about Lynette.

facebook.com/lynettebernard

Email: authornewsletterljb@gmail.com

About the Author

A New Zealand mother of two.

Lynette has found success in pursuing her love of writing with the publishing of her first fiction novel, *'Insurmountable Faith.'* She has now published her second novel *'She Finds Love,'* in response to her readers who wonder what became of Gemma.

Lynette happily divides her time between family, writing and gardening in the beautiful New Zealand climate.

www.ingramcontent.com/pod-product-compliance
Lightning Source LLC
Chambersburg PA
CBHW050239110726
47898CB00007B/2197
9780473720773